Madame Fromage's

ADVENTURES IN CHEESE

Library of Congress Cataloging-in-Publication Data is available.

ISBN 978-1-5235-0677-4

Design by Laura Palese

Workman books are available at special discounts when purchased in bulk for
premiums and sales promotions as well as for fundraising or educational use.
Special editions or book excerpts can also be created to specification.
For details, please contact special.markets@hbgusa.com.

Workman Publishing Co., Inc.,
a subsidiary of Hachette Book Group, Inc.
1290 Avenue of the Americas
New York, NY 10104
workman.com

WORKMAN is a registered trademark of Workman Publishing Co., Inc.,
a subsidiary of Hachette Book Group, Inc.

Printed in China on responsibly sourced paper.
First printing July 2023

10 9 8 7 6 5 4 3 2 1

Madame Fromage's
ADVENTURES
IN CHEESE

HOW TO EXPLORE IT, PAIR IT, AND LOVE IT, FROM THE CREAMIEST BRIES TO THE FUNKIEST BLUES

TENAYA DARLINGTON
AKA MADAME FROMAGE

Workman Publishing
New York

CONTENTS

POSTCARD

Dear Reader,

If you've picked this up, you
must be hungry for adventure.
Let's run away and eat
cheese together. This book
is dedicated to you, the next
great curd nerd!

XOXO,
Madame Fromage

PHILADELPHIA
FEB
2023

INTRODUCTION: Delicious Adventure Awaits! 1

Part One
DISCOVER
6

Template for a Great Cheese Board 8

The Secret to Great Cheese 11

Craft Cheese vs. Kraft Cheese 13

A Brief History of Cheesemaking 14

The Creative Evolution of Cheese 16

How Cheese Is Made 20

All About Milk 28

Cheese Anatomy 101 34

Part Two
EXPLORE
38

ADVENTURE 1:
Skydive into Fresh Cheese 42

ADVENTURE 2:
Soft-Ripened Safari 58

ADVENTURE 3:
Stinky Cheese Spelunking Tour 80

ADVENTURE 4:
A Transatlantic Cheddar Crossing 96

ADVENTURE 5:
Alpine Cheese Trek 114

ADVENTURE 6:
Geological Adventures in Aged Cheese
(with Crystals!) 136

ADVENTURE 7:
Smoked, Truffled, Herby, Spiced—
A Field Trip Through Flavors 156

ADVENTURE 8:
Rock 'n' Roll Blue Cheese Bus Tour 172

Part Three
ENTERTAIN
188

Shopping for Cheese 190

How to Taste Cheese Like a Pro 196

Fifty Must-Try Cheeses 200

How to Care for Your Cheeses
at Home 208

Sharing and Serving Cheese 210

Top Tips for Pairing Cheese and Drinks 224

The Lactic Lexicon 229

Part Four
KEEP LEARNING
230

Why Cheese Travel? 232

Cheese Festivals and Happenings 235

Exploring Artisan Cheesemakers Around
the United States 240

Cheesemaking Classes and Experiences 244

Twenty Wild Cheeses to Explore
Around the World 248

BOOKS FOR YOUR LACTIC LIBRARY 254
DAIRY DOSSIER: At-a-Glance Cheese Profiles 258
INDEX 274 • **ACKNOWLEDGMENTS** 281 • **ABOUT THE AUTHOR** 282

↓

Delicious ADVENTURE AWAITS!

If you've ever strolled into a cheese shop and felt gobsmacked by the sheer number of soft, pillowy surfaces and curiously craggy hunks, let me explain something. Your local cheese counter is a tiny portal into what is essentially a massive wilderness, ranging from everyday table cheeses, such as Cheddars, to extraordinary finds that are seasonal and elusive— the ghost orchids of cheese, as it were. Only those in the know, a crew of milk-thirsty caseophiles (i.e., cheese connoisseurs), ever lay eyes on them.

I'm not suggesting you quit your day job to track down rare cheeses. No. I'm here to invite you to become an explorer, right from the comfort of your own home. If you love cheese, if you are the kind of person who goes to parties to enjoy a moment of solitary bliss with a piece of runny Camembert in the corner of a stranger's kitchen while everyone else discusses real estate or their latest phone plan, well, you're one of us. You are a curd nerd. You're someone whose eyes glow a little more brightly at the mere mention of the words *triple crème*. There, did you feel it? How about if I say the phrase *cheese road trip* or *lactic vacation*?

I thought so.

You see, I'm about to launch a cheese adventure club with a series of expeditions to eight different dairy destinations. If you're into the idea of flying Air Fromage and landing in pastures to meet local makers, if you're keen to taste a wide variety of cheese styles in a way that will change how you entertain friends forever, if you're interested in hanging out with cave mistresses and cow connoisseurs, well, then follow me. Consider this book your invitation. All you need is curiosity—and a couple of cheese knives.

LET ME INTRODUCE MYSELF. MY NAME IS MADAME FROMAGE.

My life as a cheese writer and educator started when a tattooed cheesemonger handed me a piece of life-changing Roquefort. I had just moved to Philadelphia all by my lonesome, and for my first stop, I strolled into a cheese shop that had more cheeses than I'd ever seen in my life. It was the sort of old-world Italian deli that has giant provolones dangling from the ceiling like holiday baubles and 350-some cheeses facing out from the counter, glittering and shimmery and seductive. My eyes banged open like shutters. My heart turned into a thwamping accordion. My lungs filled like gills sucking in gusts of air, which smelled like warm milk and honey with pastures undulating in the background. I was, in that moment, transported.

Sure, I was in Philadelphia, but I felt like I had just been air-dropped into a small European village, and I never wanted to leave—at least not before tasting all 350 cheeses. And so I did just that. Not all at once. Every week I ventured back to this little shop for a few morsels of cheese and a wood-fired oven–baked baguette and, sometimes, a jar of truffle honey with tiny commas of dark mushrooms floating around in the amber slur. Whatever the dream team behind the counter of Di Bruno Bros. recommended, I bought and tasted. Soon, I carried a cheese notebook on these junkets. I jotted down pairing recommendations for bandaged cheeses and whiskey, for Gruyère and drizzled caramel, for briny blue cheeses and bottles of oyster stout.

As I made my way on and off subways and navigated a new city full of screaming car horns and night-shrieking stray cats, it was the quiet of the cheese shop that became my refuge. And the cheese boards I made for myself alone in my apartment, or for a few new friends who also happened to be cheese-curious like me—these moments became coveted departures from daily life, like magic carpet rides into the dairy-sphere. I began to write about these experiences on my blog under the nom de plume Madame Fromage, which led to becoming a "cheese blogger in residence" for Di Bruno Bros., then writing a book with their cheesemongers, then partnering with a travel company called Cheese Journeys to cohost luxury food tours to cheese caves around the world, and finally, becoming the cheese director for a trio of cheese-centric wine bars in Philadelphia. I currently teach writing by day, and by night I curate cheese menus and teach cheese classes.

But first, I learned to travel by taste bud. And now, so will you.

Let's go. Many lactic landscapes await!

HOW TO NAVIGATE THIS BOOK

Everything you need to know about choosing cheese, tasting it, pairing it, and sharing it is in these pages. Really, this book is a cheese adventure guide. I suggest you start treating yourself to some interesting cheeses on the regular and that you assemble a crew of co-adventurers to join you on your tasting missions. I will train you to become intrepid, to speak fluently and articulately about cheese, to track both the best cheeses on a budget and the great must-taste cheeses of a lifetime. By the time you reach the end of this book, you will be a fearless cheese adventurer who can regale friends and lovers with cheese knowledge and dazzle with spectacular cheese boards.

PART ONE is all about discovery. You'll drop into a field to learn about pasture-raised animals (page 12), pop into a creamery to watch a cheesemaker start her morning at the vat (page 24), and dart to Amsterdam to get up close to some wheels of Gouda in a cave run by the queen of Dutch cheese (page 36). Plus, there's some history (page 16) and an anatomy lesson (page 20).

PART TWO offers eight itineraries you can explore in your kitchen, from fresh cheeses to wildly flavored cheeses. Follow these chapters in order or jump around. Each itinerary is essentially a flight of cheeses that you can create on a board and taste to understand that style. While some of the cheeses in this book may be hard to track down in your hometown, many of them are available online.

PART THREE contains all my tips on shopping for cheese, creating next-level boards, and pairing cheese with beverages. You'll also find suggested cheeses for different situations you might encounter, plus a lexicon you can use to describe tastes and textures fluently.

PART FOUR includes all the resources you need to keep exploring—lists of cheese festivals, travel tips, a reading list, and more.

Ready for your first wild ride?
Let's get these wheels off the ground!

Part One

DISCO

8   Template for a
Great Cheese Board

11   The Secret to
Great Cheese

13   Craft Cheese vs.
Kraft Cheese

14   A Brief History of
Cheesemaking

16   The Creative Evolution
of Cheese

20   How Cheese Is Made

28   All About Milk

32   The Natural Wonder
of Raw Milk

34   Cheese Anatomy 101

BEING A CHEESE ADVENTURER requires a good nose and curiosity about terrain—just like a master tracker in the wilderness. How a cheese smells and tastes has everything to do with where it's made. Sniff a rustic wheel of Pecorino Sardo and you will smell thyme and lanolin from the sheep that graze freely along the rugged coast of Sardinia eating wild herbs. An aged Dutch Gouda, on the other hand, smells like a sea salt caramel—think cooked milk and ocean wind. You won't be surprised, then, if the best Goudas lead us to Holland, where much of the countryside once existed below sea level, and the cows pasture on grazing lands that were once part of the sea floor. Peel back the grass, and you'll find layers of salt and shells.

Are you ready to visit some hidden corners of the world in pursuit of great cheese? Up ahead, I've arranged a training board with three cheeses that will introduce you to key concepts every cheese scout needs. With each wheel, you'll be transported to its origin. You'll cross pastures to sip milk of different seasons, step into a creamery to meet a maker, and peer into a cheese cave run by a famous cave mistress who caresses Goudas until they reach optimum ripeness.

TEMPLATE FOR A GREAT CHEESE BOARD

Like any great trip, a good cheese board should offer a mix of adventure and comfort. I always suggest picking three cheeses in the following categories: a conversation piece, a comfort cheese, and one cheese that's local or regional. Here's a sample board to guide our first quest.

1 A CONVERSATION PIECE
(Rush Creek Reserve)

You can't look at this little Moon Pie wrapped in bark without wondering what it is and where it's from. That's what makes a conversation-piece cheese. It invites curiosity. It flirts with you. Rush Creek Reserve is a plush little stinker from Wisconsin, a cult favorite that's available only in fall and winter, usually starting in November (mark your calendar now!). To serve this, I'd peel back the top rind and suggest you dive in with some potato chips, 'cuz this cheese is a little plunge pool, and yes, that is spruce bark preventing a cheese flood. The bark infuses the cheese with a woodsy flavor and functions as a compostable container. When Rush Creek isn't in season, I'll serve a similar bark-bound beauty available year-round called Harbison from Jasper Hill Farm in Vermont.

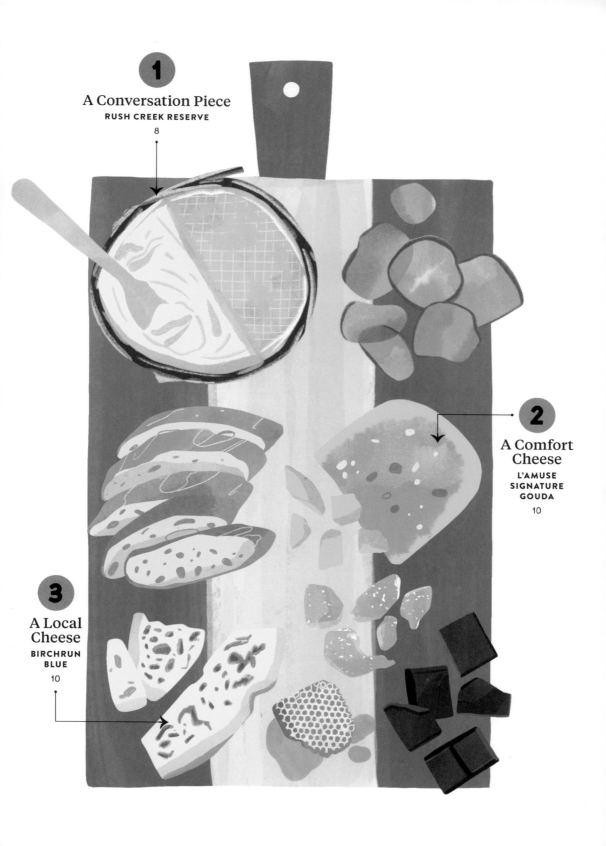

1

A Conversation Piece
RUSH CREEK RESERVE

8

2

A Comfort Cheese
L'AMUSE SIGNATURE GOUDA

10

3

A Local Cheese
BIRCHRUN BLUE

10

2 A COMFORT CHEESE
(L'Amuse Signature Gouda)

A comfort cheese should be your standby, and mine is an aged hunk with toffeelike crystals. It reminds me of my dad who is a Gouda man. This particular hunk has won over my heart because it tastes like bourbon, and it's aged by a strikingly tall blond woman with twinkly blue eyes named Betty Koster, whom you'll meet on page 36; she is famous for maturing the most crystalline Goudas of the Netherlands. She once handed me a bite of this cheese with a slice of candied ginger and a hunk of dark chocolate. It made me moan. That's how I love to serve this cheese now—it reminds me of Betty's sparkle and ingenuity.

3 A LOCAL CHEESE
(Birchrun Blue)

When you travel, it's always fun to try regional specialties, so why not do this at home? My local pick is a stunning blue cheese from a small family farm just outside Philadelphia. (Yes, it's available online, in case you'd like to try it.) Think of it as Pennsylvania Stilton, rugged but supple. If you were sitting on my stoop, I'd hand you a hunk of this blue with some oozing honeycomb and a shred of warm baguette, then tell you—while you chewed, eyes closed, bliss infused—about my friend the cheesemaker. Her name is Sue Miller, and she is the first person who ever showed me how to make cheese, after I stalked her at a farmers market. Don't worry, she'll show you, too (page 24).

While you begin nibbling, I'm going to give you an overview of what makes great cheese. It's the real reason I am writing this book, my second homage to fromage. A bite of superb cheese takes you on a journey—it's literally called *the journey*, an industry term for the way a cheese reveals complexity. When you eat divine cheese, close your eyes and imagine a curved road. Your initial impression is the first curve. When you start to chew, does the flavor take a turn? When you swallow, what do you notice up ahead, and how long does the ride last?

Like a great wine or a treasure map, great cheeses unfold. They are not simple or one note. They may not be something you can afford to enjoy every day, or every week, but once you realize they are out there, once you begin to appreciate them and search for them, you will never be bored. You will always want to try more, which is why I am still writing about cheese even after eating close to a thousand different kinds. Because the more you explore cheese, the more amazing things you discover.

THE SECRET TO GREAT CHEESE

If you're anything like most people I meet, you've spent much of your life in the Singles scene—as in, Cheese Singles. I'm not going to lie, there is something seductive about watching a processed cheese slice melt over a burger, but Singles do not contain actual cheese. They're usually made with powdered whey protein and soybean oil. They're an industrial product that's designed to last for eons. You could take them with you to a desert island.

Single and ready to mingle

Really good cheese is made with—get ready—plants!

Seriously, animals that are raised on chlorophyll-rich greens produce the most sought-after juice, known in the industry as cheese milk. When you eat cheese from animals that have eaten grass, you're basically eating a green smoothie with a rind. Cheese made from pasture-based milk is a healthy, life-giving food. In fact, there's no reason it shouldn't be part of a plant-based diet. High-quality cheese is loaded with protein and vitamins, and the better the quality of the feed, the more nutritious the cheese. In fact, cheese made from the milk of pastured animals has been shown to have higher levels of omega-3 fatty acids, beta-carotene, and vitamins A and E.

Studies also show that the fat in grass-fed dairy is different from the fat in animals raised on corn and grain, the standard at most industrial dairy farms that produce the majority of our milk supply. According to the *Journal of Clinical Nutrition*, pasture-raised dairy contains up to five times the amount of linoleic acid or CLA, a healthy fat found in the meat and milk of grazing animals. A study of over 3,500 people showed that participants with the highest levels of CLA in their tissues were 50 percent less likely to suffer a heart attack than those with the lowest levels.

This is what connects all the cheeses on the board on page 9—they taste great because they are loaded with greens. If you want the good stuff, you gotta hit up a pasture.

What Makes Great Cheese?

- **A good menu (i.e., pasture) for well-treated animals**

- **A knowledgeable artisan**

- **Aging time for complex flavors to develop**

Let's Pop by a Pasture!

Tuck into that gooey wheel of Rush Creek Reserve, then let's teleport ourselves to its origin, one of the most famous dairy farms in the United States. Spin your calendar to June, and drop your pin down on Dodgeville, Wisconsin, where a rangy guy named Andy Hatch is waiting for us in the middle of a 450-acre meadow, holding a garlic press.

Andy is the cheesemaker at Uplands Cheese, where he makes two of the most sought-after wheels in America: Pleasant Ridge Reserve and Rush Creek Reserve. Andy raises his own herd of cows—see those eighty ladies grazing over there?—and he hand-makes and ages all the cheese himself in a modest building in the middle of the field.

The secret to his success? Nope, it's not his habit of playing mandolin in his aging cave (fact!). It's the sweetness of his milk.

"It's almost like someone dropped a tablespoon of sugar into it," Andy says.

If you look closely at Andy's grass, you'll see it's lush—juicy and full of chlorophyll. Andy moves his cows to different parts of the pasture each day, depending on where the grass is sweetest. That's why he's carrying a garlic press. He kneels down, extracts some juice from the tips of some grass blades, and looks at the liquid through a Brix meter, another tool he carries in his pocket.

A Brix meter is a digital tool that measures sugar. It looks like a stopwatch.

"When we bring the cows out, we want the grass to be bursting with energy," Andy says, looking up. When the grass is about to go to seed, it contains the most sugar. Reader, look down, right here, where you're standing. Do you see all those different types of grass? There are also a dozen different types of legumes and wildflowers, like purple chicory and feathery Queen Anne's lace. They're the other secret to Andy's stellar cheese. The more varied the plants in a pasture, the more flavors and aromas you'll find in a cheese.

CRAFT CHEESE VS. KRAFT CHEESE

Craft cheeses, like the ones Andy makes, are produced on a small scale, often by a single maker who seeks to follow traditional recipes and uses the best milk possible, likely from a single herd. These cheeses are usually labeled handcrafted or small batch. Or, in Andy's case, farmstead, because his cheeses are made on the farm where the animals are raised. Farmstead cheese and handcrafted cheeses are unique because they capture the flavors of the farms where they are produced in the same way that great wines are bursting with terroir—the taste of a place.

As Andy will tell you when he hands you a bite of his award-winning Pleasant Ridge or Rush Creek Reserve "Cheesemaking is the way we distill our farm's pasture."

Stellar cheeses like Andy's take your taste buds on a wild trip. The first time I ate a scoop of Rush Creek Reserve, the experience was akin to seeing the northern lights. It had a glowing orange rind and a ring of dark bark, and when I scooped its paste into my mouth on a spoon, it filled my mind with stars and what felt like shimmering fingers reaching in different directions toward savory meatiness and green-oniony freshness. It was so alive-tasting and so different from anything I'd ever eaten that I could barely put words to it. In my little cheese notebook where I record all my tasting notes, I wrote, *Imagine plucking a tiny onion sprout, a seedling bursting with fresh oniony zest, then set it on a snail glistening in butter.*

> "Cheesemaking is the way we distill our farm's pasture."

Finding a life-changing cheese, like finding that perfect cup of coffee or otherworldly chocolate bar, is an unforgettable experience. Such cheeses are rare and usually require a professional guide or some serious sleuthing, but here's what's exciting: There are more craft cheeses available globally than ever before, especially in the United States, where, at last count, there were more than a thousand licensed artisan and specialty cheesemakers—a number that has doubled since 2000.

The Price of Grass-Feeding Cows

If you're wondering why all cheese isn't made from pasture-raised cows, here's a little lesson in economics: Pastured cows produce half the amount of milk that grain-fed cows produce at industrial dairy farms. Also, raising cows on pasture requires a lot of land, about two acres per cow. If the cows eat a pasture down to the soil, the grass won't regrow—the plants will think that it's winter and put all of their energy into the roots—and that's a big problem for a product that relies on grass for its exceptional flavor. Great cheese made from great milk demands a whole lotta effort—and with it, money.

People like Andy, a skinny guy in a feed cap with a garlic press in his pocket, have returned to old ways of farming and cheesemaking because they're passionate about carrying on tradition, caring for their land, and creating really cool cheese that can't be re-created on a massive scale. Hang around long enough and he'll tell you how he produces cheese only when his cows are on pasture, and how his two cheeses are based on a centuries-old model from France, where cheesemakers in the Jura Mountains switch up their recipes seasonally to account for subtle changes in the milk. Andy makes his firm, flavor-rich wheels of Pleasant Ridge Reserve in summer when his grasses are most tender and the milk is sweetest, and he switches to making soft, scoopy Rush Creek Reserve in fall when the grasses turn dry and the milk becomes richer (less water in the grass means more concentrated fats and proteins).

A BRIEF HISTORY OF CHEESEMAKING

Grab your walking stick and prepare for a trek through time, all the way back to the Neolithic era. According to an often-told legend, the first cheese was accidentally created when a Mesopotamian shepherd put some milk in a bag made from a dried goat stomach, which would have contained the cheesemaking enzyme called rennet, opened the bag on his lunch break, and found some cheese curds. The only trouble with this story? Early nomads were lactose intolerant, according to cheese historian and scientist Paul Kindstedt (whom you'll meet on page 152), so it's unlikely that a shepherd would have slung a goatskin bag full of milk over his shoulder. Though we'll never know for sure, the first Neolithic cheese was probably discovered by heating milk over a fire and accidentally dropping in something acidic that made it separate, resulting in an "aha" moment for a nomad who would have ended up with a cauldron of something much like ricotta.

Either way, long before refrigeration was invented, cheesemaking became a convenient way to preserve milk. Once nomadic cultures figured out how to acidify milk to create curds and whey, they collected the solid curds and eventually pressed them into cakes. By salting these cakes and drying them, the first cheesemakers figured out how to store cheese without it spoiling. When they stacked the curd cakes in a clay urn full of oil or salt water, the cakes lasted even longer. Think feta. Then, when they stored the salted, dried cakes in the back of a cool, damp cave, something else happened. Rinds formed, thanks to natural molds and microbes floating in the air. These landed on the cheeses and helped create a lovely little husk around them. Plus, they added flavor. The first cheesemakers must have had a field day—and risked their lives eating a lot of disgusting moldy blobs—to further their studies in affinage (the art of aging cheese).

Each sort of cheese reveals a pasture of a different green, under a different sky.

—ITALO CALVINO

Since those early efforts, cheese has become both sustenance and a symbol. It's been traded like gold bars, presented as wedding gifts, used to fuel Roman Olympians, and served on royal tables. It's also been turned into a mass-produced wartime staple and processed into a flummoxing spray-can situation, which is handy on a hike as long as you don't examine its list of ingredients. Amid the many inexpensive and uniform factory-made cheeses today, there is still a reverence for tradition that keeps unique, artisan-made cheeses alive—like Salers, for example, a legendary French cheese made in tiny huts high up in the mountains of the Auvergne, using the milk of a rare and very woolly cow of the same name.

Thanks to a budding maker movement, there are also unique new cheeses appearing in unlikely places. In the heart of Paris, I once stumbled across a wonderful and enterprising goat herder named Pierre Coulon (page 77), who kick-started the city's first urban micro-creamery and makes beautiful cheeses and yogurts seven days a week from incredible milk that he sources just outside the city. In Mumbai, India, a pair of brothers have launched the Spotted Cow Fromagerie, where they make French-inspired rounds of Bombrie and Camembey. Look around: Chances are, there is a small-batch cheesemaker living practically in your own backyard. Not sure? Give a Google. You may be surprised. Not far from my office in a busy city neighborhood, there is a pediatrician who operates a licensed raw-milk creamery (Merion Park Cheese) right out of his basement. I can walk to my favorite bar and eat his hyper-local cheese any night of the week.

THE CREATIVE
Evolution of Cheese

2900 BCE
The remains of a funeral meal entombed in a burial site near Cairo include a white mass made from the milk of sheep and goats. (The material is analyzed in 2018, and it makes the news because it's the first time that evidence of early cheesemaking has been found in Egypt.)

5000–6000 BCE
Ceramic sieves unearthed in Poland and, later, in Croatia are found to have fatty milk residue—probably because they were used in early cheesemaking to separate curds from whey.

77 CE
Pliny the Elder records the art of making Pecorino Toscano in his *Naturalis Historia*, a ten-volume encyclopedia.

1184
The first mention of Gouda appears, named after the Dutch city where it is traded.

Around 750 BCE
Homer's epic poem *The Odyssey* includes a description of the Cyclops's cave where Odysseus discovers "wicker trays full of cheeses." Homer's *Iliad* also includes cheese references—including a recipe for grated goat cheese and barley meal served in a goblet of wine by the sorceress Circe.

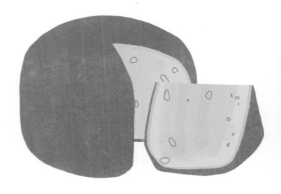

1815
The first cheese factory opens in Switzerland.

Circa 1390
The first published recipe for macaroni and cheese appears in *The Forme of Cury*, a French cookbook used in royal kitchens across Europe. It calls for butter, Parmigiano-Reggiano, and pasta. In 1802, Thomas Jefferson will serve it for dinner at the White House, securing its popularity as an American staple.

1615
Of the many paintings that feature cheese, few are as striking as those by Flemish artist Clara Peeters, which date back to 1615. Little is known about her, but she left six still lifes in her wake, including *Cheeses, Almonds, and Pretzels*. Each painting includes the same engraved silver knife from Antwerp. At the time, guests often brought their own knives to parties. By the 1650s, "breakfast paintings" featuring spreads of cheese and butter will be wildly popular.

1635
The name *Cheddar* appears for the first time as a delicacy in the English court of Charles I. Note that the town of Cheddar in the area of Somerset began producing cheeses in the eleventh century, and cheeses were aged in nearby Cheddar Gorge.

There has been cheese since the earth was new.

—PIERRE ANDROUËT, *GUIDE DU FROMAGE*

1841

Anne Pickett establishes Wisconsin's first "cottage industry cheese factory," sourcing milk from her neighbors to make cheese and butter in her log cabin. Until this point, most cheese is made in small batches by farm women as part of daily life.

1860s

Aurora, Ohio, earns the title of Cheesedom because it produces and ships more cheese than anywhere else in the United States—more than four million pounds of cheese per year. This is thanks to the Hurd brothers, who amassed an empire of eight cheese plants, starting with the Silver Creek Cheese Factory in 1862. (It burned down but is still commemorated by a historical marker.)

1851

Dairy farmer Jesse Williams builds the first American cheese factory, powered by a waterwheel, in Rome, New York, inaugurating "factory Cheddar."

1923

The iconic cheese slicer is invented by Norwegian carpenter Thor Bjørklund, who developed it in his workshop and patented it a few years later.

1862

Louis Pasteur conducts the first experiments involving pasteurization. (For more on the process, see page 22.)

Late 1800s

Taste buds are detected by a pair of German scientists (George Meissner and Rudolf Wagner). Each bud is notably shaped like an onion and made of overlapping taste cells.

1925

Roquefort becomes the first product in France to receive governmental protection to preserve its regional integrity, known as AOC status (AOC stands for Appellation d'Origine Contrôlée).

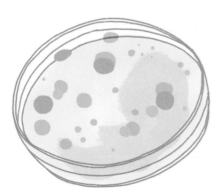

Cheese is one of the great achievements of humankind. Not any cheese in particular, but cheese in its astonishing multiplicity, created anew every day in the dairies of the world.

—HAROLD MCGEE, *ON FOOD AND COOKING*

1949

Kraft cheese slices are introduced to the market by James Lewis Kraft, an entrepreneur from a farm in Ontario. *Note:* He launched his business in 1903 by selling cheese from the back of a horse-drawn wagon.

1980s

A countercultural cheese renaissance emerges in the United States, thanks to a group of pioneering "goat ladies," including Mary Keehn, a self-proclaimed hippie and single mother of four, who launches a little company called Cypress Grove in California. Inspired by the foggy coastline, she creates an ash-lined goat cheese, Humboldt Fog, now regarded by many as the first iconic artisan cheese in the United States.

1997

Slow Food recognizes that traditional cheeses are in danger of extinction and launches its first global dairy festival. Called simply Cheese, it is held every other year in the small town of Bra in Piedmont, Italy.

1969

La Guilde Internationale des Fromagers is established in Paris as a global organization to unite cheese industry professionals. Guild members are inducted in a private ceremony and wear brown robes—a nod to monastic traditions.

1983

The American Cheese Society forms as a national grassroots organization to support home and farm cheesemaking and cheese appreciation, thanks to Dr. Frank V. Kosikowski of Cornell University.

2006

The late Anne Saxelby opens the first-ever cheese shop devoted solely to artisan American cheese in Manhattan's historic Essex Street Market. In 2017, she expands and moves Saxelby Cheesemongers to Chelsea Market. A visit to her epic shop is the American dairy equivalent to visiting Lady Liberty.

HOW CHEESE IS MADE

Cheese is alive. Just as wine is made from fermented grapes, and beer is made from fermented grains, cheese is made by fermenting milk—which makes it more delicious and digestible. Whether we're talking provolone or Pecorino, a wheel of cheese is basically a jetpack of microbes working inside milk to help it withstand time.

Milk that comes straight from the udder, aka raw milk, contains a natural community of microbes that can be used to jump-start the natural process of fermentation. Microbes can also be added to the milk in the form of a starter culture—just as you would add starter cultures to make yogurt or sourdough bread. It all depends on the recipe.

To give you a window into microbe wrangling, a term coined by cheese scientist Michael Tunick (see page 255), I'm going to introduce you to my friend Sue Miller, the first person ever to invite me to watch the cheesemaking process, who has a tiny creamery outside Philadelphia. Unlike Andy Hatch in Wisconsin (page 12), who always wanted to be a cheesemaker, Sue Miller found this vocation by chance. She's an animal lover, and after college, she and her husband, Ken, moved to the country and started a small dairy farm with a herd of Holsteins that Sue calls by name. (My favorites: Brie, Prosecco, and Little Chardy.)

Before we suit up in hairnets and rubber boots, here's a quick crash course in the basics of cheesemaking. The most important thing you'll need to know is that cheese is made from four basic ingredients: milk, cultures (aka beneficial microbes), rennet, and salt. The following is a basic blueprint for how cheese is made. If it helps, think about the fact that fromage, the French word for "cheese," comes from the word *form* (forma, in Latin), so the cheesemaking process is all about forming milk into a solid.

Lifecycle of Cheese

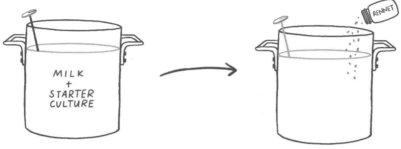

1. Heat milk and add starter culture.

2. Add coagulent (rennet) . . .

3. Gather the curds into molds to form wheels, then drain and salt them . . .

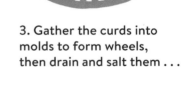

4. Mature the wheels in a cool, cave-like environment for a few days or years, depending on the style.

. . . to separate curds and whey.

Four Ingredients, Endless Possibilities

"How do we get thousands of different cheeses from just four ingredients and a few steps?" you ask. You wouldn't be the first person to marvel at this feat. Here's the deal: Cheese is all about massive variables. Here are some questions you can ask when you approach an unfamiliar cheese. The more you learn about these variables, the more you'll understand how they affect flavor.

1 **What animal?** Cheese can be made from the milk of any animal: cow, goat, sheep, buffalo, even humans (oh yes, it's been done—though not commercially—although human milk has only 1 percent protein, so it must be combined with another milk to form curds). All milks taste different and have different ratios of protein and butterfat, which affect cheese taste and texture. (For more about milk, see page 28.)

2 **What region?** The particularities of where a cheese is made—from the climate to the soil to the weather, even down to the water that the animals drink—affect its flavor. Cheeses that intentionally reflect the place where they are made are said to have terroir.

3 **Is it pasteurized?** Pasteurization involves heating milk to kill all bacteria, both undesirable and desirable. It affects the flavor and texture of cheeses. This is why some cheesemakers prefer to work with unpasteurized (aka raw) milk—or "milk with personality," as Bronwen Percival, a cheese buyer for London's Neal's Yard Dairy, calls it. For more about raw milk—a conversation that could last to the moon and back—check out the raw-milk FAQ on page 32.

4 **Whose hands?** The way an artisan handles the curds during the cheesemaking process affects the final texture of the cheese. I was surprised to learn this, but in the cheesemaking world, people really do talk about a maker's "touch." For instance, a very light set of hands is needed to stir and scoop delicate, creamy cheeses, like Brie. If you like to stir and you have a tender touch, you would probably be a good maker of Brie. Cheese shop owner Lou Di Palo, who runs Di Palo's in New York's Little Italy neighborhood, told me that he can tell which of his employees made the house mozzarella each day, based on its chew.

5 **Which cultures?** Starter cultures are an ingredient in cheesemaking that help convert lactose (milk sugar) into lactic acid. These beneficial bacteria also contribute aroma and flavor to the final cheese. Different cheese recipes call for different cultures. These days, most cultures are purchased from labs in freeze-dried packs, much like commercial yeast, though a few hard-core US cheesemakers make their own native starter cultures. Before the 1880s, native starter cultures were made by souring milk or whey from the previous day's cheesemaking, then adding it to fresh milk—much as homemade yogurt was made.

6 **What kind of rennet?** Cheesemakers can choose between animal or vegetable rennet, an enzyme that helps milk separate into curds and whey. Animal rennet, harvested from the stomach of a baby ruminant, was traditionally used in cheesemaking and is still necessary to achieve the desired taste of some cheeses, especially cheeses that are aged, like Parmigiano-Reggiano. Today, many makers purchase vegetable rennet (aka microbial rennet), which is produced in a lab, though you can also find some really interesting vegetarian cheeses from Portugal and Spain that are made with thistles (page 206).

7 **How long was it aged?** The art of aging cheese is called affinage, as you know. Affineurs—people who specialize in maturing cheeses—are responsible for bringing wheels to maturity by various processes that can include turning, flipping, brushing, washing, salting, inoculating, and testing. Time also plays a role; as moisture evaporates from wheels, flavors concentrate. For this reason, aged cheeses usually have the most complexity.

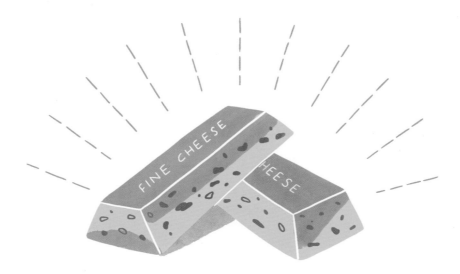

FIELD GUIDE

* Meet a *
CHEESEMAKER

A Day in the Life of
Sue Miller

When Sue Miller first decided to make cheese, in 2007, it was the middle of the night. Her family's dairy farm, Birchrun Hills an hour outside Philadelphia, had fallen on hard times because of declining milk prices. The thought of losing her home—an old stagecoach inn that has been in the family for three generations—had kept her up at night for weeks. Selling milk from her family's small herd to the local bottling plant was no longer paying the bills.

"I was literally lying in bed when the idea came to me," Sue recalls. "I thought, *I'm going to make cheese*." The next morning, she phoned the Pennsylvania Association of Sustainable Agriculture and talked her way into a cheesemaking class even though it was full. She told the person on the phone, "I have to learn how to make cheese! My family's farm depends on it."

Sue's family includes her husband, Ken, who raises crops and maintains pastures, and her twentysomething sons, Randy and Jesse, who take care of the herd. Both sons graduated from Cornell University, where they studied agriculture. Today, the Millers milk around eighty black-and-white Holstein cows (plus a few little Jerseys), and much of the milk is made into cheese, which Sue sells at local farmers markets and to restaurants along the East Coast.

Sue's cheeses are made from raw milk. She makes several styles, including a blue, and takes pride in creating cheeses that reflect her farm and the region. As she'll tell you, Chester County is the mushroom capital of the world, producing more than a million pounds of mushrooms per year. "I swear I can taste a little mushroominess in our cheeses," Sue says. "I call it Chester County terroir."

In Her Own Words: Morning to Night

Here's how Sue describes her day on the farm, which begins with a quick family breakfast before she heads to the creamery just outside her back door.

5:30 A.M.
Our day starts with the whole family drinking coffee at the kitchen table, and we always begin by checking in about the cows. Before I make cheese, I like to know if there have been any changes to the feed. Our cows graze on pasture and eat a mix of supplemental feed for extra nutrition.

6:00 A.M.
Ken heads to the milking barn, and I go to the creamery behind our house to suit up in my boots, apron, and hairnet. Then I check the temperature in the aging caves and sanitize the vats and the pipeline that brings milk in from the barn.

7:00 A.M.

I text Ken that I'm ready for the milk. We have a gravity-fed pipeline from a bulk tank that leads right into my cheese room. I like to make cheese with milk that is very fresh, less than twenty-four hours old. I always drink a cup of it so that I know what flavors are coming through before I make cheese.

7:30 A.M.

When the milk comes into the vat, I begin warming it very gently. It comes in between 30°F and 48°F, and I need to get it to 90°F.

8:30 A.M.

At 80°F, I add the cultures. The warm milk wakes them up, basically, so that they can begin the fermentation process. I'll stir the milk gently with a paddle for about an hour, and I'll keep checking the pH, because the cultures increase the acidity of the milk. We call this the ripening time.

9:30 A.M.

I add the rennet, which will set the milk into a yogurtlike consistency. We always use calf's rennet because we're trying to practice making traditional cheese, and calf's rennet is at the core of tradition. At this point, I'm still stirring slowly and checking the pH constantly. It's kind of like a meditation. I don't like any distraction, not even music. I'm using all my senses to pay attention to the milk—visual, aroma, taste, touch. Cheesemaking is really a blend of science, craft, and intuition.

10:30 A.M.

When the milk sets into a gel-like consistency, it's time to cut it. This is called cutting the curd. I use a long curd knife, and it takes only about five minutes. After I cut the curd, there's about another hour of stirring, and then I'll drain off the whey.

11:30 A.M.

Hooping begins. That's the term for gathering the curds from the vat and putting them into forms. I'll fluff the curds on a table first to remove any residual whey, then I'll fill the forms, which are round, to create wheels.

NOON

I never eat lunch. I'll nibble one of our meat sticks, or I'll eat some cheese on the fly in our break room between turning cheeses. The cheese needs turning every thirty minutes for the next hour and a half. The forms are perforated so that excess whey can escape each time I flip them.

2:30–6:30 P.M.

After cleaning up, I'll spend the afternoon down in the aging caves. All the blues get turned once a week. My two washed rinds, Red Cat and Fat Cat, need to be washed with brine three to four times a week so they stay moist.

6:30 P.M.
Finally, I'll check emails and texts
and fulfill any orders. I'm always
apologizing because I am hard to get
ahold of during the day. Usually, I
don't leave the creamery until around
8:00 p.m., and then I'll visit the barn
to see if any new calves were born.
If I can't make it, one of my boys will
bring a new calf by my window.

8:30 P.M.
Dinner. Generally, we'll have our own
meat or eggs, and I'll cook the produce
we've bartered for at market. In the
summer, nobody comes in to eat before
dark. Sometimes my son Jesse will grill.

10:00 P.M.
I fall into bed!

ALL ABOUT MILK

Four Glasses of Milk: Sip Through the Seasons

Just as the best farm-to-table chefs are obsessed with seasonal produce, the best cheesemakers work with the seasons. When Sue Miller drinks a cup of milk from her family's herd each morning, she tastes different flavors, depending on the time of year. Spring milk is usually the most flavorful because the pastures are full of tender new grasses and wildflowers, but late summer milk is usually richer because the grass is drier and denser. When Sue's cows move onto locally sourced hay in the fall, their milk changes again. If we were to sit down to a flight of milks from different seasons on Sue's farm, here's what we might notice.

GLASS NO. 1: SPRING MILK

Spring wildflowers and the first tender grass blades contribute the most delicate flavors to milk. Think of this glass as the Champagne of milks: fresh tasting, a little floral, full of zippy energy from emerald-green chlorophyll. Traditionally, spring also marks the beginning of the lactation cycle, resulting in milk with a thick, rich consistency.

  FACT: The greatest nutritional value lies in the first centimeters of plant growth.

GLASS NO. 2: SUMMER MILK

Second-growth grasses in the pasture yield another wave of flavorful milk, especially around June. As long as there's good rainfall, the pasture remains dense and lush. You should taste grassy notes but also notice that this glass of milk is thinner because there is more water in it—thanks to rainfall but also the shift in the lactation cycle.

  FACT: Milk from pasture-raised cows is golden in color because of beta-carotene in the grass. When you see a cheese with a golden tinge, like a straw-colored wedge of Montgomery's Cheddar, you're most likely looking at cheese made from pastured spring or summer milk.

GLASS NO. 3: FALL MILK

As the fields turn from bright emerald to brown, the color of harvest season, you'll taste less of a fresh grassy taste and notice more richness. As the grass dries, the milk turns high in butterfat again, perfect for making creamy cheeses. This is why Andy Hatch stops producing wheels of Pleasant Ridge Reserve, made with flavorful summer milk, and switches to making his lush Rush Creek Reserve, beloved for its soft, creamy texture. His seasonal approach to cheesemaking is inspired by centuries of Alpine cheesemakers, who did the same.

FACT: The most nutritious hay is cut when it's still green—it's harvested at the peak moment for grazing, so it still contains chlorophyll.

GLASS NO. 4: WINTER MILK

Winter milk is mild; you may taste straw. Most animals are fed hay, grains, and cereals during the winter months. Their milk grows richer from fattier feed, but it is much less complex in terms of flavor and aroma. Some makers let their cows go dry at this stage and stop making cheese altogether.

FACT: Winter marks the end of the lactation cycle. Animal milk contains the most richness at the beginning of lactation and is mostly water by the end.

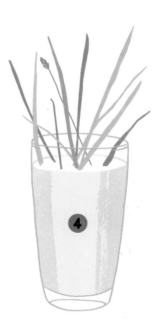

The closer you peer through the magnifying glass at milk, the more extraordinary it becomes. We throw around the expression "superfood," crowning new ingredients on a monthly basis for their nutrient-rich profile, and yet I cannot think of a single one that comes anywhere close to matching milk.

—NUTRITIONIST ANNIE BELL, *THE MODERN DAIRY*

The Four Main Milks

The easiest way to distinguish between milks? At a glance, they vary in thickness, from watery cow's milk to smoothie-like water buffalo milk. What makes a milk thick and rich? Butterfat. The thicker the milk, the richer the cheese. *Note:* The yields below are averages; milk production is affected by the seasons and the animal's lactation cycle.

MILK NO. 1: COW

About the milk: One cow can produce six to eight gallons of milk per day. Here's the rub: 87 percent of it is water, which means it takes a lot of milk to get enough solids (curds) to make a single wheel of cheese. Milk production does vary by breed. In fact, breeds are a bit like grape varietals. Some cows, like Jerseys, produce exceptionally rich milk, so they're referred to as "ice cream cows," whereas black-and-white Holsteins produce milk that's less rich, although they produce more of it. Each cheesemaker has a breed preference.

Taste: mild and sweet

Sample cheeses: Cheddar, Havarti, Gruyère, Gouda

MILK NO. 2: GOAT

About the milk: One goat produces just over half a gallon of milk a day, on average. That's a tiny amount, which is why you don't see as much goat's milk on the market. Like cows, however, goats have a long lactation period, about 284 days. Their milk tastes less sweet than cow's milk because it contains less lactose (sugar), but it has 13 percent more calcium and 134 percent more potassium. Goat's milk is naturally homogenized, which means that no cream separates to the top—this is thanks to its small, pearl-like fat globules, which are easy to digest.

Taste: High-quality goat's milk tastes like fresh grass with a slight lemony hook on the finish that is bright in flavor but not sour. If the milk smells or tastes like "animal," it's probably because a buck hung out too close to the does and caused them to release sexy hormones into the milk. Surely, we can all agree that sexy hormones are good, but not in milk or cheese.

Sample cheeses: chèvre, Valençay, Nababbo, aged goat Gouda

MILK NO. 3: SHEEP

About the milk: Like the goat, one sheep produces around half a gallon of milk per day. Sheep have the shortest lactation cycle—around 180 days—but their wonderfully rich milk produces great cheese. It contains twice the fat of cow's milk and 75 percent to 100 percent more protein, so it's basically liquid gold. Like in goat's milk, the cream in sheep's milk does not separate, and small fat globules make it easy to digest.

Taste: mild, slightly herbaceous, with a silky mouthfeel

Sample cheeses: Manchego, Pecorino, feta

MILK NO. 4: WATER BUFFALO

About the milk: One water buffalo can produce around one gallon of milk per day. A buffalo weighs 1,600 pounds, yet makes hardly any milk for its size. The quality of that milk, however, is superb. It's twice as rich as cow's milk, and it contains less cholesterol, 30 percent more protein, and loads of minerals. Some people call it a dairy superfood.

Taste: sweetly delicate in flavor and extremely silky

Sample cheeses: Mozzarella di Bufala, Casatica di Bufala, Blu di Bufala

THE NATURAL
Wonder of Raw Milk

Raw or pasteurized?

Raw milk comes straight from
the udder of a cow, just as freshly
squeezed orange juice comes straight
from oranges. Although there's no
guarantee that a raw-milk cheese
will taste better than a pasteurized
cheese, many cheesemakers will
tell you that high-quality raw milk
offers a more interesting canvas,
thanks to the natural flavors and
the diversity of its microflora. You
could say that cheesemakers who
use raw milk are traditionalists,
following age-old recipes in much the
same way that natural winemakers
are traditionalists—keen to draw
flavors from the soil and use minimal
intervention. Pasteurized milk, which
is heat treated, essentially erases the
pasture from milk. Its aim is to destroy
any potentially harmful bacteria, but
it kills everything—even taste.

What's the 60-Day Rule?

Raw-milk cheeses in the United States
are highly regulated and have been
since 1949, when a law was passed

that required them to be aged for at least sixty days before they could be sold. That's the length of time deemed necessary for potentially harmful pathogens to be destroyed, according to the Food and Drug Administration. This is why you don't see raw-milk Brie or Camembert at cheese counters in the United States—it's illegal to import them. These cheeses typically ripen in less than sixty days, so all the Brie and other "bloomy" rind cheeses sold in the United States are pasteurized. It's a real shock to taste these same cheeses in Europe, because the flavors and textures are so different. A well-made raw-milk Brie is a revelation, nuanced in flavor and lush in texture—it is unrecognizable from the many bland, rubber-band-like Bries sold in the United States.

What's pasteurization?

Named after scientist Louis Pasteur, pasteurization involves slowly heating milk to 145°F (63°C) and holding it there for thirty minutes. This is known as vat pasteurization and is most common in the cheese industry. If you want to get really geeky, there's also a heat process called thermization, an in-between route that some makers are opting for, especially European cheesemakers who want to export their cheeses without a lot of red tape. The process destroys some but not all of the natural bacteria and enzymes in the milk. Thermized milk is heated to

somewhere between 135°F and 154.4°F (57°C to 68°C) for just fifteen seconds. The milk is neither technically raw nor technically pasteurized.

How exactly does pasteurization affect cheese?

Think about freshly squeezed OJ—it tastes very different from industrially produced orange juice that you buy in a carton. Pasteurization affects the taste and texture of milk, and that means it handles differently when you make cheese from it. Because pasteurized milk is nearly flavorless, a cheesemaker has to add more freeze-dried cultures to develop a complex flavor profile. In practical terms, pasteurization makes total sense when it comes to large-scale cheesemakers who often collect milk from multiple farms and transport it over many miles. Pasteurization ensures safety, and it also extends shelf life, so there is less spoilage.

Why are some cheeses made only with raw milk?

Traditionally, cheese was made on farms from fresh raw milk. Many countries require cheesemakers to use raw milk for certain recipes in order to preserve the cultural heritage (and depth of flavor) of traditional cheeses, such as French Comté. Raw milk also contains beneficial bacteria that increase dramatically through the process of fermentation.

CHEESE ANATOMY 101

Talk Like a Curd Nerd

To expand your dairy vocabulary, here are a few useful terms. Keep in mind that no one expects you to talk about cheese like a pro when you order at a cheese counter or restaurant, but it can be helpful to know a few words in the local dialect.

AFFINEUR: A well-trained cheese babysitter who oversees the cheese-ripening process, usually in a cavelike environment. The process of maturing cheese is called affinage.

CHEESEMONGER: A person who sells cheese, just as a fishmonger sells fish.

CREAMERY: A cheese nursery, i.e., the place where cheese is made. Typically, this is a sterile room with a vat and sometimes a pasteurizer. Milk may be pumped into the room through a pipe directly from a dairy or brought in by hand, using milk cans, depending on the scale of the operation.

CHEESE CAVE: A controlled environment where cheese is aged. Temperature and humidity are adjusted, depending on the style of cheese. Yes, at one time, early civilizations aged cheeses in actual stone caves that were dark and cool and damp. Today, cheeses are aged in everything from limestone tunnels to walk-in coolers.

CREAMLINE: A milky layer that forms under the rind of soft cheeses as they ripen.

CRYSTALS: Feel that crunch between your teeth? Many cheeses develop crystals as they age. It usually takes the better part of a year for this to happen. (For more about identifying crystals, see page 138.)

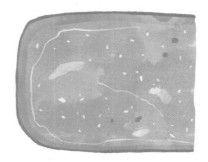

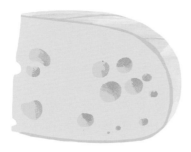

CURDS AND WHEY: When you heat milk and add an acidifier—like vinegar or rennet—you get curds and whey. Curds are lumpy milk solids that sink to the bottom of a pan or vat, and whey is the liquid that rises to the top. Whey is usually drained off (and fed to plants or pigs) so that the curds can be packed into forms to create wheels of cheese.

EYES: Holes in cheese. A cheese without holes is called a blind cheese.

NOSE: The tip or point of a cheese wedge. It's bad luck, or at least bad form, to cut it off and eat it first. Always cut round wheels of cheese from nose to rind, like a cake, to form triangular wedges. That way, each guest can taste all parts of the cheese.

PASTE: The interior, or body, of a cheese under the rind.

PEAK RIPENESS: The optimum stage for eating a cheese, usually determined by an affineur. Peak ripeness indicates that a cheese has reached its ideal flavor and texture. Since cheeses ripen over time, just like peaches, ripeness is a spectrum. A soft, runny Brie, for example, is considered at peak ripeness by many eaters, whereas some might prefer a Brie that's a bit firmer, at a younger stage.

PROTECTED DESIGNATION OF ORIGIN (PDO): An umbrella term for cheeses that have legal protection to preserve their authenticity or geographical connection to a region, like Parmigiano-Reggiano, for example. In general, a cheese with a PDO monogram is special and usually of good quality. In this book, PDO cheeses are noted in the Dairy Dossier (page 258).

RAW MILK: Milk in its natural state, unpasteurized.

RIND: The exterior of any aged cheese.

VEIN: A streak of blue, typically found in blue cheeses, although you will also find the occasional vein of blue in other cheeses, like aged Cheddar.

FIELD GUIDE

Meet an
AFFINEUR

Betty Koster

FROMAGERIE L'AMUSE, AMSTERDAM

At the doorway to L'Amuse, an expansive cheese shop overlooking a busy Amsterdam canal full of fishing boats, prepare to be greeted by Betty Koster, "the queen of Dutch cheese." She is tall with a huge smile, striking periwinkle eyes, and a blond bob the color of Brabander—her signature goat Gouda. Step through the door into Betty's brightly lit shop, and you can't help but smell a note of butterscotch—a scent that pervades her flagship store, which is also a warehouse for storing cheese before she ships it from the port. Look behind the counter: There is a wall of golden Goudas, like a bookcase full of glowing suns.

Head to the counter, and Betty will break out her black cheese plane and offer you some slices from her collection. The first bite tastes sweet and milky, like nougat. The next sample, like candied pineapple. The third, like caramelized bacon with a rum chaser. Each wheel is aged to perfection because Betty has a knack for discovering the best cheeses in the Netherlands. When she finds a batch she adores, she drives the wheels home in her truck and ages them herself. That way, she can be sure that they mature to her liking—full of sweet, milky notes and glittering crystals.

Now look past the charcuterie case and through a window into a small, dark room where heavy wooden boards support more golden wheels. That's Betty's mini–cheese cave. It holds a fraction of what she actually ages in a larger cave system behind the shop, but you get the idea. In the cheese world, Betty is famous for aging her cheeses at higher temperatures than other Gouda affineurs in order to create more crystals, and yet the paste remains miraculously buttery—never dry, like many other aged Goudas can become.

> There is a wall of golden Goudas, like a bookcase full of glowing suns.

What happens in a cheese cave? Wheels are turned and flipped regularly so that they mature evenly. They're also tasted at different stages. The longer the wheels mature, the more moisture evaporates and the more concentrated the milk flavors become. It's very much a waiting game. Cheeses ripen from the outside in, so the larger the wheel, the longer it takes to reach peak ripeness. Betty attends to some of her cheeses for several years. Her L'Amuse Signature is aged for two. Once you factor in labor costs and the price of cave real estate, you begin to understand why hard cheeses usually have a higher price tag than soft, fresh cheeses that require little or no aging.

Before we depart, Betty waves us into the café attached to her shop, where she offers cups of tea. Tea is her favorite thing to pair with cheese. "Heat," she says, "warms and opens the palate, preparing it for tasting." She might also hand you her favorite accompaniment for L'Amuse Signature—a sliver of candied ginger and a square of dark chocolate. Sweet, spicy, bitter, crunchy, creamy. Close your eyes and wait for it. First one flavor unfolds, then another. Can you taste "the journey?" Now you've been initiated.

Part Two

EXPLO

42   **ADVENTURE 1:**
Skydive into Fresh Cheese

58   **ADVENTURE 2:**
Soft-Ripened Safari

80   **ADVENTURE 3:**
Stinky Cheese
Spelunking Tour

96   **ADVENTURE 4:**
A Transatlantic
Cheddar Crossing

114   **ADVENTURE 5:**
Alpine Cheese Trek

136   **ADVENTURE 6:**
Geological Adventures
in Aged Cheese
(with Crystals!)

156   **ADVENTURE 7:**
Smoked, Truffled,
Herby, Spiced

172   **ADVENTURE 8:**
Rock 'n' Roll Blue
Cheese Bus Tour

ORE

GRAB YOUR BACKPACKS and binoculars! In this section of the book, we'll parachute into a brine bath full of fresh mozzarella (it's better than swimming with dolphins; page 58), go spelunking for pungent cave-aged stinkers the color of a Maui sunset (page 80), and rappel down the side of a mountain cheese (page 114). Prepare for some scenic surface molds (page 60), and get ready to taste lots of fromage alfresco. Whether you plan to journey solo or travel with friends, you're about to embark upon an action-packed lactic vacation that will awaken your taste buds and invigorate your intrepid side.

HOW TO TASTE YOUR WAY THROUGH THIS BOOK

The eight chapters ahead are a tour of different cheese styles. Keep in mind that there isn't an official classification system for cheese, since makers often group wheels according to rinds or recipes, and cheese shops generally arrange their selections by texture. In this book, we'll roam from milky fresh cheeses to aged (hard) cheeses, and to keep navigation simple I've used easy-to-identify cheeses as markers, like Cheddars and blues. The large category of Soft-Ripened Cheeses includes triple crèmes and gooey goat rounds.

The eight chapters ahead are a tour of different cheese styles. We'll roam from milky fresh cheeses to aged (hard) cheeses.

To start each expedition, I'll guide you through a little history, point out common tastes and textures, offer tips for using this style in the kitchen, plus roll out an itinerary of cheeses for you to try with drinks and accompaniments. Use the illustrated boards to host a cheese adventure night around your table that explores one style all at once, or meander through an adventure over the course of a month and make time for some detours (i.e., other cheeses that pair well). If you're on a budget or flying solo, scale back. You can definitely have a cheese romp even if it's just with one really good morsel. Or just buy very small hunks.

Whether you're an experienced trekker with a daredevil attitude or a slow-moving, stop-and-smell-the-robiolas kind of rambler, you're going to develop a new appreciation for cheese and discover at least one wheel that takes your taste buds to new heights.

CHOOSE YOUR OWN CHEESE ADVENTURE

Not sure how to tackle the next sections of the book? Here are a few options for planning your approach, depending on the kind of experience you're looking for.

THRILL SEEKER: Explore each style by building the entire cheese board in each adventure and going wild with all the recommended accompaniments.

JUST CURIOUS: Try a couple of cheeses in each chapter, along with a detour cheese so there's a little more variety. Sprinkle some accompaniments around the edge.

ON A BUDGET: Pick one cheese, one drink, and one condiment, and enjoy a splurge-y snack all week.

MAKING THE MOST OF THESE TRIPS
- Shopping for cheese—page 190
- Building boards—page 210
- Lexicon of tasting terms—page 229

ADVENTURE

№

1

Skydive into

FRESH
CHEESE

GETTING ORIENTED

Grab your parachutes and prepare to enter some high-moisture territory. Picture yourself dropping through clouds of feathery ricotta toward a vast horizon of mozzarella balls bobbing in an ocean. During your descent into this environment, you will smell cooked milk and salt water, which is pretty much what fresh cheeses are. They taste best right after they have been made, so put your cameras away, prepare for a soft landing, and get ready to plunge in with your spoons.

WHAT TO KNOW

Pretty much all cheeses without rinds are fresh cheeses. They are new looking, usually glistening and enticingly plush. Think burrata, ricotta, fromage blanc, chèvre, cottage cheese, cream cheese—all of these are either scoopy or spreadably soft. Among your rindless wanderings, however, you'll also find fresh cheeses that are dry and crumbly, like queso fresco, or even brined, like feta. (Cleverly, the Greeks stored feta in barrels of seawater to preserve its freshness. It's essentially a pickled cheese.) If you're keen to explore the world of fresh cheeses in a deep way, know that there are hundreds of varieties that have evolved over centuries. Remember: Fresh cheeses are the original style of cheese (need to revisit your cheese history on page 14?), and many cultures have at least one iconic freshie that is woven into their national identity, from Indian paneer to Italian mozzarella to Halloumi from the island nation of Cyprus.

If you've ever stood in a garden devouring a still-warm tomato, you know the pleasure of eating at the source. Same goes for fresh cheeses.

Why are there are so many? These tend to be easy cheeses to make, and they require little to no aging, so they go from udder to eater within days. That's a real boon for cheesemakers who might not have the storage space to hold cheeses for months or years.

WHERE TO FIND
THE BEST FRESHIES

If you've ever stood in a garden devouring a still-warm tomato, you know the pleasure of eating at the source; the taste of a refrigerated tomato from the grocery store just isn't the same. Same goes for fresh cheeses. When you're exploring this style, try to drop in on a place where exploring them are made: a cheese shop with a mozzarella bar where you can see a cheesemonger stretch and shape steaming hot curds, a farmstand at a creamery, or even a farmers market where cheesemakers often bring homemade cheese spreads or fresh cheese curds. Yes, those are fresh cheeses that have likely just been made that morning or the day before! Sure, supermarkets carry fresh cheeses, too, and those can be delicious, but they'll never be as amazing as diving right into a dish of still-warm sheep's milk ricotta in, say, rural Italy, where locals buy it fresh from the farm and the tiny curds are so pillowy, they melt the moment they hit your tongue. To eat fresh cheeses from pasture-raised animals in the environment where the cheese is made . . . that is a transportive experience—one I will tell you all about in my travel notes (see Grate Escape, page 54).

Fresh cheeses can be made from any milk, and the real key to identifying quality is looking for a clean, milky taste. They should never taste sour or like plastic—a sign that they are poor quality or that they have been sitting in shrink wrap for waaayyy too long. For example, if you find yourself frowning when you bite into an overly tangy goat cheese log from the supermarket that has been vacuum sealed like a cured sausage, you're not eating chèvre—the French word for goat cheese—as it was intended. Make a note to taste some fresh goat cheese at a farmers market, or go straight to France in spring and ogle the incredible range of fresh goat cheeses—shaped into teardrops, flowers, crosses, and even

Fresh cheeses can be made from any milk, and the real key to identifying quality is looking for a clean, milky taste.

Easter lambs. You'll take one bite of that clean, lightly herbaceous, snow-white freshness and never want to eat another goat cheese log stuffed in a plastic sock again.

ADVENTURE № 1
CHEESE BOARD

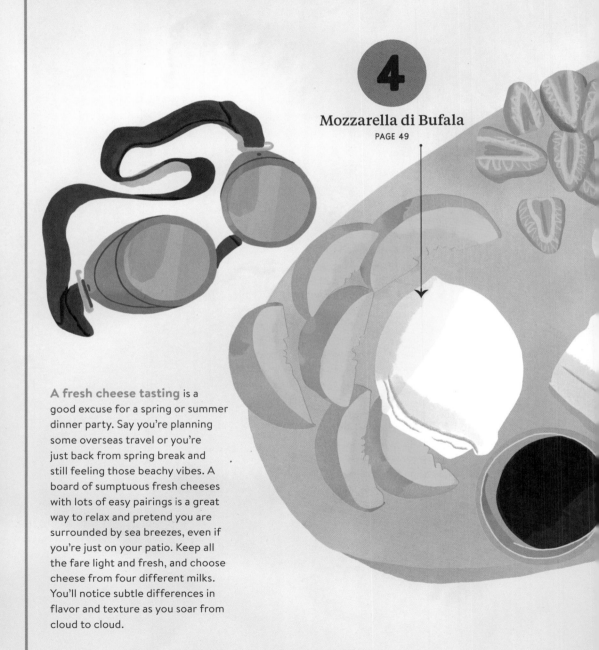

4

Mozzarella di Bufala
PAGE 49

A fresh cheese tasting is a good excuse for a spring or summer dinner party. Say you're planning some overseas travel or you're just back from spring break and still feeling those beachy vibes. A board of sumptuous fresh cheeses with lots of easy pairings is a great way to relax and pretend you are surrounded by sea breezes, even if you're just on your patio. Keep all the fare light and fresh, and choose cheese from four different milks. You'll notice subtle differences in flavor and texture as you soar from cloud to cloud.

3

Sheep's Milk Ricotta
PAGE 49

2

Labneh
PAGE 48

1

Chèvre
PAGE 48

1

FRESH GOAT CHEESE
(chèvre)

2

FRESH COW'S MILK CHEESE
(mascarpone, labneh, or fromage blanc)

Start your board with the lightest of all milks, like a **fresh local goat cheese** log or spread. Some national brands I often recommend: Vermont Creamery, Cypress Grove, Laura Chenel. These are all pioneering companies started by women makers who launched them from farmers markets and car trunks back in the eighties, paving the way for artisan American cheese. If you're already familiar with chèvre, jump into an **ashy French goat cheese** (in the next chapter), like Selles-sur-Cher or Valençay, two classics from France's Loire Valley—an area famous for its plush goat cheeses, but these will have a very thin rind. For your first bite of fresh goat cheese, look for a taste of lemony brightness and perhaps a touch of minerality or the faint taste of herbs. For your second bite, try this cheese with honey or berry jam.

If you crave creaminess, try decadent **mascarpone** from Italy, velvety **Lebanese labneh**, or moussey **fromage blanc**—France's version of cream cheese, basically. Mascarpone is the richest of the three, so if you love a luxurious mouthfeel, this is the soft cheese for you. Try a spoonful of any of these cheeses, and you should notice the taste of fresh cream. Cow's milk doesn't have the tang of goat's milk or the herby notes often found in sheep's milk. It's like the foam on a latte, fluffy with a cooked cream taste. For a transportive bite, slather this cheese on crusty bread and top it with a ribbon of salty prosciutto, a slice of tart peach, and a basil leaf.

FRESH SHEEP'S MILK CHEESE
(sheep's milk ricotta or sheep's milk feta)

If you've never eaten **sheep's milk ricotta**, it's essential that you try it now. You may need to call an Italian cheese shop to find it, or order it online from Bellwether Farms in California—my favorite source. Traditionally, ricotta was made by recooking whey that was left over from cheesemaking earlier in the day (ricotta, in fact, means recooked), and that's how Bellwether Farms still makes it—drained in baskets, just as Italian grandmothers used to do, which gives the cheese its domed shape. Serve it alongside a dish of good olive oil and some sea salt. Or try **Greek sheep's milk feta**—like the exceptional Essex Feta made from sheep on the island of Lesbos. In 2005, the Greeks won a battle to retain ownership of their national cheese, so although feta is made in many other countries—Turkey, France, and Bulgaria, for example—many of these labels now refer to it as marinated sheep cheese.

FRESH BUFFALO MILK CHEESE
(Mozzarella di Bufala)

Authentic **Mozzarella di Bufala** really is made from the milk of water buffalo. These pillowy orbs are usually flown in from buffalo farms in Italy, although there is a fabulous brand from Colombia—another country that raises buffalo—called **BUF**. You'll see it in high-end grocery stores, including Whole Foods. Buffalo milk is mild in flavor and incredibly rich, so you'll notice that the texture is much softer and more supple than cow's milk mozzarella. When you cut into mozzarella, you'll notice that it's made up of threadlike layers, and that's because the curds are stretched to give them a springy texture. Officially, mozzarella is called a a pasta filata cheese, which in Italian means spun paste. All pasta filata cheeses are great for melting because their thready texture turns stringy and gooey when exposed to heat.

Navigating PAIRINGS

Fresh cheeses love other fresh things;
anything sparkling always works, but for
a real surprise try a cup of sencha tea,
which is light and grassy—a perfect pairing.

**Light white
or rosé**

Pilsner

Vodka tonic

Green tea

ACCOMPANIMENTS

Serve this board with a lightly dressed salad and grilled fish,
chicken, or veggie skewers, if you want to make a meal. To play off the
freshness of these cheeses, deck out the board with as much fresh
produce as possible, along with anything drizzle-able.

- Honey
- Olive oil and aged balsamic vinegar
- Berries and peaches
- Fresh tomatoes or melon
- Herbs, such as fresh basil and thyme
- Ribbony cured meats, such as prosciutto or speck
- A dish of pistachios

Possible DETOURS

If you want to sightsee with a couple of aged cheeses for texture, expand your fresh cheese tour to include a craggy hunk of **Parmigiano-Reggiano.** It will pair beautifully with the honey and aged balsamic, and its crystalline paste will provide you with summer fireworks of a sort. Then add a point of interest, like a **wine-marinated cheese,** such as **Ubriaco,** or a **truffled Pecorino.**

OFF THE
BEATEN
PATH

BREAD CHEESE

If you like pizza, you may love this toasty, chewy Finnish specialty that was originally made with reindeer milk. Known in Finland as juustoleipä or leipäjuusto (which roughly translates to bread cheese), this fresh cheese was dried for easy storage, then warmed over a fire to soften it. Today, several American makers produce versions made with cow's milk, including Carr Valley and Brunkow Cheese in Wisconsin; the makers take fresh cheese curds, press and dry them in slabs, then broil them in a hot oven. What you see in the store looks like a piece of French toast, and it can be eaten in much the same way, with maple syrup or jam. Bread cheese doesn't contain any bread, so it's touted as a good gluten-free pizza base—just top with red sauce and fixings, and the cheese forms your crust.

TIPS FOR EXPLORING

* IN THE KITCHEN *

Spoon 'em, schmear 'em, crumble 'em, grill 'em. It all depends on the texture. Most fresh cheeses are mild in taste, so there are countless ways to explore them on picnics, on your patio, or on a breakfast plate. Try a different fresh cheese every week, and you'll soon know this terrain well. Here are some of my favorite ways to explore fresh cheese on the daily.

↓

Make a CREAMY LABNEH BOWL

↓

Use fresh cheese AS A DIP

Labneh, a Lebanese cream dream, is made by straining and salting yogurt (sometimes a small amount of rennet is added to thicken it). It's especially good as the base of a breakfast bowl, topped with fruit, chopped dates, nuts, mint, and honey. Or, slather a thin layer of this creamy fresh cheese into a salad bowl before adding greens and veg. Simply dress the salad with olive oil and fresh lemon juice. The creamy bottom layer will form the rest of the dressing.

Fresh cheeses love other fresh ingredients, like herbs from your garden and a liberal pinch of lemon zest. For a super-fresh-tasting dip to serve on a tray with fresh veggies and potato chips, fill a bowl with fresh ricotta, labneh, or chèvre, then drizzle it with extra virgin olive oil and sprinkle it with chopped herbs, citrus zest, and a pinch of salt. You can mash the ricotta mixture together with a fork or just offer it up as a mountain of goodness—which is what I like to do.

Bake or grill
SOLID FRESH CHEESES

For a vegetarian appetizer or main course, you can use blocky feta, Halloumi, or paneer to make a glorious treat. For baked feta, add a block of it to a baking pan and drizzle it with plenty of olive oil, add some fresh or dried herbs, like thyme or rosemary, and bake at 350°F (177°C) until the edges brown. Serve this with roasted red peppers, olives, and toasted baguette rounds for a quick happy hour. For the grill, you can brush a rectangle of Halloumi or paneer with olive oil and grill it like fish, alongside lemon halves and skewers of zucchini, cherry tomatoes, and onions. The cheese will get grill marks and turn crispy on the outside, oozy on the inside. It's a thousand times more decadent than grilled tofu.

Smoothie
IT UP

To add protein and body to a shake or fruit smoothie, try using a scoop of soft cheese. I often use quark, a dairy powerhouse I learned to love in Germany (quark has fourteen grams of protein per hundred-gram serving, compared with yogurt's four grams). For a quark shake, blend one large frozen banana, half a cup of quark, plus a pinch of cinnamon and nutmeg. Puree it until smooth, and you'll have a delicious treat.

Squeaky Cheese Curds

If you visit a farmers market or county fair in Wisconsin, make sure you buy a bag of fresh cheese curds, a state specialty. Curds are the building blocks of cheese, and when they are less than a day old, the casein network—or protein network in cheese—is springy and porous, so trapped air lets out a squeaking sound when you bite down. After about a day, the casein network knits together more tightly, becoming compact, so the curds lose their delightful squeak.

GRATE ESCAPE

My First Cheese Adventure
CHASING RICOTTA IN PUGLIA

If you dream of learning to make real ricotta in a field of figs with a little old man

who will hand you a spoonful of still-warm curds with a smile as wide as Italy, plan

a trip to Puglia—the country's boot heel, which is mostly farmland. No, it doesn't

seem like you should have to travel to understand such a simple, simple cheese,

but trust me. You'll learn how to pronounce it ("reeeeekot-tah!"—roll your *R* and

spit your *T*), and you'll taste it so often, you'll become a connoisseur. After that,

you'll never buy a tub of wallpaper-paste-like ricotta again. Because in Puglia, fresh

cheeses like ricotta and burrata are made every day and sold in the village cheese

shops, and locals would never deign to eat anything but the most perfect versions, which are supple and herbaceous, thanks to the diversity of wild

herbs and grasses that grow in the area's centuries-old pastures.

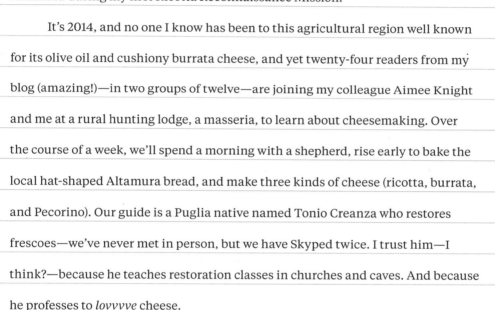

The smell of fresh thyme. Sheep grazing around stone

ruins. These are the things I notice driving through the Italian

countryside from the harbor city of Bari to the small town of

Altamura during my first Ricotta Reconnaissance Mission.

It's 2014, and no one I know has been to this agricultural region well known

for its olive oil and cushiony burrata cheese, and yet twenty-four readers from my

blog (amazing!)—in two groups of twelve—are joining my colleague Aimee Knight

and me at a rural hunting lodge, a masseria, to learn about cheesemaking. Over

the course of a week, we'll spend a morning with a shepherd, rise early to bake the

local hat-shaped Altamura bread, and make three kinds of cheese (ricotta, burrata,

and Pecorino). Our guide is a Puglia native named Tonio Creanza who restores

frescoes—we've never met in person, but we have Skyped twice. I trust him—I

think?—because he teaches restoration classes in churches and caves. And because

he professes to *lovvvve* cheese.

Still, I'm nervous when he picks us up in a rickety van, a suntanned man with

silvery stubble, his poet's shirt half open. He's friendly and relaxed, but so nonchalant

that he arrives at the airport without any signage to flag our group and just stands

by the doorway with his cowskin shoulder bag until we ask him, "Are *you* our host?"

"Sure," he says, shrugging. "I'm Tonio. I knew you'd find me."

It's just past sunset when Tonio's van rumbles through a wrought-iron gate

and stops before a dark structure that looks like the wing of a bombed-out castle.

The exterior is weather-beaten, unadorned except for an enormous rusty bell that looks like a broken wedding-cake topper. Our tired crew slips wordlessly out of the van, and we roll our suitcases across the dry grass toward a pair of large double doors. No porch lights. No lit windows. I feel an itch in the back of my throat as I wonder if I'm about to lead my readers (many of them strangers) into a situation we will all regret.

Then, we push through the large double doors into the entryway, and just past a basket full of walking sticks and a set of bull horns, I see a second chamber with a candlelit table covered with bowls and platters. A cheese table, all laid out for the evening! Two long-haired women wearing headscarves are carrying baskets of bread in from the kitchen. When they see us, they smile broadly and wave.

"Formaggio! Formaggio!" they call to us, laughing. "Cheese! Cheese!"

I'm pretty sure we are the first cheese tourists to grace this hall. The women peer at us delighted, then slip away to the kitchen, leaving us in a glowing room surrounded by heavenly cheeses from surrounding farms. There are long braids of mozzarella, rounds of burrata filled with billowy cream, triangles of ivory Pecorino that are soft and pliable, and jars of an unusual fermented cheese so acrid it makes our mouths go dry, except that it tastes delicious slathered on hot anchovy fritters. And there is ricotta. Sheep's milk ricotta, freshly made that morning from the milk of the sheep down the road—the ones that the shepherd tends. Yes, Tonio tells us, trailing into the room, it's the same shepherd we'll meet in a few days.

The ricotta before us looks unlike anything I have seen. It's plated like a beautiful pudding, and its surface looks woven. Someone has slipped it out of a round form and decorated it with fresh herbs and small purple flowers. It's "basket ricotta," we learn, which is still made locally in real baskets made from woven reeds. Today, most Italians make ricotta in plastic forms, but Tonio has seen to it that we're greeted with real basket ricotta, made the old way. In a few days, he will take us to meet an old man who still makes ricotta in a copper cauldron over a fire. Instead of purchasing rennet, he'll walk up to a fig tree, withdraw his pocketknife, and cut off a branch. An oozy white sap inside the fig branch will coagulate the milk—to our amazement, he'll toss the entire branch (leaves and all) into the hot cauldron, so that the fleecy liquid turns to curds and whey. The old man, wearing high-waisted pants and a billowy rayon shirt, will ladle soft hot curds right into our palms, then grin toothlessly as we marvel at the fresh taste. And how pillowy it is.

It will take me all week to find the right word to describe that ricotta.

When I close my eyes during the last meal of our stay, a vision finally fills my mind as I taste it. By request, we are eating ricotta for dinner, again. Tonight, I savor it. I want to paint it on the inside of my mind. As I hold the tiny curds on my tongue, a vision drops down: a cloud full of tiny, cool rain droplets.

That's what it feels like to eat fresh sheep's milk at Tonio's masseria in Puglia: like pressing a cloud to the roof of my mouth and feeling individual raindrops inside. Eating ricotta will never be the same, I tell Tonio, who is sitting next to me, drinking wine by candlelight and beginning to warm up on his guitar, which he plays late into the evening. I will always equate Puglia with a mouthful of sweet summer rain.

ADVENTURE

Nº

2

SOFT-
RIPENED

Safari

GETTING ORIENTED

Okay, explorers, we're headed into a field of soft-ripened cheeses. Expect to see downy Brie and Camembert, some very moussey triple crèmes, and packs of wrinkly-rind French goat cheeses. This trek is all about identifying the lushest, plushest cheeses on the planet, plus you're going to learn about their coats (aka surface molds) and why some of these creatures turn colors and form stripes as they age, or express rumpled features. Yes, I will help you overcome your phobia of furry rinds. If you're lucky, you'll also see some robiolas aged in leaves.

WHAT TO KNOW

Everyone loves a soft-ripened cheese. They tend to be gooey, oozy, decadent, and just a little wild—at least on the surface. In this category, there are two rind styles to look out for: velvety white "bloomy" cheeses and wrinkly-rind cheeses that come in shades of white, off-white, or koala-bear gray.

> In this category, there are two rind styles to look out for: velvety white "bloomy" cheeses and wrinkly-rind cheeses.

BLOOMY-RIND CHEESES

What exactly is a bloomy rind? I like to explain it as a very thin carpet of little mushrooms—fungus would be the appropriate term for this culture, but mushrooms sound a little more palatable, right? To make cheeses like Brie and Camembert, cheesemakers typically stir freeze-dried spores of either *Penicillium candidum* or *Penicillium camemberti* into a vat of milk during the cheesemaking process. Once the cheese is formed into wheels and set on boards to mature for a couple of weeks in a cheese cave, the spores literally bloom.

If you ever get to peer into an aging cave full of bloomy cheeses, you'll see dozens of moonish rounds covered in feathery fluff. The bloom can grow several inches tall, so cheesemakers rub the rinds to keep the bloom from going totally wild. Tamping down the bloom on these cheeses creates their plush, velvet-antler-like surfaces.

WRINKLY-RIND CHEESES

If you come across a bloomy cheese with wrinkles, a cheesemaker has likely added *Geotrichum candidum*, yet another mycological delight, to their cheese vat. Geo cheeses or brainy cheeses, as you'll often hear them called, have a crinkly

brainlike look. If you peer into a cheese cave to watch these rinds form, you may see them puffed up like little balloons. I was amazed to see this process in action during a visit to Vermont Creamery, when cheesemaker Allison Hooper showed me her aging cave. Her little geotrichum-rinded goat cheeses, called Coupole, were all puffed up on trays, much like bread dough rising; when they collapsed, the surface took on a rumpled texture, a bit like the skin on a rhinoceros.

Geotrichum is often used for goat cheeses and mixed-milk cheeses. Sometimes a dash of ash is sprinkled on the surface right after these cheeses are formed, a touch that encourages rind growth. Once the surface develops, the ash appears like a soft silver coat. Is this kind of rind edible? By now you know: of course. To me, these rinds smell and taste a bit like a yeast doughnut.

Should I eat a bloomy rind?

Yes! The rinds on cheeses like Brie and Camembert are usually the most flavorful part of these cream bombs, and cheesemakers take great pride in them. When you taste a bloomy cheese, the paste will often taste grassy and mushroomy. Try the rind separately next time you're on a Brie spree, and you'll notice it tastes peppery, like black pepper. When you eat the two together, it almost tastes like eating sautéed mushrooms. In fact, sautéed mushrooms of any kind are a great pairing for these cheeses. Just slather the cheeses on bread and top them with sautéed 'shrooms and fresh herbs. Add a glass of Champagne, and you'll be transported.

Fun fact: Most of the calcium in bloomy-style cheeses migrates to the rind. So, please eat it—the rind is part of this cheese's deliciousness and nutrition.

TRIPLE CRÈMES

Bloomy rind cheese with extra cream stirred into the vat yields a special species of moussey deluxe-ness. If you've ever been in the presence of Saint Angel, from France, or St. Stephen, from New York State, you've probably found them irresistible. These are the gazelles of a cheese case, furry and soft, the epitome of elegance.

FUN FACT: A triple crème is labeled 75 percent fat, but that industry measurement is for its dry weight only (a measure of its solids, once you take out the moisture). So, a triple crème is not as fattening as it sounds. In fact, hard cheeses are much higher in fat. So go bombs away on soft cheese!

SEE STRIPES? IT'S RIPE.

Luscious cheeses are creamy, and for the most part they'll get creamier over time. In fact, they "ripen" just like bananas do, darkening along the edges. When you see beige lines form on the surface of a Brie and the edges turn slightly brown, that's a sign of ripeness. A ripe, luscious cheese is a wonderful thing, but if the edges get very brown and the cheese starts to smell strongly of ammonia, the cheese may be overripe. If the smell of ammonia dissipates, try the cheese. It may be perfect. If the ammonia smell remains strong, the cheese may not be good to eat. A little taste will tell you for sure.

LOOK FOR LEAF-WRAPPED ROBIOLAS

Many people love Brie, and you can thank Charlemagne—the medieval emperor who ruled much of Western Europe from 768 to 814—for that (he ordered many for his court and made Brie a royally beloved cheese for centuries). But if you want to broaden your horizons, look for a robiola.

The Italians are the masters of this decadent softie. Also, if you're not a rind queen, this may be the cheese for you, because robiolas tend to have veil-thin white rinds you can almost see through, and their centers are wickedly sumptuous. Robiolas are so delicate that they're sometimes wrapped in leaves—fig leaves, chestnut leaves, even cabbage leaves—to keep the rind from splitting (a genius no-waste hack), but the leaf wrap also imparts delicate flavor.

My favorite is Robiola la Rossa, a small earthy-tasting bundle wrapped in cherry leaves. "It brings happiness," as a cheesemonger once posted on Instagram for Bedford Cheese Shop in Brooklyn.

To explore robiola, you could start with La Tur, an easy-to-spot example in most cheese shops, or crane your neck a little farther on this safari and try to find Robiola di Roccaverano, an ancient goat cheese from northern Italy's Piedmont region that likely dates back twelve hundred years, to the Arab invasions when goats were introduced to the area. Robiola di Roccaverano is now a heritage cheese recognized by Slow Food.

HOW TO TELL BRIE FROM CAMEMBERT

Many people get flummoxed when pressed to distinguish a Brie from a Camembert. Keep in mind, they have similar markings, but Brie is much older (the recipe dates back to the 700s) and is associated with villages around Paris where it's made: Brie de Meaux (from the village of Meaux) and Brie de Melun (from the village of Melun) are both name protected. Anything else called a Brie can be, well, made anywhere. Camembert evolved much later, in the 1700s, near the village of Camembert in Normandy. Traditionally, Camembert is made in a smaller format and sold in a little wooden box, one of the things that made it so popular—it was easy to ship, and the boxes were often decorated with cherubic milkmaids. At the Camembert Museum in Normandy, France, you can see a historic display of cheese boxes. Camembert de Normandie is name protected and must be made in Normandy using the raw milk of local cows.

ADVENTURE № 2
CHEESE BOARD

3

Triple crème
PAGE 67

If you need an excuse to drink
bubbly—a birthday, an anniversary,
a sexy brunch—break out the soft
cheeses. You could make this a Paris
send-off as you plan a honeymoon,
say, and lean heavily on French
bloomies (suggestions ahead!),
or you could use this opportunity
to focus on American creamies,
as many makers produce jaw-
droppingly good cheeses in this
style. For this board, I've offered
a mix of the two.

4

Robiola
PAGE 67

2

Brie
PAGE 66

1

Valençay
PAGE 66

1

WRINKLY-RIND CHEESE

*(Valençay, Selles-sur-Cher,
Coupole, Sofia)*

Start your board with a classic rumpled French goat cheese, such as **Valençay** or **Selles-sur-Cher**, from France's Loire Valley—an area famous for its plush goat cheeses in this style. The ash encourages a bridal-veil-like rind to form around the surface, adding a layer of silky texture to an already silky cheese. Ash also helps neutralize the acidity (think yogurty-ness) of goat's milk. For an un-ashed American version, try Vermont Creamery's **Coupole**, a soft cheese that looks like a scoop of melting vanilla ice cream, or for one of the most elegant goat cheeses you'll ever see on a board, try Capriole Farm's **Sofia**, a splendid ice-white bar bisected with stripes of ash. Call it the "zebra of a cheese." Any of these goat's milk selections are stellar with a hunk of honeycomb, berries, or, for a superlative combo, rose petal jam.

2

CLASSIC FRENCH BLOOMY-RIND CHEESE

(Brie fermier, Camembert d'Isigny)

France's **Brie de Meaux** and **Camembert de Normandie** are the classics in this category, but you won't find them Stateside, since these young honeys must be made with raw milk (the sixty-day law in the United States prohibits importing them). For the best French Brie available in the United States, look for **Brie fermier**—or farmstead Brie. Although the milk will be pasteurized, the fermier label means that the cheese is made on a farm, rather than in a factory, so the milk is usually of better quality. Note that you may also find bloomy cheeses made by makers in your area—always worth exploring. Now for Camembert: Since authentic Camembert de Normandie must be made with raw milk from special French cows in the Normandy region, your best bet for a French import is the **Isigny Sainte-Mère** brand, available at many supermarkets.

3
TRIPLE CRÈME
(Délice de Bourgogne,
Crémeux des Citeaux, Kunik)

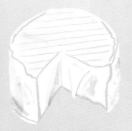

4
ROBIOLA
(Robiola la Rossa, Robiola Tre Latti,
Rocket's Robiola)

Consider **Délice** (day-LEESE) the ultimate party cheese. Although it's an industrially produced cheese made just outside Paris, it's one of the best easy-to-source French triple crèmes you can find at a cheese shop or grocery dairy case. It looks like a cheesecake, and it has a whipped consistency that makes grown men swoon. Trust me, you will purr. For a cheesemonger favorite, try **Crémeux** (Krem-OH), a triple crème made at a small creamery in Burgundy, France, then sent to star affineur Rodolphe Le Meunier, who ages these rounds under his careful watch. From the Adirondacks, there's also **Kunik** (rhymes with *tunic*), a mixed-milk triple crème named after the Inuit word for nuzzling noses.

It can be challenging to find a leaf-wrapped robiola—they're the wildebeests of the soft cheese realm—but if you can find one, such as the rare **Robiola la Rossa** wrapped in cherry leaves, you will be moved to tears. Your best bet is to call around to cheese shops that carry special imports. No luck? Ask instead for the wonderful **Robiola Tre Latti** made with three milks (goat, cow, sheep). This is a splendid cheese, and you really can taste all three milks—a tart flicker of goat's milk, sweet cow's milk, and herbaceous sheep's milk. See if you can find all of these notes as you taste at the table. For a fun variation made Stateside, look for **Rocket's Robiola** from Boxcarr Handmade Cheese, a brother-sister creamery in North Carolina; this velvety silver square has a rumpled ashy surface and looks like something you'd serve a rock star.

Navigating PAIRINGS

Break out your Champagne, Cava, Prosecco, or
sparkling rosé. These cheeses were made for palate-cleansing
bubbles. Fruited beers or a simple pilsner can also be fun.
For brunch or a festive occasion, a French 75 cocktail made
with lemon, gin, and bubbly is the ideal beverage.

Bubbly

Pilsner

**Gin
(French 75)**

**Sparkling
water**

ACCOMPANIMENTS

To offset your board's creaminess, stage it with plenty of fresh fruit and
jams or jellies. In fact, this is an excellent moment to raid your pantry or ask friends
to bring homemade preserves, especially any made with berries, stone fruit,
or flowers (rose petal and lavender are terrific with goat cheeses, and, randomly,
so is lemon curd). A hunk of honeycomb—literally honey inside beeswax—looks
beautiful on this board, and you can eat the entire thing. I love how the wax adds
texture. If you serve food, make a crunchy salad with some endive and a cold
soup. Then don't be surprised if your tasting mates huddle around your table like
animals at a watering hole; this is one helluva feast.

- Honeycomb
- Raspberries, strawberries,
  figs, grapes
- Rose petal jam or berry jam

- Walnuts
- Baguette and fruited bread
- Saucisson sec or other
  dried salami

Possible DETOURS

Want to add a little more visual interest to this landscape? Snag a bark-wrapped wheel of **Harbison** from Jasper Hill Farm—it's a bloomy cheese from Vermont with a wonderful dark, woodsy note from its spruce girdle. To stay lush but expand in style, run wild with salty, sheepy French **Roquefort** or with **Red Hawk**, a funky triple crème from Cowgirl Creamery in California. There, you've just added a salty blue and a stink bomb!

Fujiyama

You might be surprised to learn that there are more than two hundred cheesemakers in Japan, something I learned from a young American-born Tokyo-based cheesemonger named Malory Lane at a cheese conference in Pittsburgh, after I spotted her in a hotel lobby toting a small refrigerated cheese case that looked like a cat carrier. Inside was a menagerie of delicate Japanese cheeses, each one more beautiful than the last, including a goat cheese shaped like Mount Fuji with a bloomy white peak and an ashy base. Fujiyama is made by one of the most famous cheesemakers in Japan, Hiroshima-based Masanori Matsubara of Mirasaka Fromage, who makes iconic goat's milk and cow's milk cheeses inspired by the season. (He's also well known for a russet stinker in the shape of a persimmon.) To taste Fujiyama, you'll have to visit one of Tokyo's fine cheese shops, or seek out Malory Lane at japancheese.com.

TIPS FOR EXPLORING

* IN THE KITCHEN *

Softies are ideal for entertaining, but they're also terrific personal cheeses, because many of them are the size of a cupcake or saucer. Buy one every other week or so, and even if you live alone, you won't get bored as long you vary the pairings. Luckily, these cheeses are on the mild side, especially when they're young, so you can literally slip a wedge into any situation, from a bite at first light to a soft cheese nightcap.

Breakfast WITH YOUNG BRIE

Lunch IN THE PARK

Stuff a few slices into an egg dish, like an omelet or quiche, along with sautéed mushrooms, asparagus, and fresh chives. Or serve it with lox and bagels in place of cream cheese. Or (stop me now!) slather any of these soft cheeses on toast and top it with berry jam.

Spread your softie on a sandwich— I like a bloomy cheese tucked into a crisp baguette with sliced green apples, toasted walnuts, a crank of black pepper, and a drizzle of light-colored honey. Bam, done!

Bake or grill
A CAMEMBERT
FOR DINNER

Heat your oven to 300°F (149°C), and drop your cheese into a small oven-safe dish (such as a pie plate or small crock). Bake it for about twenty minutes, or until the center of the cheese feels soft to the touch, then top it with toasted slivered almonds, and serve fig jam on the side. This is great with baguette rounds and celery sticks. On the grill: Set a bloomy round into a cast-iron pan and warm that sucker up for your friends over medium heat, just until it starts to ooze. If you toast some bread on the grill, along with a skewer of fresh figs brushed with olive oil, then set out some honey and rosemary sprigs for garnish, no one at your party will ever forget you.

Use a
Cheese Dome
TO PLAY AFFINEUR

If you find a bloomy cheese that's unripe—say, the surface is very white without any beige stripes and the center is firm to the touch—you can age it yourself by setting it under a cheese dome. It works just like a humidor. The best ones have a marble base, which keeps a cheese cool. For a hack, you can always use a dinner plate and cover it with a glass bowl. Unwrap your soft cheese, cover it with the dome, and let it rest on your counter for a day before you serve it. It will age quickly, so keep an eye on it, and make sure the temperature in your house is below 70°F (21°C) so it doesn't spoil. If you feel nervous leaving cheese out, you can also set the whole dome in your fridge—it will just take a day or two longer. You'll see humidity inside the glass, creating a cavelike environment. If condensation builds up and you can't see the cheese, wipe down the inside with a paper towel so the cheese doesn't get wet. Flip the cheese every day so it matures evenly. See, you're a home affineur!

GRATE ESCAPE

How to
BRIE IN PARIS

To immerse yourself in wild rinds, you should come with me to Paris. We'll go in spring. Last time I was there, it happened to be Fashion Week, and the clothes on the street hardly rivaled what I was seeing in cheese shops, such as Chez Virginie, run by an affineuse known for her small-batch goat cheeses that she displays in her window amid tufts of blossoming rosemary. Popping inside her tiny Montmartre location was like flittering into a fairy warren. I expected the rustle of wings, but instead there was Virginie herself, who was a little brusque at first but then warm once I mentioned I was in Paris for the sole purpose of traipsing to a different cheese shop every day.

Then there was Fromagerie Laurent Dubois, where sparkling selections are displayed in glass cases like jewelry, a veritable Tiffany's of fine cheese. Next to the Saint-Germain location, you can eat a croissant made with exquisite French butter and drink a noisette—an espresso with a drop of foam the size of a hazelnut. Here, I rendezvoused with a wine-and-cheese blogger named Veronica, who had built an impressive career around food tours and cheese curation. She agreed to take me to her favorite shop, and in exchange I offered to buy as much cheese as she and any of her friends could possibly eat in an afternoon. We made sixteen purchases.

Afterward, she graciously invited me back to her flat for a feast with her French bulldog and a few chatty cheese-loving expats for what will live on in my mind as perhaps the best afternoon of my life. Champagne, crusty bread, preserves galore, and sixteen cheeses that we ate one by one while making copious tasting notes. It was an all-day affair, and I still think of Veronica as The Person Who Baptized Me with Real French Brie, because in addition to the sixteen cheeses I bought, she presented a platter of five different village Bries from a recent junket she'd taken. It included a unicorn cheese, one I had only ever read about: Brie Noir. And yes, it really is black Brie. What makes it black? It's aged beyond peak ripeness until it turns into something resembling petrified caramel, which, I'd been told, was best enjoyed dipped in coffee.

Shall I keep going? During my Paris pilgrimage, I hit eight different fromageries, which I learned is approximately one-tenth of the total number of Paris cheese shops. One industry professional told me there were at least a hundred. I'm going to hazard that Paris has more cheese shops than any city in the world, a detail I would expect the French to tout in tourist guides, and yet they don't. Perhaps they don't find the number surprising. Or they may just want to keep it secret so they can enjoy the country's more than 1,500 cheeses themselves.

If you go—and you really must—here are my recommendations for a few favorite shops, along with some not-to-miss French cheeses you won't find Stateside.

FROMAGERIE LAURENT DUBOIS Laurent Dubois, perhaps the city's most renowned cheesemonger, owns four shops where he famously displays layer cakes of Roquefort and quince paste, birds'-nest-like triple crèmes stuffed with glistening cherries, and a hundred-day Saint Maure de Touraine—a beloved French goat log with a straw running through it, which he cave-ages longer than other affineurs to bring out unusual flavors. If you buy a log, slice it penny-thin, and savor each round like a Communion wafer.

CHEZ VIRGINIE At this raw-milk enclave in Montmartre, you won't find many pasteurized cheeses—just beautiful hand-selected wheels in the shadow of the Sacré-Coeur. (*Note:* There are three locations, all very close to one another.) Virginie is a third-generation affineur who learned the art of selecting and aging cheese from her father and prides herself in building relationships with small makers. Her original location at 54 rue Damrémont has been a fromagerie for more than a century, and it's charming. In spring, the front window looks like a bonsai garden of goat cheeses topped with rosemary sprigs and strewn with flower petals. Go to Chez Virginie if you want to bliss out in cheese fairyland.

FROMAGERIE NICOLE BARTHÉLÉMY Run by the revered Madame Nicole Barthélémy, this quintessential Parisian cheese shop in the Saint-Germain neighborhood has an incredible selection, if slightly brisk service. So, do brush up on your French and offer a "Bonjour, Madame," at the very least. Don't be alarmed if you knock elbows with Catherine Deneuve or the prime minister of France alongside the towering pyramids of cheese. This shop is reputedly the preferred celebrity cheese haunt. Just around the corner you'll find Beaupassage, a modern allée of gastronomy and a wonderful open-air space for grabbing a bite or offering a few sun salutations.

The New Counter-Free Cheese Shop

In addition to long-standing cheese shops that ooze old-world charm, you'll find a number of small, sleek shops that embody a new French spirit. These spaces stand out for their counter-less design, where cheesemongers are free to roam rather than anchor themselves behind a cheese display. Susan Sturman, who leads Paris cheese shop tours for industry professionals from around the world, explained, "Behind a counter, you're in a position of dominance, working as the expert." In the new style of shop, she says, "You're with the customer, sharing the experience. It's very validating." Sturman points out that this style of selling is more inclusive and also a better use of space, since Paris rents are high. Taka & Vermo (see page 76) is a great example. Longtime brands Androuët and Fromagerie Laurent Dubois have followed suit at some of their outposts. You'll notice how different it feels to be approached and guided through a shop by a cheese docent, instead of waiting at a counter to be helped. Also, don't expect samples! As Sturman explains, "There's no sampling, because if a French person is offered a sample, they feel obliged to buy it."

How to Pick a Cheese-Perfect Baguette

Because no French cheese experience is complete without one, make sure you look for a "baguette tradition." This indicates that it's hand-rolled (notice the pointy ends!) and made with just the four basic ingredients (wheat flour, water, salt, and yeast). No additives. A commercially produced baguette is a "baguette ordinaire" and has uniformly round ends. If you are really on a baguette quest, there's an annual award for the best (the Grand Prix de la Baguette), and winning bakeries will note this on their storefronts. Look for the words *Prix de Pain*.

TAKA & VERMO Surrounded by kabob shops in the tenth arrondissement, Taka & Vermo is a hipstery zendo the size of a shipping container, tucked into a graffiti wall. Inside, you'll find shelves of exquisitely maintained cheese neatly set out on trays like a buffet of bar cookies—from oozy, ashy goat cheeses like Saint Clément, to Brie stuffed with honey and almonds, to little rounds of Belval aux Fleurs—a monastic cheese rolled in hot pink and purple petals. For picnickers, there's a well-curated selection of crackers, jams, and wines. Be sure to reach for a sundae cup of Fontainebleau Ardéchois, a traditional whipped cream cheese with chestnut mousse, the favorite dessert of Paris superblogger Lindsey Tramuta (Lostincheeseland.com).

ANDROUËT This shop is notable for being the first to source cheese from around France and bring it to the city. It is, in a sense, the original French cheese shop, founded by cheese visionary Henri Androuët in 1909. The business has changed hands a number of times (it was once owned by Air France), but it's been resurrected to fabulousness with locations across the city and beyond. I was impressed that the small shop on rue Mouffetard featured a list of seasonal selections handwritten on the front window. Inside, the mongers were friendly, and they offered bottles of biodynamic wine to pair. Pick up a hunk of Tomme au Foin, a beautiful firm cow's milk cheese aged in hay, and a half-moon of the ultra-rich triple crème Brillat Savarin layered with shaved truffles.

LA LAITERIE DE PARIS Make a pilgrimage to this urban creamery in the eighteenth arrondissement early in your trip so you can stock your minifridge with the city's best yogurt. It's runny in style and without any kicky acidity—just milky bliss blended with seasonal flavors like fig and wild strawberry. Run by Pierre Coulon, a goat breeder who spent a decade working in cheese shops and running his own goat farm outside the city, La Laiterie purchases the best milk from outside the city and produces yogurt and handmade cheese every damn day. You can peer through the windows right into his production room as you moon over beautiful wheels made and aged right here in the city, from goat cheeses stippled with fresh shallots and chives to Excelsior, a triple crème made with raw milk and organic cream. Pierre sometimes tops these with roasted hazelnuts. Bonus: The neighborhood is loaded with African textile shops and street-food vendors, plus it's not far from the Sacré-Coeur if you want to pick up some cheese to enjoy on the cathedral steps.

FROMAGERIE HARDOUIN-LANGLET Located inside the vibrant Marché d'Aligre—a neighborhood market open six days a week—this stand within the market's

covered area is the perfect spot to pick up a wide range of cheeses and groceries for the week. Plan to spend the whole morning here. First troll the flea market area for cheese knives and trinkets, snag a crêpe, and load up on produce and fresh dates (you'll see them hanging on branches in many stalls). Then, hit the cheese counter run by Madame and Monsieur Hardouin for a wedge of Saint Nectaire or a gooey Vacherin Mont d'Or in a box, if it's in season. Note that there's a second cheese shop in the market that carries a good selection of craft beer. **TIP**: Before you go, hop online and look up David Lebovitz's blog post (davidlebovitz.com) about this marché. You can follow his itinerary (which I did) and find all sorts of hidden treasures.

SAISONS The charming Mariette and Frédéric, a couple passionate about seasonal cheese, are the friendly faces behind this modern shop in the Marais neighborhood. Here, you'll find beautiful classics, like Vacherin Fribourgeois, sourced from a small maker, alongside wonderful new finds, such as Briquette du Nord, a wrinkly rectangle of goat cheese that is partially dipped in ash for zebra-esque effect. Frédéric, a classical cellist, can often be found warming up for a concert in the corner by the wine selection while Mariette chats with customers. Bonus: Saisons rents out fondue and Raclette equipment and provides kits with all the fixings!

FIVE MUST-TRY SOFT CHEESES

Because people ask me all the time what cheeses they should eat in Paris, here are five decadent raw-milk wonders that you will not find in the United States and that typify the soft cheeses for which the French are known. Pick up a couple and enjoy them on the banks of the Seine, along with a baguette.

1. BRIE DE MEAUX: The classic. Rich and mushroomy, made just outside Paris.

2. BRIE DE MELUN: Similar to Brie de Meaux, but made in the neighboring town of Melun (and often preferred by Parisians).

3. CAMEMBERT DE NORMANDIE: Creamy, with notes of roasted cauliflower. Look for Le Camembert du Champ Secret, one of the last small-batch producers of organic, raw-milk Camembert.

4. COULOMMIERS: Imagine an extra-thick Brie, a veritable cheesecake that is savory, creamy, and utterly irresistible.

5. SAINT NECTAIRE: Imagine a nutty Brie with shag carpet. The furry rind is coveted by the French and tastes like hazelnut.

ADVENTURE

Nº

3

STINKY
CHEESE

Spelunking Tour

GETTING ORIENTED

Fearless ones, grab your galoshes. This trek involves washed rinds. In other words, damp cave environments. You will meet a cave specialist named Olivia on this tour (page 93), and you will get your feet wet, because these cheeses like a sponge bath. As we trek deeper into this scenario, you may want to hold your nose (things are going to get dank), but you probably won't need your headlamp, because these cheeses glow. Well, practically. Washed rinds are easy to spot against dark cave walls because they are vibrant in color, ranging from bioluminescent peach to glowing tangerine. Get your stinko-meters out, because the brighter the rind, the bolder the odor. And taste.

WHAT TO KNOW

Why Stinky Cheeses Are Known as Washed Rinds

Ask any heavy-into-the-scene curd nerd and they will probably tell you that washed rinds are one of their favorite styles of cheese. That's because washed rinds contain so much flavor. And there are so many good ones. They also range in texture from fudgy firmness to runny custard, and when you heat them (gently), they melt beautifully. The secret to all this funky plushness is in the wash itself, which is often a saltwater solution or a combination of brine and booze (beer, wine, spirits, or whatever is local). Applying this wash every few days keeps the paste of the cheese moist and also encourages some friendly orange bacteria to party on the rind.

About That Aroma

The sticky surface bacteria of these whiffy wonders is called *Brevibacterium linens* (*B. linens* for short). Washing the rinds encourages this beneficial bacteria to flourish as the cheese matures, but why does it smell like the inside of your shoes? I hate to tell you this, especially on a group tour, but the thing about *B. linens* is that it's closely related to a bacteria that lives on the skin, called *Brevibacterium epidermis*, often on one's feet.

What Monks Have to Do with It

By now you might be wondering, who ever thought of washing cheese anyway? Bring on some guys who walked around barefoot and wore robes during the Middle Ages. Benedictine monks created these beefy creatures, probably because one of them was drinking a monastic beer in the cheese cave and got a little sloppy. These monks, who took a vow of poverty, were very good at making beer and cheese, but they didn't eat meat. So, when somebody realized that soaking a cheese with beer resulted in a treat that tasted vaguely like slow-braised beef stew and onions, you can imagine the excitement that rippled through the dining hall. Prayers answered!

In case you are a bit squeamish about eating bacteria, remember that your body has ten times as many bacterial cells as human ones.

—MICHAEL TUNICK, *THE SCIENCE OF CHEESE*

Today, many stinky cheeses can be traced back to monastic orders, from French Époisses to Switzerland's Tête de Moine (literally "head of a monk"). Around the United States, many artisans have developed interesting cheeses in this style, too, borrowing from monastic traditions to create signature stink bombs, often with great names. A few favorites: Hooligan, Drunken Hooligan, Humble Pie, Tiger Lily, Red Cat, Good Thunder.

Break out the monastic beers with this style, and you're going to see some golden light at the end of the tunnel for sure. Just keep in mind that the stronger the funk, the more you'll want to dial up the ABV (alcohol by volume)—that's because potent beers tend to be big on flavor (think of a malty imperial stout or a Belgian tripel with heavy honey notes), so they can stand up to bold beasts. Plus, beers that are high in alcohol are fab at cutting through rich fats, so they are terrific for cleansing your palate between bites of unctuous funk bombs.

Ripening Wizardry—and Why You Should Open a Window

These cheeses, like the softies in Adventure No. 2, continue to ripen over time, so you will notice that they taste (and smell) stronger the longer they linger in the refrigerator. If you find the smell becoming overpowering, stage an intervention. An overripe cheese, like an overripe banana, can be unpleasant. Open a window, and give your cheese (and yourself) a little air. The smell should dissipate a bit, but stinky cheeses will, generally, not stop stinking. If the cheese smells strongly of ammonia, it may be a sign of overripeness. It's safe to eat, but it's not optimal—not what the cheesemaker intended to showcase, flavor-wise. Taste it if you wish, but any cheese with a strong smell of ammonia is usually not very appetizing. It's a sad thing to toss a cheese into the trash bin, but sometimes that's fate.

Also, note that these cheeses do need to stay moist, so if the rind dries and cracks, it needs some TLC. You can revive a dry surface by dipping the corner of a clean towel in a little white wine or water (now who's an affineur!?), then dabbing the surface of the cheese until the rind looks rehydrated. Just know that you will want to eat the cheese tout de suite, because it probably won't taste good if you wait much longer.

ADVENTURE № 3
CHEESE BOARD

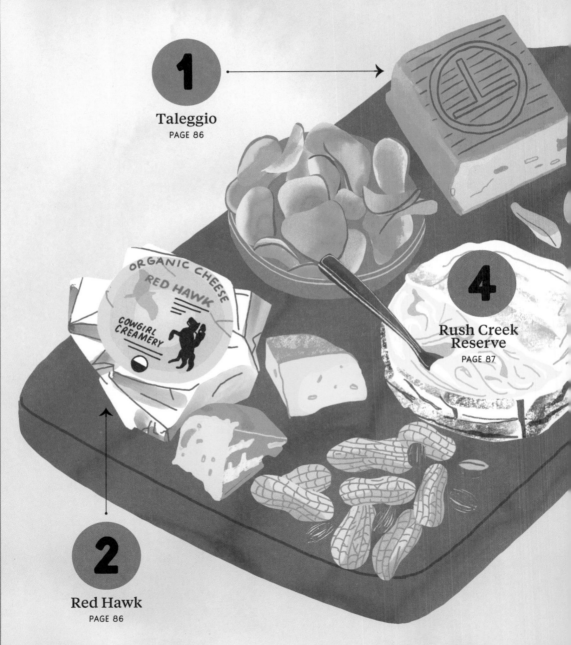

1

Taleggio
PAGE 86

2

Red Hawk
PAGE 86

ORGANIC CHEESE
RED HAWK
COWGIRL
CREAMERY

4

Rush Creek
Reserve
PAGE 87

3

Époisses
PAGE 87

Camping trip? Beach party? Backyard soiree? This adventure is ripe for outdoor gathering and grilling. Otherwise, open the windows, Ma, and prepare to burn a little incense. Since these cheeses are bold and creamy, think of this as an opportunity to do lots of dipping and schmearing (crackers, crusty bread, fresh veg) plus try out a variety of bold beverage pairings. You'll find that this style loves dark beer and dark spirits in particular.

EPOISSES
Appellation d'origine protégée
BERTAUT
1
Fromage au Bourgogne
250g
FR ce

1

MILDLY WHIFFY
(Port Salut, Taleggio, Nababbo)

2

CERTIFIABLY STINKY
(Grayson, Red Hawk, Pont-l'Évêque)

If you need some training wheels here, start with **Port Salut**, a budget-friendly crowd pleaser that originates with the Trappist monks of Port du Salut Abbey in northern France. The monks sold the name to a French industrial cheese company that now produces a friendly homage to the original. For a little more whiff, the real classic here is **Taleggio** from Italy's Lombardy region, a thick square that is springy like focaccia and with the same bread-doughy appeal. Look at the rind of a traditional Taleggio DOP and you'll see it bears a stamp of four circles; with its terra-cotta coloring, it looks like the tile of a church floor. Locals love to eat this cheese with mostarda, a mustard-oil-laced fruit condiment that's worth seeking out. For a mellow goat's milk version of Taleggio with a beautiful rose rind, try **Nababbo**.

Level up with one of two American sweethearts (stinkhearts?), or go for a French icon. **Grayson** is revered as the first real artisan American stink bomb; inspired by Taleggio, this glorious creature from Meadow Creek Dairy in Virginia is so sensuous, you may not be able to eat it in public without moaning. **Red Hawk**, from California's Cowgirl Creamery, is a triple crème stinker, making it a veritable cupcake of stinky suppleness. **Pont-l'Évêque**, one of Normandy's oldest cheeses, is an easy-to-find French classic that's great for picnics because it comes in a balsa-wood box. It was also Hemingway's favorite cheese. Note that all stinkers vary with age, so you may find these cheeses not as strong as you expect if they are on the young side or, in fact, rather feral if they have enjoyed some longevity.

3

RANK
(Époisses, Hooligan, Langres)

4

BONUS! BARK-WRAPPED STINKERS
*(Vacherin Mont d'Or,
Rush Creek Reserve, Winnimere)*

Easy-to-find **Époisses** is one of the great all-time French stinkers! The best way to enjoy this famous Burgundy cheese is to remove the top (or lid) and scoop out spoonfuls of the paste onto hunks of bread, alongside a bottle of white Burgundy. For a deeper spelunk Stateside, look for **Hooligan**— it's as wild as it sounds. This beefcake is made in Connecticut by mother-son team Elizabeth MacAlister (the herdswoman) and Mark Gillman (the cheesemaker). Their signature raw-milk stinker is made in the style of an Alsatian Munster using the milk of their small pasture-raised Jersey herd. For stinky decadence, look for **Langres**, which hails from the Champagne region of France and is shaped like a little cup that is intended to hold a splash of Champagne.

Cheese shops often have a limited supply of seasonal bark-wrapped cheeses from October through the winter. Traditional bark-bound cheeses are associated with the Jura Mountains of France, where forests of spruce trees grow in dense feathery swaths along the hillsides. Cheesemakers would peel thin strips of bark from the trunks of these enormous trees (don't worry, the bark grows back), then "girdle" their pudding-soft moons to keep them intact. The most famous of these bark-bound beauties are **Vacherin Mont d'Or** from Switzerland and France's **Mont D'Or** (there are slight variations in each country's recipe and regulations, hence the slightly different names). For raw-milk American artisan versions of this cheese, try Jasper Hill's **Winnimere** (page 273). Both are exquisite.

Navigating PAIRINGS

Funky cheeses pair well with wines that have strong
notes of honeyed fruit. High ABV beers work well,
too, so don't hesitate to try a Belgian tripel.

Gewürtztraminer

Stout, Belgian
styles

Bourbon

Kombucha

ACCOMPANIMENTS

Serve your meaty washed rinds with anything that you'd serve alongside beef stew or
bacon. Pickles and crudités add snap and palate-cleansing goodness between bites.

- Whole roasted garlic or onion jam
- Pickles (cornichons)
- Radishes
- Celery and carrot sticks
- Mostarda
- Dried apricots or figs
- Roasted peanuts or smoked nuts
- Potato chips
- Rustic bread

Possible DETOURS

Since these cheeses are all fairly bold, you may
want to add a breath-freshening **herbed chèvre** or
a **rosemary-encrusted Manchego** to the board. To vary texture,
add a crystalline Gouda, such as **L'Amuse Signature Gouda**
or **Beemster XO**; this will give you some sweetness but still
work with all the drink pairings and accompaniments.

**OFF THE
BEATEN
PATH**

UBRIACO OR "DRUNK" CHEESE

Now that you know rinds can be washed
with brine, beer, wine, or spirits, you might
want to explore the world of Ubriaco or
"drunk" cheeses. Imagine whole wheels
of hard cheese marinated in wine. Legend
has it that this style was invented long ago
when Italian cheesemakers wanted to avoid
paying tax collectors who charged tariffs
on each wheel, so the makers hid some
of their cheeses in barrels of wine. For a
stellar example, look for Occelli al Barolo, a
delicious "drunk" cheese that is packed in
Nebbiolo grape skins and seeds from making
Barolo wine. The Occelli family is beloved
for their line of drunk cheeses, so ask for
them at cheese shops. They also make a
cheese soaked in grapa (Occelli Testun con
Frutta e Grappa di Moscato) and another in
whiskey (Occelli al Malto D'Orzo e Whiskey).
For a popular alternative often available at
supermarkets, look for Drunken Goat.

TIPS FOR EXPLORING
* IN THE KITCHEN *

The pâté-like nature of these cheeses makes them ideal for a Meatless Monday board. Or use washed rinds to add big flavor to a loaded baked potato, other potato dishes, or sandwiches.

Drop-kick
A STINKER INTO HOT STARCH

Make like the Italians and drop a slab of Taleggio onto a bowl of warm polenta. Or push a piece into a hot baked potato with some caramelized onions. If you're like me, you use Limburger in your mac 'n' cheese, because if you know, you know. That's right, you can stir any stinker into hot pasta, and it'll melt into a rich, silky sauce. Add some bacon, and buh-bye! You may want to cut off the rind, but for crying out loud, don't toss it (read on)!

Toast those
STINKY CHEESE RINDS

The rinds on these cheeses can be a little gritty thanks to crystals (see page 153). Many people don't mind a bit of texture, but if you do, simply peel the rind back with a paring knife, then toast it on a slice of crusty bread under the broiler for just a few seconds. It curls up like bacon and tastes fabulous—the heat diminishes the funk, I often find.

Use stinky cheese
AS YOU WOULD
MEAT

In a vegetarian BLT, with or without
some sort of fake bacon situation.
You can also roll it in sushi—try a
very young, mild Taleggio alongside
cucumber and scallion. Or try subbing
it in place of tofu on a bánh mì.

Make fondue
IN A BOX

For the easiest, cheesiest appetizer or
meal in the world, buy a bark-bound
cheese and place it in an oven-safe
dish. You can use Rush Creek Reserve,
Winnimere, Harbison, or Vacherin
Mont d'Or. Preheat your oven to 300°F,
and warm the whole cheese until it
feels soft on top and very warm to the
touch, about 20 minutes. Remove the
dish from the oven and use a knife
to slice around the top of the rind.
Then peel the top rind back, like the
lid of a can. You now have a warm,
gooey cheese plunge pool for dunking
toasted bread, boiled new potatoes, or
a steamed veg.

FIELD GUIDE

* Meet a *

WASHED-RIND
CHEESE SPECIALIST

Olivia Haver

THE CELLARS AT JASPER HILL FARM, GREENSBORO, VT

Curious about how to get a job in the cheese world? In 2015, Olivia Haver followed her love of stinky cheese to the Cellars at Jasper Hill in Vermont, a 22,000-square-foot underground cave system built by a pair of entrepreneurial brothers, Andy and Mateo Kehler, in 2008. Together, the Kehler brothers have been at the forefront of developing new artisan cheeses from the milk of their own herd, along with skillfully maturing cheeses for other makers around their home state. Some of the best American cheeses, including several of the country's best stinkers, are aged here on their farm in Greensboro, in one of seven vaulted chambers built into an idyllic hillside.

Olivia spent two years working in Vault 6 at Jasper Hill, a dank space with a cathedral ceiling and sprayers that maintain humidity. As an affineur, she suited up in a chef coat, rubber boots, and a hairnet to begin caring for thousands of washed rinds, namely Oma ("grandmother"), a pungent little round made at nearby Von Trapp Farmstead in Waitsfield, and Winnimere, Jasper Hill's prizewinning raw-milk, bark-bound stink cushion. Here's a glimpse of how Olivia entered the field of affinage and learned to maintain rind control on some of the most deliciously funky cheeses in the United States. *Note:* Since our interview, Olivia has moved on to a new position, but she still has fond memories of getting her start in Vault 6.

What did your life look like before you started working at Jasper Hill?

I have a music degree—I'm an upright bass player—so that's basically the fastest way into a restaurant job! After college, I managed a butcher shop in Washington, DC, and got very burnt out. I took a few months off, moved to Red Bank, New Jersey, with my husband, and there was this cheese shop [The Cheese Cave] down the street, so I started cheesemongering and got sucked in just like everybody does. That's where I learned about Jasper Hill, and I fell in love with their cheese. I love Oma. I love Winnimere. Winnimere rocked my world. It's like Harbison's badass big sister.

How did you land a job as an affineur?

I looked up Jasper Hill online, and I liked their mission, so I applied for an internship. It was supposed to be two months. Within a few weeks of being here, I felt like I was home.

What gave you that feeling?

I think it was the smell! You smell bark, you smell bacteria, you smell mold, you smell all of the cheeses and their personalities. And the people here, they're so passionate. It's not just a job, it's a community. My husband didn't want to come up, so I got divorced for cheese. He said, "You know it's just cheese, right?" And I said, "No, it's not just cheese." That's when I knew how much a part of me it was.

Can you describe what it's like to work in a cheese cave?

The cellars are below ground, and when you walk into The Ellipse—the room that connects all the vaults—you smell boiling bark and you also hear the bass of someone's music coming from somewhere. Everyone's playing music in every corner.

What music do you like to play while you're washing rinds?

I like to listen to the Grateful Dead. Good vibes all around. The cheese is a living thing. It's bacteria, mold, and yeast—all living things—so I like to play it nice music.

What's the first thing that happens at Vault 6 each day?

You start looking at the cheese and assessing. You're smelling and feeling. The minute you walk into the vault, you can tell if the humidity and temperature are right. The vault, in a way, is its own living thing, so you're always thinking about the health of the space. Then you begin caring for the cheese. You might start turning Willoughby or barking Harbison. It just depends what's ready.

Washed rinds are tricky because soft cheeses are so sensitive. Anything you do to a soft cheese will stay with it for the rest of its life. If you don't turn it that day, it might slouch to one side. If you don't wash it enough, you'll see it get dry. Too much wash, and it will be too wet. Anything you do to it, you cannot take back.

What tools do you use to wash cheese?

I love my brush collection. It is awesome. We have brushes for everything. When the cheeses are younger, I'm using a shorter, more compact bristled brush. As they get older, I opt for a softer brush—one that's a little more uneven so you can softly graze the rinds with the brine. Sometimes you have to excite the rinds—you want to make little micro-scars in the surface, so you might want a brush with more bristles so you can get more bristle contact.

I also think a lot about how much pressure I apply. Washing cheese is so detailed. I'm also thinking about which kind of stroke. Do you want to go in circles? Up and down? Back and forth? You have to hit every inch of that cheese with brine or that one little inch you missed will be dry the next day.

Are there job opportunities in affinage for curious cave queens like yourself?

Yes, definitely. You just have to commit to the lifestyle. There's not a lot of cell service up here, and everything is very spread out, so you have to get used to that. If you like using your body and learning about cheese, though, you'd like it. There are about twenty-five or thirty cellar workers. We all stretch together every morning! And we hang out. Hill Farmstead Brewery is right up the street, so it's nice to go grab a beer after work.

What's the most interesting part of your job?

When you feel every cheese within a batch, you feel their personalities, so I'm always thinking, *What does this exact cheese need?* A consumer may only buy one Willoughby, but if I get a batch, that's a thousand pieces! So, I want every cheese to be cared for to the best of my ability. I'm really into Danny Meyer's book about hospitality [*Setting the Table*]. I want every person who buys one of the cheeses I've touched to be happy with it.

What do you like to drink with your washed rinds?

I'm a Cicerone-certified beer server, so I like a dark beer or a wild sour—like a gueuze. I like them with a rich, fatty cheese. The roastier beers bring out meatier flavors. You can almost mimic a grilled hamburger.

What's the first cheese that changed your life?

The first cheese I fell in love with was Taleggio. I got it at Wegmans, where I used to work. The texture is so great. It's soft but it has a little structure to it. You can melt it or just shove it right into your face. I like to eat it at room temperature with bread, crackers, whatever I can scrounge up. After you get into washed rinds, there's no going back.

ADVENTURE

№

4

A Transatlantic

CHEDDAR
CROSSING

GETTING ORIENTED

Why are some Cheddars orange and others white? Why are some mild and others sharp, and what's a clothbound Cheddar? Pack your steamer trunk. We're going to talk about American Cheddars, starting with Vermont, and then we'll set sail for Cheddar's birthplace—England—to check out the vibrant world of traditional Cheddars around a popular destination in Somerset called Cheddar Gorge. Yes, this is where Cheddar originates. The recipe made it to the Americas in the pockets of the colonists, so we're essentially tracing the route backward across the Atlantic. Along the way, you'll be served plenty of hard cider and beer, two great pairings for Cheddar. All you need for the cruise? A hearty temperament and deck shoes.

WHAT TO KNOW

Cheddaring

The first thing you should know about Cheddar is that it's a verb. You may have broken a piece in half and noticed that it's both crumbly and moist. That's because this cheese is "Cheddared" and then milled. Let me explain. When the curds are formed in the cheesemaking vat, cheesemakers drain all the liquid whey and let the warm curds knit together to form a spongy mat. Then they cut the mat into slabs and stack them to expel as much moisture as possible. Cheesemakers then stack and restack these slippery slabs (it's like watching someone flip fish in a bathtub) until the curds reach the desired acidity level (pH). Then, they're fed through a chipper vac of sorts—imagine a sausage mill for cheese—where they are salted and shredded into bits called "fingers." This labor-intensive process gives Cheddar its signature texture and bite.

> Look closely at your next bite of Cheddar, and you should see that it's made up of crumblike grains that break apart easily and yet hold together like a good scone.

If you get a chance to peer into a Cheddar room someday, you'll see that Cheddar-making is something of a sport requiring muscle and a good sense of timing. Every little action counts toward making a cheese that is texturally perfect and tasty. Look closely at your next bite of Cheddar, and you should see that it's made up of crumblike grains that break apart easily and yet hold together like a good scone.

Block Cheddar

Every supermarket in North America is loaded with block Cheddar. Why so much Cheddar and not, say, Danish Havarti? Keep in mind that British colonists brought over cows, along with recipes for their favorite cheeses. Cheddar was a fan favorite,

> A great block Cheddar, and there are many, should be crumbly but supple, and taste balanced in its saltiness and acidity.

a style beloved by the crown, from Henry II, who ordered loads of it for his table, to Queen Victoria, who received a nine-foot wheel at her wedding (who needs cake?). In fact, the first American cheese factory, which opened in Rome, New York, in 1851, made Cheddar. Like all recipes, it evolved over time, and much has been written about the shape-shifting nature of its look and taste since it was first produced in the twelfth century. What's important to know is that the two world wars consolidated cheesemaking, and that means that Cheddar—once handmade on small farms—became a factory product. Most of today's Cheddar is made on a large scale, popped out in blocks, shrink-wrapped, and aged in plastic, where it remains moist and stackable until it's time to cut and repack it for consumers. The key, for you, is to try a variety of Cheddars and take note of their texture and taste.

A great block Cheddar, and there are many, should be crumbly but supple, and taste balanced in its saltiness and acidity. If it's rubbery or bitter, or if it makes you shrug and go "meh," move on. Block Cheddars can be white or orange (from annatto, a flavorless plant-based dye), so don't judge a Cheddar by those hues; however, if you see a Cheddar that is the color of butter, nab it. That's usually a sign that the cows were raised on pasture, and the pale golden color you see is actually beta-carotene, which cows can't break down when they graze on grass. Hence, it ends up in the milk, becoming a pale gold bar of cheese.

Clothbound Cheddar

Sail over to the UK, and you'll find what's often called farmhouse Cheddar and meet bands of Cheddar heads eager to tell you that real Cheddar is made in large drums, not blocks. The quickest route to understanding this kind of Cheddar is to head to Somerset in southwest England where a handful of families have revived the area's recipe, hand-making cheese using local starter cultures and grass-fed raw milk from their farms. These cheeses are Cheddared and milled, then wrapped in muslin, smeared with lard, and cave-aged. We're talking about clothbound Cheddar—the mummy of the cheese world. Wrapping and larding these cheeses locks in moisture and allows them to age gracefully, let's just say. Exactly when the process of bandaging Cheddar was introduced is up for debate, since early Cheddars—a cheese once aged in the local Cheddar Gorge—did not have a uniform recipe initially. Today, Somerset's clothbound Cheddars are to the cheese world what the village wines of Burgundy are to the wine world.

Start with the three legendary family-made stalwarts: Montgomery's Cheddar, Westcombe Cheddar, and Keen's Cheddar. Then, seek out the newest clothbound prizewinner, Pitchfork, created by the Trethowan brothers near the village of

Signs of a Good Block of Cheddar

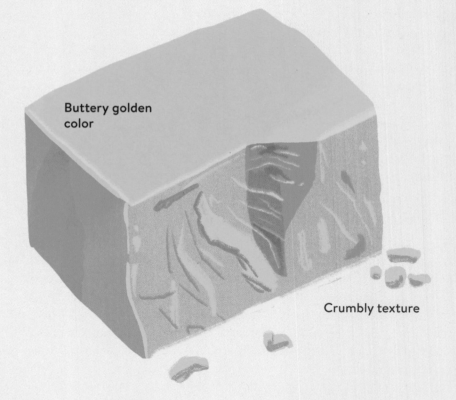

Buttery golden color

Crumbly texture

Cheddar. These cheeses, known as West Country Farmhouse Cheddars, are now a protected category of Cheddars, and the artisans of Somerset have been recognized by Slow Food. According to tradition, these Cheddars must be made in small batches on the farms where the milk is produced, using untreated raw milk of the same day, traditional animal rennet, and local starter cultures. The cheesemaking process is done entirely by hand and takes three days.

Once the drums enter the cave, the flavors of these labor-intensive Cheddars require over a year to develop. You really need to close your eyes to enjoy them. Talk to the Somerset Cheddar makers, and they'll tell you that they aspire to create cheeses with round, rather than linear, flavor. Terms such as earthy, nutty, and fruity are often used to describe them, along with premier Cheddar master James Montgomery's favorite flavor note: Marmite-y, as in the polarizing British condiment that tastes meaty, yeasty, and umami—a flavor profile that he looks for when he grades batches of Montgomery's Cheddar at his Manor Farm.

On a recent Cheddar odyssey to Somerset, I observed James Montgomery prowl around his aging cave one afternoon in his tall boots and tweed jacket as he pointed out some very painterly blue-green molds growing on the surface of his cheeses. "Ahh! This is what I love to see," he bellowed, raising a broad-knuckled finger. He explained that the molds growing on the surface break down the lard over about two months, allowing the cheese to begin to breathe through the cloth. He discovered this after a new employee accidentally applied too much lard to a batch of Montgomery's Cheddar. "I began stripping the cheese, and as the last layer of cloth came off, it looked weird. It was white—the

> These Cheddars must be made in small batches on the farms where the milk is produced, using untreated raw milk of the same day, traditional animal rennet, and local starter cultures.

lard was still intact. And the cheese tasted completely different. Very brassy," Montgomery observed pensively. "It told me that the cheese hadn't breathed—none of the Marmite-y flavors had developed. That mistake taught me an enormous lesson. Now I *love* to see mold on the surface of my cheese."

There you have it: Mold is gold.

ADVENTURE № 4
CHEESE BOARD

2

Isle of Mull Cheddar
PAGE 104

2

Keen's Cheddar
PAGE 104

A Cheddar tasting is a great excuse for a cold supper with apples, pears, and fall preserves. To add something warm, serve a stew or mugs of hot apple cider. This is a very festive tasting, a great way to celebrate the change in seasons or the birthday of someone who loves Cheddar; you can delight them with the many surprising and wonderful things that pair with this iconic cheese. Ask your friends to bring a variety of hard ciders, IPAs, dark beers, Scotch, or even ginger beer. The only thing I find challenging to pair with Cheddar is wine, because Cheddar tends to be acidic and salty, so it can render a subtle wine flavorless. Most sommeliers I know recommend a buttery Chardonnay (oaked) or a dry Cabernet Sauvignon.

1

Hook's 12-Year Cheddar
PAGE 104

Bleu Mont Dairy Bandaged Cheddar
PAGE 105

3

2

Quicke's Cheddar
PAGE 104

4

The MoonRabbit
PAGE 105

4

Red Rock
PAGE 105

A TRIO OF BLOCK CHEDDARS

*(Single-source 6-month,
1-year, 2-year blocks)*

Start this epic tasting with three block Cheddars at different ages so you can see how flavors evolve—at, say, **six months, one year, and two years.** You'll see how a mild cheese turns bolder in flavor and denser in texture. I like to pick Cheddars from a single farm so that I can taste the milk from one place and see how it evolves over a few months to a few years. There are many creameries to recommend, but one standout is **Shelburne Farms** in Vermont, a sustainable pasture-based operation that's also an educational nonprofit and inn. Other sources: **Hook's** in Wisconsin, **Cabot** in Vermont, and **Beecher's**, which has urban creameries on both coasts (Seattle and Manhattan).

TRADITIONAL BRITISH CLOTHBOUND

(Montgomery's, Keen's, Westcombe, Pitchfork, Quicke's, Isle of Mull)

Next step: Familiarize yourself with a couple of world-class cheeses from Cheddar's birthplace. Montgomery's is arguably the "king of Cheddars." If you want to try all the great Cheddars of Somerset, look for **Montgomery's, Keen's, Westcombe,** and **Pitchfork**— each one is stunning in its own right. Although they're all made in the same area, using the same basic recipe (raw pasture-raised milk, animal rennet, local cultures), each of these artisan Cheddars displays slightly different nuances and varies from season to season. If you see **Quicke's Traditional,** a pasteurized clothbound made in Devon, try it, too. It's quite different, with a touch of horseradish on the finish. And **Isle of Mull Cheddar** from the Inner Hebrides, where the cows at Sgriob-ruadh Farm are fed the spent barley from whiskey production.

3
NEW AMERICAN CLOTHBOUND

*(Cabot Clothbound, Flory's Truckle,
Bleu Mont Dairy Bandaged Cheddar)*

4
FASCINATING CHEDDAR VARIATIONS

*(Red Rock, Marco Polo Reserve,
The MoonRabbit)*

For your third stop, try one of the clothbound Cheddars that England has inspired in recent years as artisan cheesemaking in the United States has expanded. **Cabot Clothbound** is wildly popular, a collaboration cheese made by Cabot Cooperative and aged at the Cellars at Jasper Hill Farm. **Flory's Truckle** is a collaboration between makers in Iowa and an aging cave in Missouri; it's a cheesemonger favorite. It's also sweeter than the traditional English clothbounds, perhaps more suited to the American palate. **Bleu Mont Dairy Bandaged Cheddar** from Wisconsin is a mythical creature—hard to find but so worth it (try ordering it online). Willi Lehner hand-makes this clothbound Cheddar in small batches and ages it behind his house in a beautiful hobbit cave he built himself.

If you're still going strong, try one of the wild Cheddars that breaks from tradition. **Red Rock**, a Cheddar/blue hybrid created by Roelli Cheese in Wisconsin, is bright orange in color with lightning-like blue streaks. It adds vibrance to a board, plus it's truly unique in taste—all toasty Cheddar embedded with bolts of blue intensity. **Marco Polo Reserve** from Beecher's Handmade Cheese in Seattle is a clothbound Cheddar studded with green and black cracked peppercorns, which add delightful crunch and brightness to this beautifully aged cheese. **The MoonRabbit**, from Wisconsin, is a sweet, creamy Cheddar bathed in Green Chartreuse liqueur, which adds a touch of herbaceousness to the rind. It's wrapped in green foil, making it easy to spot in a cheese case.

Navigating PAIRINGS

From my many tastings, I find Cheddars best with beers—
saisons, stouts, and especially IPAs. Just match the strength
of the hops to the strength of the cheese. If you like hard
cider, a hopped cider or tart cider can be wonderful.

Cabernet
Sauvignon

IPA

Scotch

Ginger beer

ACCOMPANIMENTS

Cheddars are fun cheeses to pair because they work so well with unexpected things,
like marmalade and guava paste. Anything slightly tart or sharp is often a good
match. Chutney is a classic English pairing, and so are oatcakes, an oaty cracker found
in every British cheese shop. If you can't find a traditional oatcake, use Carr's Whole
Wheat Crackers. They're fabulous topped with Cheddars and a spot of apple chutney.

- Chutney
- Marmalade
- Quince or guava paste
- Apple or pear butter
- Walnuts
- Dried apricots
- Candied ginger
- Dehydrated orange slices

- Grapes
- Sliced green apples
- Cured meats
- Grainy mustard
- Bread-and-butter pickles
- Oaty crackers
- Toasted sourdough

Possible DETOURS

If you prefer a little variety on board, look for some other British fascinators, such as **Tunworth**, a gorgeous Camembert-style cheese made by Stacey Hedges of Hampshire Cheese Co. Or pick up a nub of **Wensleydale**, a cheese popularized by the Claymation series *Wallace and Gromit*. It's produced in North Yorkshire, England, and is one of those gentle, likable cheeses you can eat with an oatmeal cookie and a cup of tea to feel totally comforted on a dreary day. While you're at it, snag a glowing-orange hunk of **Sparkenhoe Red Leicester**, a mild-mannered beauty named after a raging bull, plus a nub of **Colston Bassett Stilton**. Now you have a cheese board worthy of British royalty.

OFF THE BEATEN PATH

APPLEBY'S CHESHIRE

If you want to travel back in time to a cheese that influenced Cheddar production, seek out Cheshire, England's first recorded cheese. It appears in the Domesday Book of 1086, a chronicle of England and much of Wales that was commissioned by William the Conqueror. At one time, thousands of makers across the countryside produced this delicate, slightly tart cheese that, like Cheddar, was milled and wrapped in cloth. (*Note:* It's milled differently and uses different starter cultures than Cheddar.) Today, Sarah Appleby and her husband, Paul, are some of the last people to make a traditional raw-milk clothbound Cheshire, which they form into drums and wrap in calico. When I'm in England, it's my favorite breakfast cheese, alongside scones and plum jam.

TIPS FOR EXPLORING
* IN THE KITCHEN *

Cheddars are one of the all-time great table cheeses. They're easy snackers and they're so simple to pair, especially with tart or tangy flavors like pickles and mustard. For some fun, why not try a different Cheddar every few weeks or so in your lunch? Just keep a stash of preserves on a shelf, along with a desk drawer full of nuts, dried fruit, and crackers.

Make a
TUNA MELT OR GRILLED CHEESE

Just be sure to choose a young Cheddar for melting, as aged versions are less moist and often turn oily. The acidity in Cheddar makes it great on any sandwich with a tomato. A tuna melt on rye bread—tuna salad, a slice of ripe tomato, and some grated Cheddar—is terrific if you pop it under the broiler.

Try a
PLOUGHMAN'S LUNCH

Eating a Cheddar alongside a pint was popularized by a UK milk marketing campaign in the 1960s, encouraging Brits to hit pubs for lunch. Bizarre, but true. Still, there's nothing quite like a good Cheddar, a hunk of rustic bread, some pickles and mustard, plus an IPA.

Make a
SKILLET SUPPER

Roast a bunch of potatoes, mushrooms, onions, and red peppers in a skillet, along with a couple of sausages, if you like. When it's piping hot, top it with grated Cheddar and chopped scallions.

Take
A HIKE

Somerset, England, isn't just Cheddar country, it's also cider country. The landscape is full of mossy-green pastures and rows of tangled orchard trees. There's a reason Cheddar and apples go together—pack both on your next outing!

FIELD GUIDE

* Meet a *
SECOND-CAREER CHEESEMONGER

Greselda Powell

MURRAY'S CHEESE SHOP, NEW YORK, NY

Many people who work at cheese counters land there by accident or, you might say, fate. For engineer Greselda Powell, it started with a trip to the famous Cheddar-making state of Vermont. In January 2015 she was laid off from her telecommunications company after twenty-five years, so she took a rented car and went exploring, only to discover some wonderful Vermont cheeses and cheesemakers. The experience led her to switch careers. Today, she's a full-time cheesemonger at Murray's in New York City, where she sells the very cheeses that inspired her life's detour.

Describe your cheese adventure. How did you become a cheesemonger?

After I got laid off, I went to a spa up in Ludlow, Vermont, and I found a Vermont cheese trail map. It was January, and there I was driving around in a rear-wheel-drive Mustang, visiting cheesemakers. I had an amazing time. I got to meet cheesemakers and their families and their kids and neighbors. I could see that they loved getting up in the morning and creating. I just loved the vibe. Plus, those cheeses just blew me away—their tastes and textures—so I just kept on driving, hoping I wouldn't get stuck in a ditch.

After two weeks in Vermont, I thought that instead of going back to my world of engineering, I should continue down the path of cheese, so that's what I did. I began returning to Vermont. I went to the Vermont Cheesemakers Festival, and that really blew me away. To see the cheesemakers amid the cider makers and condiment makers, I saw how interconnected everything was. I also went to Shelburne Farms—they have a pasture-to-palate program that I did. Then, I went over to Sterling College for a Fundamentals in Cheesemaking class that was in conjunction with Jasper Hill Farm. By the summer of 2017, I felt like I had taken everything except affinage, and I knew Murray's had an affinage program. They knew me as a volunteer, so they accepted me.

What was your first day like behind the cheese counter at Murray's?

I started the week before Thanksgiving 2017. It was fun. I really enjoyed giving good service to people. I was nervous, but I knew enough to be dangerous! I was familiar with all the cheeses from Jasper Hill Farm in Vermont, and I had been a Murray's intern, plus I'd worked at Whole Foods in the specialty department for nine months, so I had plenty of things to recommend.

Describe what you do every day now.

As a monger, I want you as a customer to find a cheese you will enjoy so you will come back. Or a condiment that you enjoy so you will come back. I try to convey my joy. To me, it's all about establishing a rapport with my customers, to give them different cheeses and to give their kids cheeses to try. If you convey your passion, people come back!

How do you help people navigate so many cheeses?

At a place like Murray's, the cheese case can be very daunting. We have two goals as cheesemongers: One is to convey our passion and the passion of the cheesemaker (Why do they get up and make cheese every morning?). Two, we want to make going into a cheese store an enjoyable experience and an entertaining experience. Trying different cheeses and different pairings—having that orgasmic moment, right? I've heard people say, "This cheese is friggin' better than sex." [*laughs*] A cheese should make you want to run home and retaste it. A lot of people are like my good friend Phyllis—they know only Cheddar, Gouda, and Manchego—but there's so much more to life than that!

> I've heard people say, "This cheese is friggin' better than sex."

Can you describe the first pairing that blew your mind?

Yes, I took a class with educator Christine Clark, and I still remember that she paired Camembert with some kimchi—two things that you'd never think to put together. That's the fun part. I have to admit, my time at Murray's as a student and volunteer gave me such great exposure to what's out there.

What have you discovered since you started?

Cheese is variable. You can get the same cheese, and it can taste different through the seasons. Or because of breeds. Or because of terroir, so I always emphasize that you may think you've discovered your favorite cheese, but you may not taste it again, because it's like a special bottle of wine. It can be once in a lifetime.

What do you find challenging about your job?

As cheesemongers, we all have our comfort points, and we have to learn to sell the cheeses we're not comfortable with. You may not like a cheese, but you should still learn how to appreciate it and talk about it. That's something I am trying to work on every day.

So, how do you talk to people about cheese?

I'm trying to use wonderful adjectives to describe cheese in order to give people insight into what they're about to taste. It's a challenge. Taste and flavor and aroma are all connected to memory. I'm learning to really taste things outside of cheese in order to build more taste descriptors.

For example, Puigpédros! It's a Spanish cheese that tastes like broccoli rabe to me. Now I'll ask customers who come to the counter, "Do you like broccoli rabe?" And if they say yes, I'll offer them a taste of Puigpédros.

What cheese do you like to take home after work?

One of my favorite cheeses is Rogue River Blue. Especially with a bottle of twenty-year port. Whenever somebody wants a blue, I give them a taste of Rogue River, and I tell them, "Get yourself a good bottle of port, go home, turn down the lights, get your significant other, and turn on some Al Green. Let *this* be your Friday night." That's exactly what I tell my customers!

Do you have a go-to cheese that you recommend to new cheese explorers?

It's probably Flory's Truckle (page 263). It starts off sharp, then you get floral notes, then a finish of Parmigiano. It gives you a different experience as you go along for the ride. When I talk about football, I can get really animated, and I feel the same way when I talk about that Flory's Truckle! It's not one note, it's many notes. For people who are used to one-note Cheddar, I feel like Flory's Truckle opens them up to possibilities in cheese—like if this cheese is so interesting, what else is out there?

ADVENTURE

Nº

5

ALPINE CHEESE

Trek

GETTING ORIENTED

Ready for some serious mountain cheese? Grab your climbing boots and glacier glasses. We're headed to the Alps, the highest mountain range in Europe, and its nearby sub-Alpine range: the Jura. At high elevation, you'll find some of the world's most flavorful cheeses. Shepherds in Switzerland, France, Italy, and Austria still carry on the tradition of moving their animals up the mountains every spring to the best bovine buffets, and the cheeses made from high-mountain milk are some of Europe's most prized. I'll explain why once we reach the summit. So, stretch your legs, strap a canteen to your chest, and prepare to feast on what some would call Alpine power bars.

WHAT TO KNOW

Fondue Cheeses

There's more than one reason why the regions these types of cheeses hail from are also known for fondue. First of all, the bold, savory Alpine wheels melt well, but have you ever thought about why people eat fondue—a dish so simple it requires little more than fire, cheese, a jug of wine, and some crusty bread? It's the kind of dish you'd eat if you lived in the Alps, far from grocery stores but close to cheesemakers with cellars full of cheese. As we start our ascent, you'll begin to notice small Alpine huts that often look like Swiss music boxes, with timber walls, sloped roofs, and painted shutters. This style of house was traditionally the summer home of mountain cheesemaking families. Some are still in use by cheesemakers, though many have been converted into tiny restaurants that serve hearty meals to hikers.

SWISS FONDUE

• Serves 4 •

My Swiss grandmother used to make this recipe every winter and serve it alongside pickles, a salad of butter lettuce dressed with tart vinaigrette, and a plate of thinly sliced cured meats. The key to making fondue is adding the cheese slowly and using a wooden spoon to stir it constantly in a figure eight pattern so it doesn't stick to the pot. *Note:* If you don't have a fondue pot, just use a saucepan.

½ pound (225 grams) Gruyère cheese, grated

½ pound (225 grams) Emmentaler cheese, grated

1 teaspoon (2.6 grams) all-purpose flour

1 garlic clove, peeled and halved

1¼ cups (295 ml) dry white wine

Freshly ground pepper

Freshly grated nutmeg

3 tablespoons (44 ml) brandy or kirsch

1 crusty baguette, cubed

1. Place the grated Gruyère and Emmentaler in a large mixing bowl and toss it with the flour so that all the cheese is lightly dusted. Then, rub the inside of your fondue pot with the garlic clove, pressing firmly so that the juice coats the walls of the pot.

2. Place your fondue pot or saucepan on the stove and pour in the wine. Bring to a boil over medium heat, then lower the heat and begin adding cheese a pinch at a time. Use a wooden spoon to stir vigorously in figure eights and wait until each pinch of cheese melts before you add more (this will prevent it from clumping).

3. When all the cheese has been incorporated into the mixture, move the pot from the stove to a heating element on the table. Add a dash of pepper, a dash of nutmeg, and the brandy or kirsch.

4. Serve immediately. Don't forget, anyone who loses a piece of bread in the pot has to kiss the person who retrieves it.

Traditional Alpage vs. Alpine Style

What I've just described is the setting for true Alpine cheese, known in the industry as Alpage cheese (ahl-paj—rhymes with massage). The word refers to both the cheesemaking hut and the pristine Alpine pastures where animals are brought to graze each spring and summer, a practice of seasonal migration known as transhumance. Cheeses such as Gruyère, Emmentaler, L'Etivaz, Vacherin Fribourgeois, Comté, and Beaufort originate high in the Alps. Today, you can still find traditional high-mountain Alpage versions, but most are industrially produced in the valleys on a much larger scale, where it's more cost-effective and less labor-intensive to raise animals and make cheese. Industrial Alpine cheeses can be delicious, but they're approximations of true Alpage cheeses.

Traditional Alpage cheeses are highly prized because they must meet two requirements: First, the cheese must be made seasonally, only in summer months when animals are feeding exclusively on high-mountain pastures. Second, there can be no transportation of milk. Alpage cheese must be made in the Alps from body temperature milk, straight from the animal—just as it has been done for centuries. Alpage cheesemakers often produce no more than three or four large wheels per day, and house them in their cellars or in village caves. Because the wheels are large and dense, they can be matured for several years, until it's convenient to transport them. A long maturation period makes for complex flavors, which is another reason why Alpage cheeses are revered.

> Industrial Alpine cheeses can be delicious, but they're approximations of true Alpage cheeses.

High Mountain Cheeses = High Protein and Wild Flavor

If you're an athlete or maximizing protein, know that high-mountain cheeses are some of the most nutrient-dense cheeses on the planet. Cows feeding on high-quality Alpine pastures are said to devour up to twice as many nutrients as they do grazing in the valleys, and that makes for milk with a high concentration of proteins, short-chain fatty acids, minerals, and omega-3s.

> Just as old vines give the richest wines, old pastures yield the richest milk.
> —PATRICK RANCE

Curious to know how elevation contributes to high-quality pasture? Look around. We're at the summit of our Alpine cheese trek—so, spin around with your arms out like Julie Andrews in *The Sound of Music* and relish the view for a second. You're surrounded by lush meadows full of wildflowers, clean streams, and unpolluted air. Because the land has never been tilled or manipulated by humans, the root systems of the plants run deep, making for extra-hearty vegetation that draws from deep groundwater. It's a chlorophyll-rich, cow-dotted patch of serenity. When you kneel down to look at what's growing, as some botanists have, you're apt to find 150 or more different herbs, grasses, and wildflowers.

Pretty wild, right?!

Exactly! As Edward Behr explains in *The Oxford Companion to Cheese*, wild pastures have more plant diversity than cultivated land and also more broad-leaved plant species. This also means more terpenes—the aromatic organic compounds that contribute distinctive aromas and flavor. (For example, a pine tree smells like pine, thanks to a terpene called pinene.) Terpenes also lend wines their distinct aromas and flavors. So, the magic of Alpine pastures is this: They contain more nutrients and terpenes, resulting in cheeses that are extra rich in energy and flavor. Hence, Alpine Power Bars.

Who's ready to do some trail running?

ADVENTURE № 5
CHEESE BOARD

3 Raclette
PAGE 123

2 Comté
PAGE 122

5 Alp Blossom
PAGE 125

Appenze

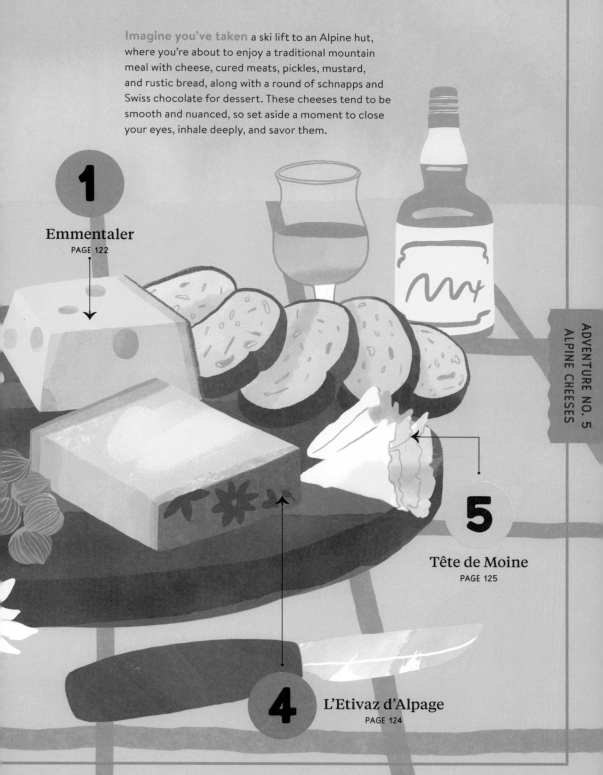

Imagine you've taken a ski lift to an Alpine hut, where you're about to enjoy a traditional mountain meal with cheese, cured meats, pickles, mustard, and rustic bread, along with a round of schnapps and Swiss chocolate for dessert. These cheeses tend to be smooth and nuanced, so set aside a moment to close your eyes, inhale deeply, and savor them.

1

Emmentaler
PAGE 122

5

Tête de Moine
PAGE 125

4

L'Etivaz d'Alpage
PAGE 124

EMMENTALER

Start your ascent by understanding the difference between American Swiss cheese—a ubiquitous deli counter staple with holes—and real Emmentaler, the actual cheese with holes that inspired it. Real **Emmentaler AOP** has been made in Switzerland's Emme Valley since the thirteenth century, and it's known for its girth. If you want some educational entertainment, cue up a video of this enormous cheese being sliced. (Just Google "how to cut an Emmentaler.") The taste of Emmentaler is mild and slightly sweet with a flicker of buttermilky tartness (think not-quite-ripe apricots), a good counterbalance to salty cured meats like speck, a lightly smoked ham that is shaved thin like prosciutto.

COMTÉ

Next, we're off to the Jura Mountains of France, to taste one of the all-time great aged French mountain cheeses, **Comté**. Comté is related to Gruyère—the onion soup cheese from Switzerland—but where **Gruyère** swings savory (think roasted garlic), Comté swings sweet (think candied nuts). Connoisseurs often favor **Marcel Petite Comté,** which is hand-selected and aged at a labyrinthine military fort deep in the Jura Mountains (see page 130). Because this cheese ages so beautifully, it's fun to taste it at different stages of maturation. If you're at a good cheese counter, ask to sample a few different wheels. A four-month Comté will taste mildly sweet and grassy, but an eighteen-month Comté can take you into a flavor zone of candied cashews, bourbon, and brown butter.

3

RACLETTE

Okay, let's say you're out on the slopes and you want to get melty. If you've heard of **Raclette**, you know that it's both a cheese and the name of a gorgeous yet simple dish the Swiss and French love to eat at ski lodges. A Raclette meal is simply boiled potatoes, melted cheeses, caramelized onions, and cornichons, all served in a mountain of gooey goodness. Raclette the cheese is a fudgy-textured wheel with slightly funky mushroomy notes that is made in the mountains of both Switzerland and France. Traditionally, a large wedge of this cheese was heated over a fire, then scraped—as it melted—over boiled potatoes, hence the name Raclette, from the French word *racler* (to scrape) Today, most

Europeans use a tabletop Raclette grill and simply plug it into a wall by the table. If you fall hard for Raclette, look for a Raclette grill at kitchen stores or online, and make the most of long winter evenings by hosting a series of Raclette parties. You'll find Raclettes made by a number of brands, so keep your eye out for **Raclette du Valais AOP** if you want to try the Alpine version—it tends to taste extra-mushroomy. If you like flavored cheeses, look to **Jumi Cheese** from Switzerland, which offers wonderful smoked and truffled versions of Raclette. Also, **Reading Raclette** is a stellar Raclette-style cheese from Vermont.

TRUE D'ALPAGE CHEESE

(L'Etivaz d'Alpage, Gruyère d'Alpage, Sbrinz d'Alpage)

Now you're at the pinnacle of this category—a true Alpage cheese made at high elevation (above 1,000 meters, according to Swiss law) in the summer by a single maker or village dairy is usually a cheese of a lifetime. The cheeses are typically made by hand and aged in mountain caves, and are an endangered species, basically. If they make it to the US market, it's because someone at a great cheese counter cares about them and knows these are bucket-list cheeses. One of my favorites, **L'Etivaz d'Alpage**, is deeply rooted in Swiss tradition. It's still made in copper cauldrons over an open woodfire, high up in remote Alpine chalets. It's sometimes described as "old-world Gruyère," so imagine a waxen cheese that tastes nutty and caramel-like with a pop of wild onions. At last count, about seventy families still make L'Etivaz. Blaise Chablaix, a

L'Etivaz cheesemaker I once visited with Cheese Journeys—a travel company focused on artisan dairy, with whom I cohost tours—took us outside where his cows graze and pointed out that there were forty-three different wildflowers per centimeter of mountain pasture (they'd just been counted by a university plant analyst). "My children know that what we make is special because of these flowers," he said. "We cannot make this cheese anywhere but here."

Gruyère d'Alpage and Sbrinz d'Alpage are two other fantastic high-mountain cheeses worth seeking out. Sometimes called "Swiss Parmesan," Sbrinz is a hard raw-milk cheese with a beautiful crystalline structure and notes of butter and wildflowers. *Note:* If you can't find an Alpage cheese, try **Le Gruyère AOP** or **Chällerhocker**, two cheeses from Switzerland with remarkable flavor.

5

TÊTE DE MOINE OR ALP BLOSSOM

("flower cheeses")

For our descent, here are two unique "flower cheeses" that illustrate ingenuity within the Alpine cheesemaking realm. Pick one or both for a board, because they are delightful and delicious—the first is a cheese that you shave into blossoms, and the second is an Alpine cheese rolled in confetti-like petals. **Tête de Moine**, from Switzerland, is the only cheese I know of that has a special accessory built to serve it, called a girolle. This rotating blade created by a Swiss engineer is inserted into the cylinder-shaped wheel, then turned to produce rosettes of tête. Tête de Moine, which means "head of a monk" in French, was a specialty of the monks of Switzerland's Bellelay Abbey,

and though the girolle was invented more recently, it makes this firm, funky cheese immediately likable. Pop a rosette into your mouth and it melts like a snowflake. You can also drop rosettes onto salads or make a gussied-up cheeseburger.

Flower-coated **Alp Blossom** from Austria's first cheese school, Sennerei Huban, is designed to draw attention to the variety of herbs and wildflowers growing in the Bregenzerwald meadows where local cows graze to produce milk for this cheese. Rose petals, marigolds, lavender, and chervil make this kaleidoscopic cheese one of the most memorable you'll ever see, and the coating contributes a wonderful floral and herbaceous taste.

Navigating PAIRINGS

Since Alpine cheeses tend to be nutty, oniony, and
herbaceous, think about what you'd pair with Thanksgiving
stuffing: A fruity white or red wine usually works well, as
does a crisp lager or malty ale. An Old-Fashioned cocktail
heavy on winter spice notes is stunning, and so is a cup of
fermented pu-erh tea, which has deep brothy notes.

Beaujolais

Nut brown ale

Old-Fashioned

Pu-erh tea

ACCOMPANIMENTS

Play off the flavors in many of these cheeses with dried fruits, nuts,
and anything herbaceous—rosemary bread is one of my favorites. All of these
cheeses pair beautifully with caramelized onions or roasted garlic.

- Dried figs or apricots
- Toasted hazelnuts
- Onion jam
- Whole roasted garlic cloves
- Roasted potatoes

- Cornichons
- Sauerkraut
- Cured meats
- Whole-grain mustard
- Rosemary bread

Possible DETOURS

Change up the landscape with **Ossau-Iraty** (OH-so EAR-ahty),
a sheep's milk cheese from the Pyrénées. Its mellow nature is perfect
for offsetting the bold flavors on an Alpine board. Weave in a truncated
peak of **Valençay** (page 272) for a soft goat cheese that adds visual play.
Or try some award-winning American cheeses inspired by Alpine
makers, such as **Uplands Pleasant Ridge Reserve** or Jasper Hill Farm's
Alpha Tolman. Both are rich, nutty, and made from pasture-raised milk.

OFF THE
BEATEN
PATH

CACIOCAVALLO

Italy's gourd-shaped caciocavallo (kotch-ee-oh-ka-va-loh) means "cheese on
horseback." These unusually shaped cheeses, mentioned by Hippocrates back
in 550 BCE, were tied on each end of a rope and carried by horse, like a pair
of saddlebags, into village markets. Similar to provolone, the easy snackers
often remind me of jerky because they are dry and thready in texture, a good
cheese for taking on a hike or a trail ride. Look for caciocavallo at Italian
specialty food stores, or hop online and order Suffolk Punch, an American
artisan version of caciocavallo from Parish Hill Creamery in Vermont.

TIPS FOR EXPLORING
* IN THE KITCHEN *

Need a super-melter? The elastic texture of Alpine cheeses renders them stretchy when they're heated, and because they're loaded with flavor, you can use them more sparingly. Some chefs treat them as finishing cheeses to add punch to pizzas or mac 'n' cheese when they come out of the oven.

Top BRUSSELS SPROUTS

The oniony notes in Alpine cheeses pair well with cruciferous vegetables like Brussels sprouts and cauliflower (or even a cauliflower pizza). When the veggies are hot, try grating a little Gruyère on top and running the dish under the broiler until the cheese browns. Then add a sprinkle of fresh nutmeg.

Load up A POTATO

If you don't have time to host a Raclette party, just make a baked potato and load it up with Raclette cheese, caramelized onions, chopped cornichons, and plenty of freshly cracked black pepper. If you want, add a little bacon or frizzled prosciutto that you've fried in a skillet, too. This makes a fabulous quick supper, alongside a leafy salad dressed with vinaigrette.

Panini
THESE CHEESES

Use any Alpine-style cheese for a
hot-sandwich fantasy. Comté and
Emmentaler are especially good
on toasted rye or sourdough with
caramelized onions, ham, and coarse-
ground mustard.

Add big flavor
TO A VEGGIE
BURGER

Top your next veggie burger with
melty, funky Raclette or grate some
aged Gruyère into your own veggie-
burger mix. It's a great binder and will
add a burst of umami.

CHECK IT
OUT

ADOPT AN ALP

Swiss cheese importer Caroline Hostettler has made it her mission to
raise awareness about the value of traditional Swiss cheese culture.
Her Adopt an Alp program pairs cheese shops with one of thirty-
four cheesemakers in the Alps so that customers can follow a single
mountain maker each season at their alpage, then order the cheese
(check out adopt-an-alp.com).

GRATE ESCAPE

Exploring Cheese in France
A VISIT TO THE COMTÉ CATHEDRAL

Inside Fort St. Antoine, a former military bunker high up in the Jura Mountains, there are stalactites in the lobby. The Comté Cathedral, as it's called among curd nerds, is built into a rural French hillside, and its underground caverns hold 100,000 wheels of the most popular cheese in France. I've come not only to see the spectacle of this lactic mecca, having heard about its vastness from cheesemongers at parties, but also to taste Comté of different ages and from the milk of different elevations. "High pasture equals high flavor," or so the saying goes. Plus, the lusher the grasses, the higher the butterfat.

Here in the mountains of France and nearby Switzerland, the great melters of the world are born. I grew up eating them with my Swiss grandparents, who migrated to Cleveland and never strayed from their heritage, menu-wise, so Comté has been part of every holiday party I can remember. Here in the Jura, it feels like home to be surrounded by a culture where everyone eats fondue and bubbling hot potato dishes served with Riesling and local sausages—even in summer.

At Fort St. Antoine, the only cheese anyone talks about is Comté. Each cheese rolls in at seventy-five pounds and is as wide as a wagon wheel. Literally, this is a cheese designed for transport. No one hauling food down a mountain wants to carry extra weight, so mountain cheeses are cooked and pressed—literally squeezed—to expel every possible drop of moisture. The result is a rich, fatty cheese that melts on your tongue like silky lardo.

At the fort, the best Comté wheels are gathered from village dairies, called fruitières, and brought here to the nursery, where they begin their residency for up to three years. The fort has five skilled cave masters who oversee salting, washing, and flipping the wheels, so that they mature evenly. Each wheel is also tasted and graded by the cave masters, who can identify the six aromatics (lactic, vegetable, spice, fruit, bread/toast, and animal/meat) that give great Comté its complexity. The best wheels exhibit more than one of these flavors, though many variables determine which

flavors stand out. Some wheels have more pronounced notes of winter spices (think nutmeg), and others taste more like toasted brioche.

"Each cheese has its own story," says Fabien DeGoulet, our cave guide but also, notably, the Best Cheesemonger of the World 2015. Fabien is French, but he spent several years at Tokyo's premier cheese shop. He's here serving as an intern because the great dream of pretty much everyone in the cheese industry is to spend time at Fort St. Antoine learning the art of affinage.

For novices, such a prospect feels daunting. The caves, once designed for giant artillery, are vast and dank. And the place reeks of ammonia, especially in the aging rooms, where thousands of cheese wheels off-gas all day, every day, making the air burn your eyes. But Fabien doesn't seem to mind. He springs over puddles in the hallways with his long legs—an albino cricket: white cap, white lab coat, knee-high white rubber boots.

At Fort St. Antoine, wheels replaced weaponry in the 1960s, when a man named Marcel Petite reenvisioned the space as a cave system where he could practice affinage lent, or slow maturing. Petite loved his local cheese and wanted to achieve more complexity in its taste by giving more attention to the aging process. It worked, and now each wheel here bears his name, Marcel Petite Comté.

It's not hard to see why the wheels from these caves are revered. The level of sophistication is mind-boggling—and it's all focused on one cheese! One. Single. Cheese. If anything, this laserlike focus reflects the seriousness and single-mindedness with which the French approach dairy, particularly when it comes to the country's heritage cheeses. Comté gained name protection in 1952, and the rules surrounding its production are stringent.

For example, the milk must be from a specific breed of cow, primarily Montébeliards, a rugged animal with russet markings. I've seen them all along the roadsides and heard their brass bells ringing across the hills. The milk of the Montbéliards must be fresh, pristine, and unpasteurized. It cannot be run through a pump—that would disturb the delicate fat globules and, ultimately, affect the texture of the cheese.

Inside the fort, wooden shelving rises from floor to ceiling, and different chambers house cheeses at various maturation stages and even elevation levels. Claude Querry, a cave master who is renowned within the cheese realm, is legendary for his palate. It's said that he can taste a cheese and pinpoint the exact meadow where the cows grazed.

Claude is a compact man with a tight stride who always carries a tool called a cheese iron in his pocket. It looks like a delicate mallet with a hollow handle. To check the ripeness of a cheese, Claude pulls a wheel of Comté halfway off the shelf and balances it against his body, then leans into it with his ear as he begins to tap the rind. As the handle of his cheese iron ricochets off the surface, Claude listens to the tone. In this tone, he can recognize the sound of an internal fracture in the cheese—a hairline crack—and he can determine when a cheese is ripe, ready for market.

"It's about resonance," Fabien explains, translating. "When Claude hears a crack, he knows it's ready and he makes his notes on the rind." Sure enough, Claude withdraws a core sample with the handle of his iron, tastes a small piece of the Comté thoughtfully, then uses the iron's pointy tip to scratch an unreadable-looking note to himself on the side of the cheese. Only the five masters know how to read these hieroglyphs.

Every day, each cave master will taste and score roughly three hundred cheeses. They're trained not just to taste where the milk has come from—which meadow, which maker—but also to assign each wheel to the best buyer. Some retail shops, for example, prefer more fruity notes or more winter spice. "Americans like sweet flavors," Fabien says.

Each year, cheese buyers fly in from around the world to visit the fort and sample the different Comté flavor profiles. The cheeses are housed in groups, depending on their origins, which means that a walk through the caves is literally a stroll through mountain pastures turned into milk turned into cheese—aged sunshine and native grasses and wildflowers.

Finally, it's off to the tasting room, where Fabien sets out four different cheeses and begins outlining the flavors, drawing from a massive flavor wheel that has been specially developed for the nuances in Comté. The first two cheeses he samples are both ten months old, but they're from different fruitières and they taste wildly different.

One is all grass and cream, whereas the other tastes brothy, like a cup of beef consommé. The last two cheeses have been aged over a year—from 2016 and 2017. Both have great depth of flavor, and when I look at the cheeses on the board, I can see how the color of the paste has darkened and how each one has become denser as moisture evaporated. In one of these last samples, crystals have begun to form, giving it the texture of toffee.

My favorite, from May 2016, is reminiscent of salted caramel. Fabien catches me rolling it around on my tongue, my eyelids starting to close dreamily. "It would be great after dinner, wouldn't it?" he asks. "With brandy or Scotch?"

Of course, I couldn't agree more.

ADVENTURE

№

6

Geological Adventures in

AGED
CHEESE

(WITH CRYSTALS!)

AGED GOUDA
Wisconsin, USA

EWEPHORIA
Netherlands

WILDE WEIDE GOUDA
Netherlands

MIMOLETTE
France

ASIAGO d'ALLEVO
Italy

AGED MANCHEGO
Spain

SBRINZ

PECORINO
Italy

SBRINZ
Switzerland

RAGUSANO
Sicily, Italy

GETTING ORIENTED

Ready your rock hammers and safety goggles: We're here to survey some aged cheeses embedded with sparkling gems. If you study the fracture face of a hard cheese, you'll notice glittering white specks. Many people mistake these diamondlike dots for salt, but they're not. They are crystals, as you'll learn from legendary scientist Dr. Paul Kindstedt (page 152), whose team has devoted years of fieldwork to cheese crystallography. No joke. First, though, we'll mine our way through history, because the cheeses in this category are ancient. Prepare to make notes in your field book as we chip into aged Gouda, real Parmigiano-Reggiano, and Pecorino as part of this excavation.

WHAT TO KNOW

Not Just Grating Cheeses

Though you might consider some of the cheeses in this adventure to be grating cheeses, keep in mind that they were developed long before anyone dreamed of smothering a Caesar salad in Parm. In the cultures where these cheeses were created, they're beloved table cheeses, enjoyed socially at family meals and often served with the local wine (red wine drinkers, this is your cue to pour a glass). Know that the world of hard cheese is vast, so there's plenty to survey on your own.

Look for dry, aged cheeses that look like you'd need a chisel to crack into them.

We'll map out three kinds—aged Gouda, grana-style cheeses, and aged sheep's milk cheeses—since these are often matured for several years to develop flavors and form intense crystals. When you break open these wheels, you'll notice that they look like rock face—dry and brittle or flaky. Look closely and you can observe how the size and quantity of the crystals vary. Pry open an aged Gouda, for example, and the face is waxy and smooth with small glistening crystals, plus a few nooks and crannies that look like geodes. Crack into a Parmigiano-Reggiano and the face is rough and shimmering—thanks to a dense structure of quartzlike grains that look like sandstone. The difference comes down to how the curds were treated early in the cheesemaking process.

Here's a general rule of thumb if you're hunting for crystalline cheeses: Look for dry, aged cheeses that look like you'd need a chisel to crack into them.

PRESSED CHEESES

What makes rock-hard cheese? The same thing that makes rock-hard muscles: weights! These cheeses are basically bench pressed. If you ever see Gouda production in action, for example, you'll observe how makers load young wheels into a cheese press with weights that squeeze the cheeses, much like sponges, to remove as much liquid as possible. The drier the cheese, the longer it keeps—just as the shelf life of a dry cracker exceeds that of fresh bread. Archaeologists have uncovered numerous Roman cheesemaking artifacts, including perforated ceramic press molds,

which are evidence that pressed cheeses date back a very long time.

Once cheeses are pressed, they can be stored for years, and with proper affinage they turn into sweet-salty rock candy. In this chapter, we're going to excavate aged cheeses that are primarily from the Netherlands and Italy because they are similar in structure—dense, rocklike, and craggy. To serve them as part of a board, you often need to chip at them with a pointy blade, called a stiletto. They can also be planed, with a cheese plane, if they're not too flaky.

For the record: Within the cheese industry, hard cheeses are often categorized as cooked pressed cheeses or uncooked pressed cheeses, depending on their recipe. Cooking the curds creates fruity notes in Alpine cheeses, like Sbrinz and Comté, and in hard Italian cheeses like Parmigiano-Reggiano and Grana Padano. Uncooked, pressed cheeses include Gouda, Pecorino, Ossau-Iraty, and also Cheddar. The one thing that unites all of these wheels is that they are pressed to remove as much moisture as possible so they can be aged without spoiling. If you want to explore aged cheeses more broadly, please be sure to mosey over to Alpines (page 114) and Cheddars (page 96), too, since they also age gracefully. This adventure focuses specifically on crystal-heavy hard cheeses outside of those two categories.

Aged Gouda

Gouda is a "high seas" cheese. Historically, the Dutch were deeply involved in trade, and their Gouda was built to endure long ocean voyages, becoming a staple source of protein on sailing ships. By the twelfth century, Gouda's popularity had spread across Europe as "an essential item on the explorer's shopping list," according to Juliet Harbutt, author of *World Cheese Book*. The tiny town of Gouda, where wheels were once traded in the market square, gives this cheese its name.

Today, most Gouda is actually marketed by a handful of Dutch brands that pool milk and produce cheese on an industrial scale. For that reason, I always recommend Beemster, a progressive dairy cooperative in North Holland that insists on pastured milk and still hand-stirs their curds. It's one of the best Goudas you can find at the supermarket. For small-batch cheese, the Dutch use the term *boerenkaas* (pronounced bore-en-koss), or farmers' cheese, which comes from a single milk source. Some good examples are Wilde Weide, Remeker, and Nylander. They're hard to find but fabulous, and all three are made by small family farms from organic, pasture-raised milk.

As you dig into aged Gouda, you'll notice that these waxen wheels are the sweetest of the hard cheeses. Here's the science behind it: Gouda is what's known as a washed curd cheese, meaning that once the whey is drained from the vat, it's replaced with hot water. This helps draw lactose, the sugar found in milk, out of the curds. As a result, bacteria have nothing to munch on, so they stop producing acid. Hence, Gouda retains its sweet, sugary profile, one of its most appealing characteristics. Young wheels have a gentle milky sweetness, and aged Goudas develop complex notes of brown sugar, bourbon, even pineapple. Many Goudas are golden or burnt orange in color, thanks to a touch of natural annatto, which makes the tiny white crystals appear especially bright, like impossibly small fossils. Keep in mind that you'll find the most crystals in wheels aged eighteen to twenty-four months.

Parmigiano-Reggiano and Grana Padano

Parmigiano-Reggiano is an Italian relic that has been around for at least nine centuries. Parm is what's called a grana cheese, which means granular. Look at a shard, and you'll see that it's made up of tightly packed grains that look like coarse sugar, or the internal structure of a geode. Made from partially skimmed milk from cows that graze in the country's fertile north, the curds of this cheese are cut into rice-size grains before they are drained, pressed, and packed into forms to become wheels. Add a year or more of aging, and pretty much every last drop of moisture evaporates, creating a pressed cheese with a dense, crystalline structure. Because of its strict production methods and limited quantity (see page 143), real Parm tends to be on the pricey end of the hard cheese spectrum. I like to savor it with a glass of Prosecco. For grating, I usually reach for Grana Padano, a hard grana-style cheese that is also from northern Italy, but less complex and less regulated. In the United States, Copper Kettle Parmesan and BelGioioso's American Grana, both made in Wisconsin, are also good-value options for topping pastas and salads, or for easy snacking.

Pecorino and Manchego

For hard sheepy treats, look no further than Italian Pecorino. (Pliny the Elder describes the stages of Pecorino Toscano in his encyclopedia, *Naturalis Historia*, which he completed in 77 CE, just to give you an idea of how long Pecorino has been around.) There's also Spanish Manchego, a cheese that appears in one of the greatest novels of all time, the early-seventeenth-century *Don Quixote*.

Aged sheep's milk cheeses are easy to recognize because the paste is as smooth as marble and the color of ivory. They taste richer and generally milder than aged cow's milk cheeses, making them easy to pair. Pecorino is sold at different ages, from fresco (fresh), which is mild and pliable—great for an antipasti plate—to stagionato (seasoned, or aged), which is hard and crumbly with concentrated flavor notes of almonds and herbs. Like Pecorino, Manchego is sold at different ages, so if you're after crystal action, look for a six- to ten-month Manchego curado.

One useful thing to know for anyone on a Pecorino excavation: In Italy, sheep's milk cheese is called Pecorino (pecora means "sheep"), and despite the generic name, every region has its local spin. Around Rome, for example, you'll find Pecorino Romano, a salt bomb that is great for accenting dishes. Around Tuscany, you'll find Pecorino Toscano, known for its sweetness and a wonderful pairing for jammy Tuscan wines. In Sicily, Pecorino Siciliano leans a little spicy, so it's sometimes accented with peppercorns or hot chilies. In short, the Pecorino that has evolved over centuries in each area of Italy fits the cuisine and represents the soil types and sheep breeds that vary from region to region. So, sampling a slew of Pecorini—the plural of Pecorino—is a damn glorious way to go deep into this style.

Will the Real Parm Please Stand Up?

There are only around three hundred producers of real Parm, some of whom produce only two or three wheels per day, following strict regulations. Parmigiano-Reggiano is such serious business that there's even a consortium—I call them the Parm police—to inspect every wheel. The inspectors stamp authentic wheels that are made according to the following standards:

Origin

Authentic Parm can be made only in certain zones of Emilia-Romagna, Italy, between April 15 and November 11, when the cows are eating the lushest grass. These zones are Parma, Reggio Emilia, Modena, Bologna (on the left bank of the Reno river), and Mantova (on the right bank of the Po river).

Milk

The diet of the animals must be grass or hay—no silage (fermented fodder)—and the milk must be delivered to the cheesemakers within two hours of milking. Per tradition, this cheese can be made only in copper vats, not stainless-steel ones, in keeping with the original recipe.

No additives

The cheese must be made of only raw milk, salt, and traditional animal rennet.

Aging

Each wheel must be stamped on the day it's made to ensure that it's aged for a minimum of one year. After twelve months, it's graded by the consortium. The best flavor develops at eighteen to twenty-four months, and some wheels are aged even longer, closer to thirty months.

Care

Affineurs turn and brush wheels of Parmigiano-Reggiano regularly. These aging experts also periodically test each wheel with a hammer to detect imperfections. Needles are used to extract core samples to ensure that each wheel is fine grained and flaky in texture, and that the developing flavors and aromas fit the profile of top-quality PR.

DECODING HIEROGLYPHS ON REAL PARMIGIANO

LOOK FOR THE FIRE-MARKED OVAL: This dark stamp is made by someone in the Parmigiano consortium. They brand the wheel with an iron only if it meets the highest standards. Rejected wheels cannot bear the seal of real Parmigiano-Reggiano. They're often sold as packaged grated cheese.

MIND THE PIN DOTS: The rind of real Parm looks like it's covered in braille, but it's actually a code. The code lists the name of the dairy and the month and year of production so that every wheel of real Parm is traceable. Lines or slashes running across the pin dots indicate that the wheel was rejected.

ADVENTURE № 6
CHEESE BOARD

4

Pecorino
PAGE 147

3

Parmigiano-Reggiano
PAGE 147

Think of this board as fieldwork for future cooking and snacking. By sampling many hard cheeses at once, you'll understand how to use these cheeses in dishes and know which ones pair well with pantry staples, such as aged balsamic, honey, and dried fruit. Note that this board is arranged from sweet to salty. If you want to accentuate the aged element of these cheeses, serve your findings on pieces of pottery.

1

L'Amuse Gouda
PAGE 146

2

Brabander Goat Gouda
PAGE 146

1

DUTCH GOUDA
(L'Amuse, Beemster, Wilde Weide)

Although "Holland Gouda" was recently granted name-protected status, you'll find Gouda made all over the world. Point your shovel toward tradition and start your dig with a high-quality Dutch Gouda such as **Beemster**, which is often found at supermarkets, or look for **L'Amuse Gouda** at a specialty cheese shop. Both companies offer Gouda at different ages, so to maximize crystalline crunch, seek out a Gouda aged at least eighteen months. For a special treat, see if you can find **Wilde Weide**, made on a tiny island in South Holland by Jan van Schie. This Dutch cheesemaker makes just six wheels of raw-milk Wilde Weide each day under the same thatched roof where his father made cheese wearing wooden clogs. The name *Wilde Weide* means wild meadow.

2

A GOUDA VARIATION
(Midnight Moon, Brabander,
Finger Lakes Gold Reserve, Ewephoria,
Marieke Gouda Smoked)

For a change of milk, look for a goat Gouda, such as **Midnight Moon, Brabander,** or **Finger Lakes Gold Reserve.** All of these have a candy-corn-like sweetness that's addictive. **Ewephoria**, made from sheep's milk, is even sweeter—it tastes like bourbon-soaked pineapple. For a good smoked or flavored Gouda, look for **Marieke Gouda**, made in Wisconsin by Dutch cheesemaker Marieke Penterman. Her Gouda laced with fenugreek seeds is a nod to traditional Goudas, which often incorporated spices—thanks to the Dutch spice trade—and her smoked Gouda is one of the few Goudas on the market that is naturally smoked over real hickory wood.

REAL PARMIGIANO-REGGIANO

(or Grana Padano, Asiago d'Allevo, or Ragusano)

Break out your excavating tools on a hunk of real Parmigiano-Reggiano, like **Cravero Parmigiano-Reggiano,** aged by fifth-generation affineur Giorgio Cravero. Naturally aged in his family's stone cave, where windows provide breezes from the countryside (there is no other air system, nothing high-tech), Cravero Parmigiano-Reggiano is exalted for its sweet taste and its unusual moistness despite intense crystallization. If you can't find real Parm, or if you've tasted it many times, try a different aged cow's milk cheese from Italy, such as **Grana Padano, Asiago d'Allevo,** or **Ragusano.**

AGED SHEEP'S MILK CHEESE

(Pecorino Sardo, Pecorino Toscano, Manchego)

If you've never tried **Pecorino Sardo (aka Fiore Sardo),** then do yourself a favor and try this smoky, salty sheep cheese from Sardinia that predates the Romans. Shepherds smoke it over balsam wood in mountain huts called pinnette—it's deeply traditional and should be experienced, especially with honey. For something sweeter and more delicate, choose **Pecorino Toscano** or a lovely Manchego, such as the wonderful farmstead **Essex Manchego,** which smells of straw and almonds.

Navigating PAIRINGS

Many wines and beers will work with these bold
cheeses. Note that sheep's milk cheeses are especially
flexible. Pecorino and a martini? Divine. Aged Gouda
loves rhum agricole or a Dark 'n' Stormy cocktail.

**Sparkling wine
or bold red**

Nut brown ale

Aged rum or gin

**Black tea or
coffee**

ACCOMPANIMENTS

Sweet aged cow's milk cheeses, such as Goudas and Parm, are especially
good with salty snacks and dried fruit. And aged sheep's milk cheeses, such as
Pecorino and Manchego, love sweet accompaniments, like honey or date syrup,
along with anything herbaceous, such as rosemary bread.

- Olives
- Almonds or candied nuts
- Charcuterie
- Cherries
- Dried figs or fig cake
- Dried apricots
- Honey or date syrup

- Aged balsamic
- Sliced fresh fennel
- Grilled vegetables
- Rosemary bread
- Pretzels
- Ginger cookies

Possible DETOURS

Mix up all this lactic crystal action with a soft slice
of goat cheese, like **Leonora** from Spain or **Bucheron** from France.
Both have bloomy rinds and are beautiful on a board, plus they'll add
a little tang. For a truly creamy detour, try **Brebirousse d'Argental**, a
silky sheep's milk purse with a blaze-orange annatto rind that looks
gorgeous among golden Goudas. All of these are young beauties that
will counterbalance the old flames. For a geologically appropriate
final bite, search for **Glacier Blue**, from Cascadia Creamery in
Washington, which is aged in a lava tube—an underground corridor
formed by lava flow. No, you can't make it up!

The Perfect Tool for Serving Hard Cheese

**Wondering how to serve hard cheese on a board? Since spreaders
and cheese planes will be useless here, pick a pointy knife and
allow guests to chunk off hunks of these cheeses. In most knife
sets designed for cheese, you'll find a pointy "stiletto." It's the
perfect tool for breaking hard slabs into shards. Then you can dredge those
bite-size shards through honey or aged balsamic. Delicious!**

TIPS FOR EXPLORING
* IN THE KITCHEN *

Hard cheeses tend to cost more than softies because they're more expensive to produce—more milk, more labor. So, buy small amounts and know that they keep well. And since they're so dense, you'll feel satiated quickly.

Pack an
AIRPORT SNACK

Mix shards of hard cheese, like aged Gouda, with nuts and raisins—or even pretzels, popcorn, or a bit of dark chocolate—for a long trip.

Add crunch
TO A SALAD

Toss sliced apples, Napa cabbage, scallions, and spinach with vinaigrette. Hunk up aged cheese in place of croutons to add richness and texture.

Make an
ANTIPASTI PLATE

Grill a bunch of veg, and set out a hunk of Parmigiano-Reggiano, sliced Pecorino, a bit of charcuterie, and a bottle of aged balsamic.

Save the rinds
FOR SOUP

Hard cheese rinds are great for making a meatless broth. Just drop them in as you would bouillon cubes and let them simmer for as long as you're cooking.

**OFF THE
BEATEN
PATH**

MIMOLETTE

With its orange color, pumpkinlike shape, and famously craggy
exterior, French Mimolette is an excellent party cheese, especially
around Halloween, when cheesemongers across the United States
like to carve it. It fits perfectly in this section because it was
originally designed, under the rule of Louis XIV, to replace popular
Dutch cheeses like Gouda and Edam with a French counterpart.
Nutty and fruity with a gentle twist of butterscotch, Mimolette often
reminds me of young Cheddar crossed with an aged Gouda. Look for
a deeply aged version, and chip at it like a geode. It's best eaten in
shards, alongside a glass of raisiny red wine and smoked almonds.

FIELD GUIDE

* Meet a *

* Meet a *

CHEESE CRYSTALOGRAPHER

Dr. Paul Kindstedt

"The American public is being exposed to cheese crystals like never before," says Dr. Paul Kindstedt jubilantly from a podium in Greensboro, Vermont, to an audience of cheesemongers and journalists. It's the anniversary weekend for the Cellars at Jasper Hill, Vermont's premier aging cave, and Kindstedt is about to lead the crowd through a "whistle-stop tour" of glittering cheese crystals found in Gouda, Parmigiano-Reggiano, Pecorino Sardo, Manchego, and Mimolette. In the cheese world, Kindstedt is the revered author of two groundbreaking books, *American Farmstead Cheese* and *Cheese and Culture: A History of Cheese and Its Place in Western Culture*. When he's not writing bibles, he teaches dairy chemistry at the University of Vermont. Recently, his lab made some fascinating discoveries, and Kindstedt—who looks like a cheese action figure (lean, bearded, intense)—is clearly elated to share it.

In 2012, Kindstedt formed a cheese crystal research team after a late-night epiphany at a cheese conference in Sicily: "Crystals could be cool," he says. "Europeans loved crystals in cheese, and yet I had been trying to eradicate them for fifteen years." Kindstedt explains how he'd worked with a group of distraught American grocers to fight calcium lactate on Cheddars—patches of white crystals that consumers mistook for mold. Some customers had even returned aged cheeses with heavy crystallization, fearing that the crunchy bits were glass shards. The grocers saw crystals as "public enemy number one," Kindstedt says, adding "and yet crystals are natural by-products of the aging process."

So, Kindstedt decided to start digging. Instead of fighting crystals, he decided he would try to make them cool. After he returned from Sicily, he reached out to Dr. John Hughes, world-renowned geologist and fellow UVM colleague. Together with Hughes and two UVM graduate students, Kindstedt began studying cheese using geological tools like a powder X-ray diffractometer and a polarized light microscope. The team discovered an array of calcium- and magnesium-based minerals, along with a variety of amino acid crystals, including L-leucine, L-tyrosine, brushite, and struvite. One crystal even attracted international attention from geologists and climatologists: the mineral ikaite, which the Kindstedt lab found on the surface of Winnimere (page 273), a bark-wrapped wheel of gooey goodness from right here at Jasper Hill Farm. In fact, the discovery was so significant that Kindstedt was awarded the Hawley Medal from the Mineralogical Association of Canada.

Turns out, ikaite, which grows on the damp surface of Winnimere, is a rare mineral first seen in nature by deep-sea divers who encountered spires of ikaite on the sea floor back in the 1960s. Until the Kindstedt lab found ikaite crystals on

Turns out, ikaite, which grows on the damp surface of Winnimere, is a rare mineral first seen in nature by deep-sea divers who encountered spires of ikaite on the sea floor back in the 1960s.

cheese rinds, geologists had seen this mineral only in laboratory samples of Arctic sea ice. Winnimere is technically a "smear-ripened cheese," meaning that a cocktail of bacteria is rubbed onto the surface to encourage rind development. For some reason, the surface encouraged ikaite to form—a fascinating discovery. "Ikaite only forms at freezing temperatures; otherwise it melts," Kindstedt says. "Why it forms on the surfaces of smear-ripened cheeses [like Winnimere] is a mystery."

Today, Kindstedt is on fire as he flips through slides of fluffy white calcium lactate patches on the surface of a raw-milk Cheddar and shimmering nodes of L-leucine embedded throughout Parmigiano-Reggiano. "They're like pearls," he exclaims. "If we can get people to fall in love with cheese crystals, we can strengthen the artisan cheesemaking movement."

If you dig the science of cheese crystals, check out the Cheese Science Toolkit (cheesescience.org) created by the late Pat Polowsky, a former master of science student in the Kindstedt Lab. Then, see what you can observe about crystals in the following cheeses:

What Are Those Crystals in My Cheese?

AGED GOUDA

Crystals: abundant "small pearls" of L-tyrosine

Not all Goudas contain crystals, but many aged varieties do. Look for tiny specks of the amino acid L-tyrosine. Kindstedt notes that they're smaller than the pearls found in Parm and Grana, and they offer a pleasing, sweet-salty crunch.

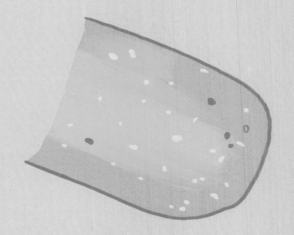

PARMIGIANO-REGGIANO AND GRANA PADANO
Crystals: large pearls of L-leucine

Both of these aged Italian cheeses are "absolutely loaded with crystals" of L-leucine, an essential amino acid. Kindstedt's team noted that these firm, perfectly round crystals were large enough to pop out of the cheese matrix and sit side by side "like a string of pearls."

MIMOLETTE
Crystals: L-tyrosine and L-leucine

Study the "eyes" (holes) in the paste of the cheese, and you'll probably see a lining of flaky L-leucine crystals. The paste of Mimolette also contains specks of crystalized L-tyrosine.

SUPERMARKET AND RAW-MILK CHEDDAR
Crystals: calcium lactate pentahydrate

Look for fluffy white crystals or a haze of calcium lactate on the surface of supermarket Cheddars. "They're visual, but not crunchy," Kindstedt notes. Crystalized calcium lactate pentahydrate can also be found in the body of aged raw-milk Cheddars, especially those with cracks or crevices; in raw-milk Cheddars, "these crystals can be a few millimeters in diameter and are crunchy."

SBRINZ
Crystals: L-tyrosine and L-leucine

"Look for amino acid crystals that are the result of Alpine starter cultures in highly cooked cheeses," Kindstedt says. These two crystals can also be found in some Gruyère and Comté.

WINNIMERE AND OTHER "SMEAR-RIPENED CHEESE"
Crystals: ikaite and struvite

You may not see these crystals immediately, Kinstedt notes, but you will notice a perceptibly gritty texture on the surface. These were once thought to be salt. In fact, they are miraculous crystals!

ADVENTURE
№
7
SMOKED, TRUFFLED, HERBY, SPICED

A Field Trip Through Flavors

GETTING ORIENTED

I'm going to let you in on a little secret: Flavored cheeses are kinda like wine coolers. True connoisseurs view them with suspicion. And with good reason. Flavorings can be cover-ups for low-quality milk. But there is some good stuff out there, too— and I'll show you how to find it. Just keep this in mind: If you find blueberries or peppermint sticks in a cheese, leave it for the gnomes.

WHAT TO KNOW

Make Sure You Can Taste the Milk

Flavored cheeses are one of the fastest-growing categories in the American cheese market, so expect to see more harissa- and Buffalo sauce–flavored cheeses coming to coolers near you. When you sample such a cheese, always ask yourself this: *Can I taste the milk? Is it balanced?* A great flavored cheese should still taste like cheese. Otherwise, what's the point?

Here's the Rub

I mean no disrespect toward flavored cheeses, but since many add-ins are overdone, your safest bet is to choose cheeses that have been rubbed. Look around, and you'll find wheels that have been caressed with rosemary, lavender, tomato paste, pepper blends, ground coffee, even cocoa. The good thing about these cheeses is that they contain surface-level complexity, which you can enjoy as you munch the rind, while the interior retains the integrity of the cheese itself. It's almost like you're getting two cheeses in one. Mahón, for example, is a fabulous cheese from the island of Minorca massaged with olive oil and paprika. Taste it and you'll notice a hint of floral pepper and a fruity kiss of olive along the edge, but the center of the wheel tastes different, like cooked sweet cow's milk. Another example: Cowboy Coffee, from Goat Rodeo in a suburb of Pittsburgh, works like a latte—it's mostly milk with a little bit of espresso. The makers use a blend of cow's and goat's milk to create a sweet, bright cheese that they rub with ground local espresso beans for a touch of smoky bitterness. Genius! Second tip: Bushwhack your way to a good cheese counter and ask a cheesemonger if you can sample the best flavored cheeses in the case. The best way to learn about flavored cheeses is to taste a lot of them. Third tip: If you fall hard for pumpkin-spice Cheddar, just own it. There's no shame in cheese love.

Look for Naturally Smoked vs. Smoked Flavor

Another dirty secret: Most smoked cheeses on the market never see any real coals (they're flavored with liquid smoke), so when makers take the time to naturally smoke their wheels over real wood, you'll notice a nuanced taste that allows the milk to shine through. One of the best smoked cheeses I've ever tasted comes from Crooked Face Creamery in Maine, where Amy Rowbottom cold-smokes her Jersey milk ricotta over real applewood to create her beautiful, spreadable smoked ricotta, called Up North. It's like eating the world's best soft-serve ice cream by a campfire. The cheese is featherlight yet luxuriant, with an unmissable milky sweetness that is made sweeter somehow by the gentle flicker of smoke—a taste you never tire of no matter how many spoonfuls of this cool, creamy wonder you devour. For another subtle smoke ring, try Idiazábal from Spain, an iconic sheep's milk cheese that is lightly smoked over cherry, hawthorne, or beech wood. It's wonderful on a camping trip, with red wine or dark beer.

Seek Out Adventurous American Makers

Look to the West and you'll find Cypress Grove in California leading the way with a line of flavored fresh goat cheeses with clever names, like Sgt. Pepper (laced with a blend of red peppers) and Purple Haze (rolled in lavender and fennel pollen). Nearby Point Reyes Creamery offers Japanese-inspired TomaRashi, a mild, buttery cheese with flecks of nori, toasted sesame, hemp seeds, and poppy seeds.

Head toward the Midwest for two nature-inspired cheeses from Wisconsin's Deer Creek Cheese. The Blue Jay is a blue dotted with juniper berries, a surprisingly delicious combination (especially with gin), and the Rattlesnake is a medium-bold Cheddar infused with tequila and habanero peppers. After a hike, I like to eat the Rattlesnake with chips and pineapple salsa. Point your compass toward Indiana and head toward Piper's Pyramide, a cloudlike goat cheese with a layer of smoked paprika. It was created by Judy Schad of Capriole Goat Cheese, who is also famous for her delicate Julianna, a soft, mushroomy wheel rolled in calendula petals, safflower, and herbes de Provence. It's better than wedding cake.

In the East, you'll find Abruzze Jawn from New Jersey, where artisan cheesemaker Paul Lawler of Cherry Grove Farm began making a raw-milk, grass-fed pepperjack using seven different kinds of peppers. In 2015, it won a medal for America's best flavored cheese.

ADVENTURE № 7
CHEESE BOARD

3

Brin d'Amour
PAGE 163

Next time you want to grill and chill, set up a flavored cheese tasting with plenty of beer, chips, and veg. Or plan this board for snack time on a camping trip. With so much big flavor, all you need is a couple of pilsners and a pocketknife.

4

Vampire Slayer
PAGE 163

Pilsner

2

Moliterno al Tartufo
PAGE 162

1

Up in
Smoke
PAGE 162

SMOKED

(Up in Smoke, Campo, Idiazábal)

TRUFFLED

(Moliterno al Tartufo, Cacio di Bosco al Tartufo, Sottocenere)

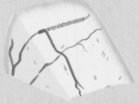

Start your board with a cheesemonger favorite: **Rivers Edge Up in Smoke**, a tender chèvre wrapped in a bourbon-misted maple leaf, then smoked over alder and hickory chips. This beauty from Oregon's central coast is produced by Pat Morford and her daughters at their farmstead creamery, Rivers Edge Chèvre. For something more meaty, look for **Campo** (it tastes like ham), a divine washed-rind cow cheese cold-smoked over pecan wood from Samantha Genke at Boxcarr Handmade Cheese in Cedar Grove, North Carolina. The name means field in Italian, but I prefer to think of Campo as the ultimate camping cheese. Eat it fireside with a flask of bourbon. For a traditional smoked sheep cheese from Spain, look no further than **Idiazábal** (iddy-ah-THAW-ball). It's lightly smoked and nutty—a terrific pairing for smoky red wines, stout, or smoked beer.

Many truffled cheeses are made with truffle flavoring, which tastes synthetic, so look for cheeses with actual bits of dark truffle, such as the truffle bomb that is **Moliterno al Tartufo**. Dry and woodsy, this dense and powerfully truffley Pecorino from Sardinia is excellent alone or grated. On a board, serve it with a mild, light-colored honey. **Cacio di Bosco al Tartufo**, from Tuscany, contains both black and white truffles and is more subtle and summery. For an interesting truffle-cheese variation, seek out **Sottocenere** (sotto-chen-NAY-ray), a creamy cheese from the Veneto region dusted with spices and stuffed with truffle slivers. It looks festive on a board and is excellent with warm potatoes (think foil packs for your next camping trip).

3

HERBY

(Brin d'Amour, Pecorino Ginepro, Cornish Yarg)

Corsica's **Brin d'Amour**, meaning "Breath of Love," is the ultimate herby cheese, made from moist sheep's milk enrobed in rosemary, fennel, and juniper. *Note:* It also goes by the name of Fleur du Maquis. Try it with a gin and tonic, alongside **Pecorino Ginepro**, a sheep's milk cheese from Italy's Emilia-Romagna region that is soaked in balsamic vinegar and pressed with juniper berries, giving it a dark, stubbly surface. For a breathtakingly beautiful cheese, look for nettle-wrapped **Cornish Yarg** from Cornwall, England. With its moss-green exterior, you can't look at this British stunner without dreaming of a picnic on a riverbank. Play off the buttery, lemony notes in this cheese with Berliner Weisse or a pilsner, and spend the afternoon cracking pistachios in the grass.

4

SPICED

(Vampire Slayer, Weinkäse Lagrein, Belper Knolle)

For an excellent pepperjack variation, look for **Vampire Slayer** from family-run Calkins Creamery in the Poconos of Pennsylvania. Clad in a black wax cloak, this mellow cow's milk cheese is armed with garlic, ginger, onion, and paprika to ward off dark spirits. For a booze-infused variation that tastes like salami, thanks to generous amounts of garlic and black pepper, **Weinkäse Lagrein** from the Alto-Adige region of Italy is soaked in Lagrein wine, which gives its rind a burgundy pop of color. Pair it with charcuterie—or don't!—it tastes like salami. For a deliciously strong grating cheese that is compact enough for a long-distance camping adventure, look for **Belper Knolle** from Switzerland. It's the size of a garlic bulb (and loaded with chopped garlic), then rolled in a thick coating of black pepper. The name means "tuber from Belp"—and it does look like an earth-covered turnip.

Navigating PAIRINGS

Keep your pairings simple and let these cheeses
lead the board. Lean toward light beers and
uncomplicated reds here, especially with spicy
and herby cheeses. For truffle cheeses,
consider a sparkling wine.

**Medium-bodied
red**

Pilsner

Vodka tonic

Sparkling water

ACCOMPANIMENTS

Lean on mild, juicy pairings here to prevent your palate from
getting fatigued when you taste a bunch of flavored cheeses. A drizzle of
honey is wonderful with truffled Pecorino.

- Soppressata
- Celery sticks
- Cucumber coins
- Grapes
- Olives

- Pickles
- Kettle chips
- Baguette
- Pistachios

Possible DETOURS

If you want to weave subtle flavors through this board,
look for **Havarti with dill**, a mild, creamy cow's milk cheese
from Denmark. There are also wonderful spice-laced Goudas,
including **Gouda with fenugreek seeds**, which has
a delicate maplelike taste. For a glorious smoked blue,
try **Rogue Creamery Smokey Blue**—an Oregon cheese
inspired by Smokey Bear.

OFF THE
BEATEN
PATH

ROCKWEED

For an unusual cheese layered with seaweed, look for award-winning
Rockweed from Maine. Allison Lakin of Lakin's Gorges was inspired by the
seaweed-covered rocks near her farm to create a bloomy cheese with an
emerald-green layer. It's creamy and full of salinity, not to mention gorgeous,
thanks to that bright green streak of chlorophyll.

TIPS FOR EXPLORING
* IN THE KITCHEN *

The cheeses in this adventure are great for snacking and for adding flavor to simple dishes. Don't hesitate to cube them like croutons and toss them onto leafy salads or pasta salads.

↓

Tuck your
HERBY CHEESES INTO AN ENDIVE BOAT

You can use this gluten-free trick for many cheeses, but herby cheeses are especially good if you set them into a taco-shaped endive leaf. Add chopped walnuts and a slice of apple for more crunch.

↓

Grate
TRUFFLE CHEESES ON PASTA OR ROASTED SQUASH

Splurge-y truffle cheeses will go far if you use them to add flavor to a simple pasta or risotto dinner. Just shave some truffle cheese, such as Moliterno al Tartufo, over the top. A little truffle cheese makes roasted butternut squash extraordinary.

Pack
FLAVORED CHEESE
ON ROAD TRIPS

Since these cheeses are both sustenance and a condiment, they're an efficient way to add jazz to a car ride. Next time you indulge your wanderlust, snag a couple of savory flavored cheeses and put them in your cooler alongside a few cukes, cherry tomatoes, and chips. They'll dazzle your travel partner when you break them out at a rest stop, and later you can pair them with whatever you find in the minibar at your hotel.

Put pepperjack
IN YOUR MAC

To add a little heat to your next dish of mac 'n' cheese, try using a pepperjack-style cheese. Try Vampire Slayer, a garlic Cheddar (page 163), especially around Halloween.

Make Your Own Flavored Brie

For a festive presentation at a party, buy a wheel of young Brie that's still a little firm in the center and slice it in half horizontally like a bagel. Then line the bottom layer with apricot or strawberry jam and toasted walnuts, or sautéed mushrooms and finely chopped chives. Place the top layer of Brie onto the filling, and wrap it in waxed paper. Refrigerate until thirty minutes before serving.

FIELD GUIDE

Meet a

CHEESE PAINTER

Mike Geno

Just as famed naturalist John James Audubon passionately painted birds and wildlife, Philadelphia oil painter Mike Geno has turned his artistic life into an homage to fromage. To date, his food-centric still lifes include more than 350 cheese portraits, as he calls them, and his subjects are often selected for their aesthetics—a ribbon of ash, a pepper-pocked interior, a scarlet rind. "I paint whatever makes me hungry," he says. "And I always paint from real life, never photos, so I can eat my subject." Follow Geno into a cheese shop, and you'll see him devour the counter with his large deerlike eyes, searching for the next hunk that makes him salivate.

> I like to translate what I find the most seductive about my subject. And cheese, it turns out, is the absolute perfect match for the way I paint. I get hungry looking at cheese.
>
> —MIKE GENO,
> *NEW YORK TIMES*

For his latest series, Geno set out to pay homage to innovative cheesemakers in the United States—a country many people associate with bland American cheese. His United States of Cheese is now a searchable map on his website (mikegeno.com) that highlights interesting cheeses from each state, including Alaska and Hawaii. Nope, you won't find Velveeta or Monterey Jack, two American icons, but you will find Morchella, a soft cheese from Wyoming studded with morel and mushrooms, along with Teahive from Utah, a hard cheese rolled in black tea and bergamot oil. "There's so much creativity within the cheese world," Geno says. "Most people have no idea."

As soon as Geno spread the word about his United States of Cheese project, wild cheeses began arriving at his studio by mail and even by personal courier. Early on, a studio visitor brought him a black wheel of Brie from Hawaii. "The cheesemaker used squid ink for color," Geno explains, pointing to a portrait of *Ocean Brie-eze* from Naked Cow Dairy on the island of Oahu. The cheese looked like a typical moon of bloomy white cheese, except when Geno cut into it, the dark paste oozed seductively, sending out a dark archipelago. That standout detail shimmers on canvas against an ocean-blue background.

One of Geno's favorites is Roth Sriracha Gouda, which he refers to as "the Jessica Rabbit of cheese." Hand-painted with bright red sriracha chili sauce and rubbed with crushed red peppers, this spicy cheese from Wisconsin appears cartoonish yet sexy in Geno's eyes. It looks garish hanging in his studio next to Big Bluff Tomme, a pale goat cheese from Missouri dusted with beige reishi mushroom powder. Nearby, Geno points to a personal favorite: Perdido, a golden wheel of cow's milk cheese with a horizontal stripe of ash and a velvety coating of moose-brown carob. "I saw it and

When sunlight streams through the long windows, the paint looks wet, each cheese almost lickable.

I knew I had to paint it," Geno says. He still loves to tell the story about how it was personally bestowed upon him by a fairy-tale-like woman with long white hair and a red cape who had been following his work from Alabama, where she made cheese for forty years. "I've been waiting for you to call me," said Alyce Birchenough, of Sweet Home Farm, as she handed him a wheel of her Perdido at a conference.

The creativity of cheesemakers like Birchenough have become a source of inspiration for Geno. "By representing their art as my art, there's a whole new level of relating to cheese and cheesemakers," he says. "I'm really lucky. I've gotten to find out how nice people are."

Geno, a former meat cutter who started sketching bacon and steaks after graduate school, has received glowing attention for his cheese portraits from *Vice Munchies*, the *New York Times*, and even *Esquire*. "My portraits of bacon and sushi have never generated this kind of interest," he says, noting that he now makes most of his living through commissions and cheese-print orders on his website. The cheese community and the delicious appeal of cheese itself breeds a unique scene and an unusual level of fervor, he says.

It also helps that at Geno's studio, in a former brush-bristle factory, his cheese portraits are spread across one giant wall like an epic floor-to-ceiling grazing board. When sunlight streams through the long windows, the paint looks wet, each cheese almost lickable.

CHEESE IS GOOD FOR YOUR TEETH

HERE'S A LITTLE DOSE OF CHEESE SCIENCE: Cheese is a great bite at the end of the night, because eating cheese slows tooth decay, according to Harold McGee, author of *On Food and Cooking*. McGee points to calcium and phosphate in cheese, which help protect your enamel from cavity-causing acid secretions that spike at the end of a meal. No wonder the French always insist on passing around a cheese plate after dinner.

ADVENTURE

№

8

Rock 'n' Roll

BLUE
CHEESE

BUS TOUR

GETTING ORIENTED

If the cheese world has rock stars, you'll find them among the blues, a band of pierced characters covered in tattoo-like markings that range from parsley green to indigo. To experience the full range of their multidimensional output, you might as well become a roadie and hop aboard their tour bus. Ready to Roquefort 'n' roll? Pack your motorcycle jacket and your best ripped T-shirt if you want to blend in, because the thing about blue cheeses is that most of them sound like heavy metal bands. Can't you just see Stilton opening for Gorgonzola Dolce? Or a headliner called Valdeón (a cheese draped in a dark cape of leaves) following bands like Black Castello and Bleu de Gex? The thing is, just like many hard-core rock musicians, blue cheeses are misunderstood. Many people write them off as too intense, too salty, but there's such a range—from spicy Cabrales (get ready to lose all feeling in your tongue) to sweet, cherry-ice-cream-like Chiriboga Blue. Prepare to party hearty, kids, this is gonna be one helluva trip!

WHAT TO KNOW

The Original Blue

Blue cheeses are the "pierced" cheeses of the world. Here's how they're made: During the process of cheesemaking, blue mold is stirred into the milk (the same blue mold that grows on bread, no less) to give the final cheese color and flavor. After the wheels are formed and aged for several weeks, the cheesemaker uses long needles to pierce the cheese. The piercings encourage the blue mold to oxidize and form visible blue veins. The more times a cheese is pierced, the more blue lines you'll find.

According to legend, blue cheese was invented by a shepherd who stashed fresh bread in a cheese cave next to some wheels of cheese and forgot about it for several weeks. While he was away, the blue mold spores "wandered" from the bread over to the cheese. Thus, French Roquefort was born, a cheese that dates back to the seventh century. At the Roquefort caves in France—the famous caves of Combalou—one family of makers (the Carles) still bake homemade rye bread to harvest blue mold for their blue cheese. Yep, pretty hard-core.

Roquefort also bears the distinction of being the first French cheese to receive Protected Designation of Origin status so that—like Champagne—it cannot be made outside the region where it originated. Roquefort is made from the milk of Lacaune sheep, and the sea caves where it ages have fissures in the rock that allow ocean spray to moisten the wheels. This gives Roquefort its naturally salty flavor.

Variations on a Theme

Although punchy Roquefort is considered the original blue, this salty slayer is just one of hundreds, if not thousands, of blue cheeses. Travel around France, not to mention the world, and you'll find both iconic as well as unusual blues everywhere. (Ever heard of Negroni Blue? It really is marinated in a Negroni cocktail.) Some blues—like Stilton—have natural rinds and thus, earthy flavors. Others are rolled in foil to lock in their moisture and make them creamy, like Roquefort and Gorgonzola. You almost need spoons to eat them. Finally, there are earthy blues wrapped in leaves, not to mention "white blues," like white Stilton, which has been inoculated with blue mold but never pierced, so it has the piquant smell and taste of a blue but no blue stripes.

Want to keep partying? Memorize this refrain: *To hell with crumbles*. If you're accustomed to buying pre-crumbled blue cheese in tubs at the grocery, get off the bus. Just kidding. Really, though, blue cheese crumbles are typically not of great quality, and they're full of anti-caking agents, like cellulose (aka wood pulp). So, next time you're in the mood for a blue on a steak or salad, bypass the plastic storage containers and crumble your own blue cheese. I'll tell you exactly what to look for, depending on your taste.

Savor the Flavor

Blues are some of the most nuanced cheeses in the case. They can be made from any milk—goat, cow, sheep, buffalo—and they vary in texture, from puddinglike to crumb-cakey to downright flaky. Their flavor range, like the voice of a talented vocalist, is wide and wild. Don't be surprised if you detect a trace of pipe tobacco or leather in a really good wheel of Colston Bassett Stilton or a note of dark chocolate and minerals in Valdeón. Some even taste grapey, like Blue des Basque, even though it is completely grape-free. And then there's Cabrales, a Spanish blue that has been compared to licking a battery. Yes, if you're the kinda person who likes doing shots of tequila, you're probably a Cabrales fan.

Get your lighters out. The bus just rolled up to the club, and we're about to party hard.

ADVENTURE № 8
CHEESE BOARD

1

Gorgonzola Dolce
PAGE 178

2

Stilton
PAGE 178

4

Rogue River Blue
PAGE 179

Plan a Blue Cheese and Black Sabbath party for your hard-core friends—a themed tasting I once hosted at my favorite bar, which had a record player. What's better than the hiss of vinyl alongside mouthfuls of blue cheese? You can ask everyone to bring a different hunk, or you can share this set list, which ranges from mellow to fierce with a couple of fun variations at the end. If you're not into super-intense flavor, dial this back and just pluck some faves from the first and last category for a striking dessert board.

3

Roquefort
PAGE 179

1

MELLOW

*(Gorgonzola Dolce, Chiriboga Blue,
Cashel Blue, Cambozola Black Label)*

Start soft. These are all creamy cheeses you can serve with a spoon. **Gorgonzola Dolce** from northern Italy and **Chiriboga Blue** from Germany are the sweetest on the blue cheese spectrum. They're seductive and have converted many long-standing anti-blue holdouts into swooning fan grrrls. Ireland's **Cashel Blue** is an easy-to-find lush leader you should be able to grab from your local supermarket, as is **Cambozola**, a cross between Camembert and Gorgonzola that is also a triple crème. It has a rad silver rind. Pair any of these cheeses with Amarena cherries in syrup, fresh figs, or sliced pears, and have a good time.

All of these cheeses are terrific with earthy walnuts, dark chocolate, and a pint of stout.

2

INTENSE

*(Colston Bassett Stilton, Stichelton,
Shropshire Blue, Bayley Hazen Blue,
Glacier Blue, Valdeón)*

Next, we get a little rugged with mostly natural rinds. The first four are all Stilton styles. **Colston Bassett**, made at one of the smallest Stilton creameries, rocks all kinds of flavor notes, from leather to toffee to bacon and tobacco. **Stichelton**, a raw-milk rock star, is a tribute to the way Stilton was originally made before regulations required English Stilton producers to pasteurize. **Shropshire Blue** is essentially Stilton with golden annatto added for color, and **Bayley Hazen Blue** from Jasper Hill Farm in Vermont is considered by many to be the best American version of the Stilton style, though **Glacier Blue** (page 263) from Cascadia Creamery in Washington vies for the title, too. For something intense but completely different, try leaf-wrapped **Valdeón**, a mixed-milk blue from Spain. It's covered in tiny blue veins, which is the secret to its strength. The face of it looks like liner notes.

3

FIERCE

*(Cabrales, Roquefort, Gorgonzola Piccante,
Point Reyes Original Blue)*

These bold blues are salty and punchy, especially Spanish **Cabrales**, which can surprise you with its wasabi-like heat. It's the one cheese I often recommend with a chaser of cold hard alcohol, such as tequila or vodka. For straight-up salty gorgeousness with lusty sheep's milk softness, **French Roquefort** is an essential experience. Its spirit animal is Sauternes, the classic French dessert wine. Italy's frisky **Gorgonzola Piccante** is less nuanced but great for a quick, swift heel kick. Soft and salty **Point Reyes Original Blue** is sharp and acidic. All of these cheeses can be tamed with honey or a hunk of honeycomb and dessert wine.

4

BOOZE-INFUSED

(Rogue River Blue, Negroni Blue, BirbaBlu)

These blues bring sweetness to a board. Lead with **Rogue River Blue** from Rogue Creamery in Oregon, a creamery that makes a wild array of blues. A stunning example of artisan American cheesemaking, Rogue River Blue is boozy and gentle with an undulating sweet-salty profile that's more mellow than "hello!" thanks to its booze-infused grape-leaf wrapping macerated in pear liqueur. Rogue River is also the first American cheese to be crowned World Champion Cheese at the World Cheese Awards. **Negroni Blue**, from Italy, is just like it sounds: a creamy blue soaked in a Negroni cocktail (made with gin, Campari, and vermouth) and topped with candied orange slices. It's a showstopper—a blast of boozy flavor with a straightforward medium strength. For beer lovers, don't miss **BirbaBlu**, a beer-forward babe soaked in blonde ale and packed in malted wheat.

Navigating PAIRINGS

Blue cheeses love dessert wines and dark beer or
IPA. They're also fabulous with bourbon drinks or
a bitter amaro. Try a Black Manhattan, made with
bourbon and an amaro in place of vermouth,
for a surprising match.

Port, Sauternes	Stout, IPA	Bourbon	Cherry soda

ACCOMPANIMENTS

Since blue cheeses tend to be salty, these pairings are mostly sweet.
Serve a simple board with dried fruit, honey, and nuts for a classic combination.
For something wild, check out Mansi Jasani's recommendations for
blue cheese and Indian sweets (page 183).

- Ripe pears
- Cherries
- Figs
- Dried apricots
- Quince paste
- Dates
- Walnuts

- Candied pecans
- Honey or honeycomb
- Chutney
- Onion jam
- Dark chocolate
- Biscotti
- Oat biscuits

Possible DETOURS

A few well-known soft goat cheeses are actually dusted with
Penicillium roqueforti, which adds a whisper of blue flavor
to their exteriors. Look for these two wonderful examples:
Monte Enebro from Spain and **Westfield Farms Classic Blue Log**
from Massachusetts. To offset the intensity of a blue cheese board,
try a hunk of **German Butterkäse**—it's the pound cake of the cheese world,
mild and buttery, a perfect non-blue bite to reset your palate.
Add a butterscotchy aged Gouda for textural variety and a hit of sweetness.

OFF THE
BEATEN
PATH

BLUE BRAIN

Imagine a snowball covered in furrowed blue mold, and you'll picture
Blue Brain, a recent offering from Jumi Cheese in Switzerland that's made
international news. When it appeared at Borough Market in London,
the *Guardian* ran a story with the headline "'Blue-brain' cheese: is this
the mouldiest cheese in Britain?" Probably not, but Blue Brain is a great
conversation starter. And a deliciously soft cream bomb that tastes like a
fruity blue when it's young (a few weeks old) and grows gradually friskier
over time, not only in its bite but in its rather morbid appearance. Try setting
this ghoulish cerebellum on a board at Halloween.

TIPS FOR EXPLORING

* IN THE KITCHEN *

Blue mold is like a feather boa—it leaves a trail wherever it goes.
So, store your blues separately from your other cheeses—
in a different bag or container—or prepare for a few indigo streaks
on your Cheddar and Camembert.

↓

Load it
ON A BURGER

Point Reyes Original Blue, from
California, is my go-to wedge for burger
night. It's creamy enough to spread,
and it's full of sea-salty savoriness
because the cows graze on pastures
close to the Pacific Ocean, so you won't
need to add any extra salt.

↓

Top
A STEAK

The minerality of Valdeón from León,
Spain, pairs well with beef. It's full of
fine indigo veins, and because it's a
leaf-wrapped cheese, there's a sweet
earthiness about its edges that forms
a perfect flavor bridge between seared
meat and a glass of Cabernet.

Build
A WEDGE SALAD

Choose a hunk of real Roquefort next time you're in the mood for a classic wedge salad of iceberg lettuce, bacon, tomatoes, and chopped chives. Douse the beast with buttermilk dressing and top it with a thin slab of Roquefort. It will fall apart beautifully and taste far more delicious than blue cheese dressing because you'll be able to apply a few crumbles to every forkful.

Serve it
FOR DESSERT

Don't bother with cake and ice cream. Serve a cakey wedge of Colston Bassett Stilton plated with figs and honey, or surprise your friends with a scoop of soft Gorgonzola Dolce in a small cup or coupe glass, then top it with Amarena cherries in syrup and a wafer cookie or pizzelle.

CHECK IT OUT

INDIAN SWEETS AND BLUE CHEESE

Mumbai-based cheesemonger Mansi Jasani loves to pair her favorite Indian snacks with blue cheese. On a visit to the States, she once stepped out of a taxi in front of my house, carrying bags laden with sweet-spicy treats and stellar cheeses for a pairing party. When she emerged from the kitchen with triangles of Bayley Hazen Blue topped with tufts of chhundo, a shredded mango pickled in a sweet-spicy syrup, I saw stars. It wasn't just beautiful to look at—like lightning bolts set against Bayley's soft indigo webbing—it was a stunning match. Imagine the twang of spicy mango against piquant blue cheese. Also memorable: aam papad, mango fruit leather with a touch of chili spice. Before your next blue cheese bash, stop by an Indian grocery for some chhundo and aam papad.

GRATE ESCAPE

A Backstage Pass to the
CHEESEMONGER INVITATIONAL

Where can you eat your weight in prizewinning cheeses from around the world while a man in a cow costume moos into a mike on a stage full of knives and rolling papers? Let me pull you through the back door of a heavy-metal-style cheese competition where dueling cheese shops are about to face off for a national title of champion cheesemonger. Here, have a beer and a cup of fondue. Then follow me through the sea of neck tattoos and the occasional person dressed in lederhosen, and you'll be in the mosh pit of the Cheesemonger Invitational (CMI), an event that started in the mid-2000s.

No, this isn't the only cheese competition of its kind—the French have the highly esteemed Meilleur Ouvrier de France, where participants in different food categories compete for honors. There are also cheese festivals around the world, including the World Cheese Awards (page 179), but the competitors at such festivals are usually cheeses, not people. CMI is one part bootcamp for cheesemongers, who train for months in advance, and two parts performance. When the show starts, you'll watch contenders try to ace a blind tasting, present original pairings in visually appealing ways, and speed-wrap hunks of cheese. That's why there are knives and wrappers on the stage.

The master of ceremonies is the country's most high-octane cheese spokesperson, and also one of its most powerful casein czars: Adam Moskowitz, whose Larkin Cold Storage facility in Long Island City, New York, is the clearinghouse for much of the imported cheese that you see in the United States. Adam likes loud beats, cow-spotted couture worn with gangsterish gold necklaces, and life on the edge. He's also an ingratiating host and a DIY guy who used to turn his storage facility upside down to host CMI in the early days. Back then, CMI was a scene where you had to wear earplugs if you wanted to hear your thoughts the next morning, but you could sneak off to a corner and eat Alpine cheeses all night long, because Adam had a line on the best stuff.

Tonight, we're in San Francisco (a few years ago, the Cheesemonger Invitational expanded with competitions on both coasts and in Chicago). It's a beautiful pre-pandemic night in January 2020, and this year's herd of hungry spectators is hanging out in a music venue made of cinder block painted matte black. The scene is less deafening, thanks to a better sound system, though still every bit as renegade. Look around the club and you'll see a Who's Who in dairy, from a crew of reps for Humboldt Fog, to Dutch cheesemaker Jan van Schie, who has traveled from a tiny island in Holland to offer samples of his Wilde Weide, to Carlos Yescas—an advocate for Latinx cheesemakers and raw milk. Owners of every major cheese shop in the United States are here, milling among groups of roving mongers wearing punny T-shirts, like *Last night a cheesemonger saved my life.* There's even Miss Cheesemonger, a longtime cheese slinger turned opera singer from San Francisco who presents arias in homage to fromage while her listeners eat cheese boards she's curated to pair with her lyrics.

Start chatting up the crowd and you'll meet plenty of PhDs, a few leather daddies, some fashion moguls who own designer creameries (yes, this is a thing), back-to-the-landers who stir curds in solar-powered spaces, a handful of midwestern dairy farmers in feed caps, and a "cheese preacher" from Chicago who goes

by "Cheese Sex Death" at her sold-out Sunday school classes.

So, sure, we're all here to see a show, the one on stage and

off. Behind the curtains, competitors are bumping fists,

gearing up to cut perfectly sized hunks of Havarti or

Cheddar or whatever is set before them. The speakers

are blasting beats. Two guys in suspenders are dancing.

Any minute now, the chanting will begin—"Moo, bahhh,

maaa"—and the stage lights will start flashing.

But first, someone hands you a toothpick with a hunk of rare Rogue

Creamery Smokey Blue. And guess what? If you eat it and smile, you're in.

That's all it takes to be one of us.

Part Three

ENTE

190   Shopping for Cheese

196   How to Taste Cheese
          Like a Pro

200   Fifty Must-Try Cheeses

204   Cheese Board Planning
          for Beginners

208   How to Care for Your
          Cheeses at Home

210   Sharing and Serving
          Cheese

212   Animal, Vegetable, or
          Mineral?

213   Tablescaping Tips

216   Tools, Boards, Knives,
          and Next-Level Gadgets

218   Going All Out

224   Top Tips for Pairing
          Cheese and Drinks

226   At-a-Glance Drink
          Pairings

229   The Lactic Lexicon

RTAIN

READY TO KICK OFF your travel boots? Let's pour some drinks and text some friends. It's time to share what you've learned from your adventures by building boards and hosting pairing parties. Everything ahead comes from a decade of throwing cheese balls (it's my thing—imagine a spring formal around a giant cheese board) and teaching Cheese 101 workshops at restaurants, shops, châteaus, and spas. Oh, yes, it's completely acceptable to eat cheese in a bathrobe.

Entertaining with cheese is easy, 'cuz no cooking. Assemble your besties, tell them you're launching a cheese adventure club, and pick a country to explore or a style of cheese to cruise around, or let a beverage like hard cider or orange wine become the anchor for a cheese-pairing-challenge night. Not feeling nerdy? No worries. A cheese party is really just an excuse for an easy-breezy celebration— great for birthdays or anniversaries. Ask each guest to bring a surprise cheese for the honoree, or build a board of decadent cheeses and ask your guests to bring bottles of bubbly. Who needs cake?

Let's zip to the store, and then I'll show you how to serve, pair, store, and converse about cheese like the lactic leader you have become. I've even got a lexicon of cheese descriptors on page 229 in case you want to host a formal tasting or write a menu or just stretch your palate at the cheese counter. Plus, if you're stumped at the store, you can refer to my bucket list of cheeses for fifty hunks to try before you die (page 200).

SHOPPING FOR CHEESE

Come on, let's grab some souvenirs. Depending on your home base, you can head to a local cheese shop or browse an array of cheese shops, cheese clubs, or makers online. It really is an amazing thing to have hunks sent right to your door. During the pandemic, many retailers and cheesemakers boosted their online inventory, so there's never been a better time to source cheese directly from makers and mongers.

Where to Buy Cheese Online

ORDER FROM A GREAT CHEESE SHOP

I always recommend buying directly from a shop where cheeses are freshly cut and wrapped. Here are some great cheese shops that offer high-quality selections with quick shipping. Pick one that's close to you so your cheese has a short flight.

- Antonelli's Cheese Shop, Austin, TX
  antonellischeese.com

- The Cheese Shop of Salem,
  Salem, MA
  thecheeseshopofsalem.com

- The Cheese Store of Beverly Hills,
  Beverly Hills, CA
  cheesestorebh.com

- Di Bruno Bros., Philadelphia, PA
  dibruno.com/cheese/

- Fairfield Cheese Company,
  Fairfield, CT
  Fairfieldcheese.com

- Formaggio Kitchen, Boston, MA
  formaggiokitchen.com

- Fromagination, Madison, WI
  fromagination.com

- Murray's Cheese, New York, NY
  murrayscheese.com

- Saxelby Cheesemongers,
  New York, NY (specializes in
  artisan American cheeses)
  saxelbycheese.com

- Zingerman's, Ann Arbor, MI
  zingermans.com

SUBSCRIBE TO A CHEESE CLUB

A number of shops offer monthly boxes, which takes the guesswork out of cheese buying. I'm partial to Curd Box (curdbox.com), created by curds&co. in Brookline, Massachusetts, for thoughtful selections and tasting notes. Also, Cheese Grotto (cheesegrotto.com) offers a club focused entirely on American artisans, and Antonelli's Cheese Shop (above) delivers splendid tasting kits with virtual classes, a fabulous gift.

BUY DIRECT FROM CHEESEMAKERS

Many great cheeses made in the United States are not available in supermarkets because distributors tend to work with large dairies, so if you want to try a variety of small-batch cheeses from a particular state, or you just want the 411 on great artisan American cheese, check out the list of mostly small-batch creameries by state (page 240).

What It Means to "Scrape the Face"

TIP

Look for this pro move! When an experienced cheesemonger prepares a sample of cheese from a wheel that's been wrapped in plastic, they'll use a knife to scrape off the surface layer of cheese that has touched plastic wrap. That's because cheese is very absorbent, and it will take on the taste of anything that's next to it. If you become a cheesemonger one day, don't forget to scrape the face!

Tips for Navigating a Cheese Counter

Okay, let's explore a cheese case. Think of it like an Island of Plenty and give yourself time to talk to the locals next time you go. If you live in a place with an independent cheese shop or a grocery with a specialty cheese counter, you're within range of paradise. Here's what you should know: Many cheesemongers who work at counters are like Greselda Powell (page 110), who fell in love with cheese and abandoned a successful career in another field to devote herself to dairy. They tend to be passionate, well-informed curd nerds, and some of them are even Certified Cheese Professionals, which is a bit like being a cheese sommelier. Feel funny chatting with them? Afraid to initiate a conversation? Don't be. I mean, are you afraid to talk to a tour guide? Or a concierge? Cheesemongers know everything that's happening in the case. They live to talk cheese and can tell you what style is in season, which Camembert is perfectly ripe, and which wheel will pair well with that special bottle of rosé in your cart.

Here's a suggestion: The magical hour of any cheese shop is right when they open, or around 10:00 a.m. on a weekday when the case is freshly stocked and you can have a conversation with the mongers. Don't be afraid to go early and ask questions.

☐ What do you have that's local or seasonal?

☐ Which cheese are you in love with right now?

☐ What's the wildest, most unusual cheese in the case?

My First Encounter with a Cheesemonger

When I first tasted Carles Roquefort, I couldn't name any of those flavors, I just experienced them like bolts of lightning.

I still get chills when I remember the first day I wandered into Di Bruno Bros. in Philadelphia, and a guy behind the counter named Hunter Fike handed me a life-changing bite of Roquefort.

First, I was smitten by the story he told me: This particular Roquefort was made by a French father-daughter team, Jacques and Delphine Carles (see page 270), who still harvest the blue mold for their cheese from homemade bread. *Say what?* Today, he told me, most makers purchase commercial *Penicillium roqueforti* from a lab, so the fact that Jacques and Delphine still use real rye bread for their blue cheese makes them the last traditional cheesemakers at the Roquefort caves of Combalou. (My eyes bugged out when I learned that there were actual caves—the kind with stalactites and stalagmites—where all French Roquefort cheeses are stored as they age.)

After telling me this story, Hunter guided me through what felt like a meditation in order to truly taste Carles Roquefort. He told me to close my eyes, warm the cheese between my fingers, and inhale deeply. Then he asked me to set the Roquefort on my tongue, close my mouth, and let the cheese soften. After a few seconds, he said, "Draw in a breath over the cheese, and then exhale through your nose." Then he waited. It was my first lesson in how to truly appreciate cheese, and it was rapture. Pure Roquefort rapture.

That sliver of iconic French blue took me on a journey of flavor, from an initial impression of sea-saltiness, to lush grapey sweetness, to vegetal notes of creamed spinach and minerals, to a mind-exploding spice punch that reminded me of the time I accidentally ate a whole peppercorn. Of course, when I first tasted Carles Roquefort, I couldn't name any of those flavors, I just experienced them like bolts of lightning. After I swallowed, I opened my eyes and just stood there, saying "wow" over and over again and laughing.

That was the beginning of my cheese life, a personal odyssey to eat every cheese in the Di Bruno Bros. case. After that, I returned to the shop every week for more lactic lessons from Hunter and other mongers, and I always brought a notebook. As we tasted cheese together, I jotted down flavor notes and pairing ideas and stories, which eventually led to a cheese blog and a book for the Di Bruno Bros company that Hunter and I wrote together. See what one bite of incredible cheese can do?

ASK THE RIGHT QUESTIONS

TIP 1

Want to feel like more than just a sightseer? Here's how to embed yourself in curd nerd culture. When you find yourself bellied up to the cheese counter, repeat after me:

- What do you have that's local or seasonal?

- My comfort cheese is X. What do you recommend that's in that style?

- If I'm going to drink X, what kind of cheese would be good to pair with it?

- I'm getting ready to travel to X. What are some cheeses I might try from there?

- Which cheese are *you* in love with right now?

- Do you have any farmstead cheeses?

- What's the wildest, most unusual cheese in the case?

BUY FRESH CUTS

TIP 2

The best cheese shops display whole wheels, and the staff handles cutting and wrapping in front of their customers. This is referred to as a cut to order counter, rather than a counter that sells pre-cuts, aka shrink-wrapped cheese. Once cheese is sliced and wrapped, it starts to suffocate (after all, cheese is a living food). You'll be able to taste this once you've developed your cheese prowess, because a "dead" cheese will taste flat in the same way that a flat soda lacks sparkle. If you do buy shrink-wrapped cheese, look for a packing date on the label. Ideally, it's been wrapped within the week. Generally, though, if you want stellar cheese, take the time to visit a cut-to-order counter. You wouldn't buy pre-poured coffee, so think twice before buying pre-cut cheese.

WHEN IN DOUBT, REACH FOR A SHEEP'S MILK CHEESE

TIP 3

Seriously, if you feel lost or indecisive, pick a firm sheep's milk cheese like Manchego or Pecorino Toscano; it will make pairing magic with just about anything you have at home—red wine, salami, dirty martinis, that jar of caramel in the door of your fridge. Sheep's milk is like the rare friend who can walk into a party, stay all evening, talk to everyone, and never offend.

CHEESE CALCULATOR

Here's a quick way to figure out how much you'll need of each cheese at a party or a cheese tasting.

NUMBER OF PEOPLE	AMOUNT OF CHEESE NEEDED (2 OZ PER PERSON)
5	¾ lb (340 g)
10	1¼ lbs (567 g)
20	2½ lbs (1.13 kilos)
30	3¾ lbs (1.7 kilos)
40	5 lbs (2.26 kilos)
50	6¼ lbs (2.8 kilos)

BUY SMALL AMOUNTS, UNLESS YOU'RE THROWING A PARTY
Purchase what you need for the week, so that your cheese stash stays fresh. For one or two people, a quarter pound each of three cheeses is usually enough for a week, if you're planning a couple of happy hours. Of course, it depends on what kind of cheese monster you are.

FOR A PARTY, PLAN ONE TO TWO OUNCES PER CHEESE, PER PERSON
As a cheesemonger once explained to me, one ounce of cheese is basically the size of your pinky or a pair of dice. There are sixteen ounces in a pound. For a nosh sesh with loads of accompaniments, like the cheese itineraries I've laid out in Part Two (page 38), plan on one to two ounces of each cheese per guest.

BE ADVENTUROUS—CHOOSE AT LEAST ONE NEW CHEESE
Remember my advice at the beginning? Try buying three cheeses at a time: a conversation piece, a comfort cheese, and something local or regional. With thousands of cheeses to explore, why get stuck circling Colby?

HOW TO
↓
Taste Cheese Like a Pro
aka THE YOGA BREATH OF CHEESE

At the counter, it's common to see cheesemongers squish a small piece of cheese between gloved fingers and inhale deeply before tasting. As any cheese professional will tell you, developing an appreciation for cheese starts with your nose. Just as wine nerds like to sink their nostrils deep into their glasses before they swirl and sip, curd nerds use a sniff test and a special "yoga breath of cheese" (my term) to fully taste each cheese. Here's how to practice this at the counter or with friends at home when you present a cheese board.

1 **Sniff.**
Take a piece of cheese and snap it in half right under your nose to make a clean break. How does it smell? Does it remind you of anything? Fresh milk? Caramel? Bacon? Hay?

2 **Set it on your tongue.**
Let it soften for a second or two. Sometimes it takes a moment for cheese—especially a hard one—to release its first flavor note. Feel free to close your eyes for this little pause. It's okay to roll the cheese around on your tongue, but don't chew it yet.

5 As you chew, pay attention to "the journey."

The best cheeses take you through three or four flavor landscapes. Usually, there's a first impression, followed by a second flavor or two as you begin to chew, and then a final note after you swallow. That final note may last several seconds, or it may curve around the bend into a new flavor and leave you with an aftertaste of citrus or herbs or hay or a burst of sweetness.

3 Open your mouth and inhale.

Take a deep breath—pretend you're at the doctor's. Inhale a big gulp of air so that it passes over the cheese on your tongue, and hold it in for a sec.

4 Close your mouth, then exhale through your nose.

Okay, you just sucked the aroma into your upper palate. As you exhale through your nose, you should experience something like "surround sound" but through taste. What flavors do you notice? Try using the Lactic Lexicon on page 229.

6 "Bunny Sniff" Your Elbow

If you're sampling a lot of different cheeses and you start to feel overwhelmed, simply roll back your sleeve and "give a bunny sniff" to the inside of your elbow. It should smell neutral, like clean skin. Then go back to the cheese.

Tips for the Budget Explorer

If you started this book at the beginning, you know that making good cheese costs money. For animals. For land. Plus, there's labor—some cheeses require daily or weekly maintenance as they age, not to mention marketing, packaging, delivering, shipping, and so on. Nobody in the world of artisan cheese is getting wealthy. Maybe they're getting a little bit famous in the way that some poets get famous, but trust me, nobody says, "I'm going to make a fortune by becoming a cheesemaker." So, like pour-over coffees and craft beers, stellar cheese costs a bit extra. Just know that. Now, here are some tips for exploring beautiful cheeses without going into hock.

SOFT CHEESES ARE USUALLY THE MOST ECONOMICAL.
This is because they contain a lot of moisture and take less time to age (read less real estate in a cave). So, your best bet for a crowd is a cheese board made up of soft and fresh cheeses of different textures or milk types, like the board described in Adventure One (page 42). Why do you think so many parties feature a giant slab of soft Brie?

USE FRESH CHEESE TO MAKE YOUR OWN DIP.
To stretch out a cheese board, pick up fresh ricotta or labneh (page 265) as your base cheese. Put it in a bowl, add a drizzle of olive oil, top it with some finely chopped herbs like basil or chives, and zest a lemon over it. Dang! You've got a terrific spread for crostini or a wicked dip for chips and celery. Set a few smaller wedges of cheese around it, along with some grapes and dried apricots or figs, and you've got a great board on a budget.

MAKE FETA YOUR EVERYDAY CHEESE.
Feta (page 270) is a pickled cheese designed to endure hot island life. It does not go bad, as long as you buy it in brine and keep it submerged and covered in your refrigerator! The best budget feta, in my opinion, is Bulgarian sheep's milk feta (I buy mine at a local Middle Eastern grocer), because it's wonderfully rich and creamy. Here's how to feta-cize your whole life: Stuff it in omelets, crumble it on salads, toss it with hot or cold pasta, sprinkle it on roasted veg, wedge nuggets of it into a baked sweet potato and then add hummus and wilted spinach, bake a slab of feta in your toaster oven for a snack and serve it with a drizzle of honey or olive oil along with pita chips. It's also good with melon or peaches or crumbled over pizza or casseroles before baking. It's even good on grilled steak or chicken, because it's salty and creamy, especially if you go for sheep's milk feta.

HARD CHEESES ARE SPENDY, SO LOOK FOR SPECIALS.

It takes a lot more milk, time, and effort to make aged cheeses, which is why they tend to cost more than young softies do. On the other hand, they pack the most flavor, so you can use a lot less. Splurge on small amounts and use them to boost salads and pasta dishes. To maximize, use a vegetable peeler and shave long, thin ribbons of hard cheese on top of simple meals for a big pop of flavor. Several good-value hard cheeses I often recommend: Piave, Grana Padano, Copper Kettle Parmesan.

SHOP AT FARMERS' MARKETS AND FARM STANDS.

Often, it costs less to buy direct. Sometimes makers need seasonal help at markets, too, so you might even be able to barter your time in exchange for cheese, especially if you become knowledgeable about the farm and can speak about it to others. Whatever you do, don't snarf all the samples and walk away without buying a piece of cheese. That will earn you a lifetime of bad dairy karma.

FIFTY
↓
Must-Try Cheeses

AN EXPLORER'S BUCKET LIST

Next time you feel a pang of wanderlust or you're unsure what to order at a counter, scan the horizon for one of these cheeses. Each wheel is a one-of-a-kind wonder. May the flavor and history of each one transport you to another time and place. And may you be inspired to keep discovering.

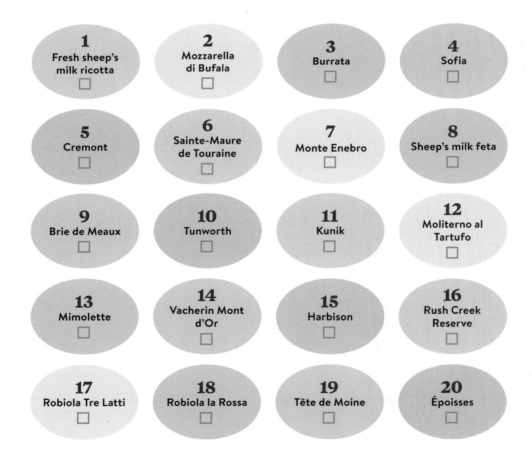

1 Fresh sheep's milk ricotta ☐

2 Mozzarella di Bufala ☐

3 Burrata ☐

4 Sofia ☐

5 Cremont ☐

6 Sainte-Maure de Touraine ☐

7 Monte Enebro ☐

8 Sheep's milk feta ☐

9 Brie de Meaux ☐

10 Tunworth ☐

11 Kunik ☐

12 Moliterno al Tartufo ☐

13 Mimolette ☐

14 Vacherin Mont d'Or ☐

15 Harbison ☐

16 Rush Creek Reserve ☐

17 Robiola Tre Latti ☐

18 Robiola la Rossa ☐

19 Tête de Moine ☐

20 Époisses ☐

21 Grayson ☐

22 Retorta ☐

23 Zimbro ☐

24 Gorwydd Caerphilly ☐

25 Appleby's Cheshire ☐

26 Montgomery's Cheddar ☐

27 Isle of Mull Cheddar ☐

28 Red Rock ☐

29 Cabot Clothbound ☐

30 Beaufort ☐

31 Pleasant Ridge Reserve ☐

32 Comté ☐

33 Chällerhocker ☐

34 Sbrinz ☐

35 L'Etivaz ☐

36 Manchego ☐

37 Taleggio ☐

38 Idiazábal ☐

39 Brabander Gouda ☐

40 L'Amuse Signature Gouda ☐

41 Wilde Weide ☐

42 Parmigiano-Reggiano ☐

43 Alp Blossom ☐

44 Pecorino Toscano ☐

45 Pecorino Ginepro ☐

46 Testun Malto d'Orzo ☐

47 Rogue River Blue ☐

48 Colston Bassett Stilton ☐

49 Stichelton ☐

50 Carles Roquefort ☐

FIELD GUIDE

* Meet a *
VEGETARIAN CHEESEMONGER

Adam Verofsky

Vegetarian cheese lover Adam Verofsky has worked at Whole Foods in various cheese departments since 2011. When I need the recs on veggie cheese, he lets me pick his brain. "I try all the cheeses that we carry, but I don't buy or bring them home unless they're made with vegetarian rennet," he says. Today, Verofsky oversees cheese teams in the mid-Atlantic region and spends his days bouncing from store to store. Of the numerous wheels and wedges he's tried, here are his go-tos for snacking and cooking, along with a couple of his favorite makers:

Torta del Casar A gooey Spanish cheese made with thistle rennet (see page 206). Verofsky says, "I grew up on burgers and fast food before I became a vegetarian in my early twenties. Torta takes the place of bacon in my life, it's so full of flavor."

Halloumi A great cheese for grilling or broiling, Halloumi is sold in blocks and can be used as a substitute for tofu. "It's got that toothiness and saltiness I crave," Verofsky says.

Cabot Cheddar All Cabot cheeses from Vermont are vegetarian, except for the company's processed American cheese slices and shredded Mexican blend cheese. Verofsky uses Cabot Cheddars for cooking and for shredding on tacos.

Catamount Hills For melting, Catamount Hills from Cabot is Verofsky's ultimate life enhancer. "Think of it like a cross between a Parm and Gruyère," he says. Verofsky loves to melt Catamount over roasted cauliflower.

Pavino This butterscotchy raw-milk crunch bomb from Roth's Private Reserve in Wisconsin is another vegetarian favorite for snacking and cooking. If you like aged Goudas with lots of little crystals, give this hunk a whirl.

Point Reyes Original Blue Original Blue (page 268) is Verofsky's go-to blue for crumbling on salads or topping a veggie burger.

TIP: If you're concerned about animal welfare on farms, look for the green-and-blue Certified Humane label or the green label from A Greener World (AGW). Both agencies are nonprofits that work to certify farms, and you can find detailed information about their standards on their websites.

CHEESE BOARD

↓

Planning for Beginners

THE CHEESE CASE MATRIX

BASIC CHEESE	MORE ADVENTUROUS		
BRIE	Délice de Bourgogne	St. Stephen	Cremont
BLOCK CHEDDAR	Cabot Clothbound	Shelburne Farms 2-Year Cheddar	Flory's Truckle
PEPPERJACK	TomaRashi	The Rattlesnake	Vampire Slayer Garlic Cheddar
GOUDA	Marieke Gouda	Ewephoria	Midnight Moon
MANCHEGO	Pecorino Toscano	Idiazábal	Pecorino Ginepro
CAMBOZOLA	Chiriboga Blue	Gorgonzola Dolce	Point Reyes Blue

Okay, let's say you've been standing at the counter for twenty minutes and you're starting to have a meltdown, literally, or maybe there isn't a cheesemonger available to answer your questions. Here are six cheeses you will probably recognize—from standard supermarket Brie to the gateway blue known as Cambozola (page 261)—with recommendations for stepping out of your comfort zone. Start with a "Basic Cheese" you know, then hop over to a "More Adventurous" option for something similar in taste and texture with a little more nuance, or jump straight over to an "Otherworldly" option if you want to taste something wild.

OTHERWORLDLY

Basic		More Adventurous		Otherworldly
Harbison	{	Tunworth	{	Robiola Tre Latti
Montgomery's Cheddar	{	Red Rock	{	Isle of Mull Cheddar
Piper's Pyramide	{	Marco Polo Reserve	{	Weinkäse Lagrein
L'Amuse Gouda	{	Wilde Weide	{	Marieke Gouda Foenegreek
Ossau-Iraty	{	Pecorino Sardo	{	Moliterno al Tartufo
Stichelton	{	Rogue River Blue	{	Roquefort

TOP PICKS FOR WHEN YOU'RE FRAZZLED

No time to browse the case? Too tired to taste the Taleggio? Here are a few fast and easy recommendations.

FOR DATE NIGHT
A triple crème like Délice de Bourgogne or Kunik. Just add bubbly.

FOR PASTA NIGHT
Pecorino Romano or Moliterno al Tartufo—both are salty and savory with big flavor, great for grating (or shaving) atop pasta.

FOR SANDWICHES
Havarti—it's plush and melts like a dream.

FOR MORE FLAVOR
Gruyère.

FOR A DESK SNACK
Aged Gouda—just grab some nuts, pretzels, and apples.

FOR LOUNGING WITH RED WINE
Piave, a nutty, fruity hard Italian cheese, or Manchego

FOR TAKING TO THE MOVIES
Pecorino Toscano—it's buttery and sweetly nutty, like popcorn.

Friends with Restrictions

Stumped by what to serve your pals who are lactose-free, vegetarian, kosher, or pregnant? Here are my top cheese picks.

LACTOSE INTOLERANT? OPT FOR AGED CHEESE, GOAT'S MILK CHEESE, AND SHEEP'S MILK CHEESE.

Here's a life-changing secret: Cheeses that are aged at least three months are virtually lactose-free. That includes Cheddars, Goudas, all of your Alpines, and hard cheeses. Avoid high-moisture cheeses, like ricotta and Brie, because they still contain a lot of whey (the carrier of lactose). Also, suss out cheeses made from goat's milk and sheep's milk—they are easy to digest—and surprise your lactose-sensitive friends with a wedge of Brabander goat Gouda (page 259) or sheepy Pecorino.

VEGETARIAN? TRY CHEESES MADE WITH MICROBIAL RENNET OR THISTLE RENNET.

Ninety percent of the rennet (page 23) used in commercial cheesemaking today is actually vegetarian. It's usually labeled on cheese packaging as microbial rennet, which is inexpensive and made in a lab to replace traditional animal rennet, which is what was used for centuries. The trick is, vegetarian rennet works best with soft cheeses, not hard ones, so it's not an easy switcheroo. Companies that excel at soft cheese, including Cyprus Grove in California (makers of the iconic Humboldt Fog) and Tulip Tree Creamery in Indiana, use exclusively vegetarian rennet. For a special treat, seek out thistle-rennet cheeses, like Zimbro or Azeitão, which are traditional in Spain and Portugal, and naturally vegetarian. You may need a cheesemonger to help you source them. A tea of flowering thistles is used to curdle the milk (cardoons naturally contain rennet), resulting in luxurious cheeses that taste vaguely vegetal, like an artichoke. For an exceptional thistle-rennet cheese, look for Retorta, an award-winning, pasture-based, raw-milk sheep cheese from Spain's Finca Pascualete, a farm that has been in the same family since the 1200s.

GO KOSHER WITH CERTIFIED CHEESES.

Kosher cheeses are clearly marked with the symbol of a certifying organization, such as STAR-K, KOF-K, Circle-K, or OU (Orthodox Union). Procuring a kosher certification can cost a cheesemaker thousands of dollars, so it's hard to find small-batch kosher cheeses. The best example I know of is 5 Spoke Creamery in New York, a small farm that offers a line of wonderful kosher cheeses, including Harvest Moon, a take on French Mimolette (page 266). Also, check out The Cheese Guy (thecheeseguy.com) for an extensive line of kosher dairy. Or, Tillamook in Oregon offers a single kosher cheese. Tillamook Kosher Medium Cheddar? It's a thing.

BABY ON BOARD? AGE UP.

Doctors often recommend avoiding raw-milk cheeses because of the slight risk of listeria, a bacteria that can cause serious (and yes, even fatal) infections in pregnant women and people with weakened immune systems. The "risky" raw-milk cheeses that doctors are worried about really center on young, high-moisture raw-milk varieties. That's because young raw-milk cheeses are more susceptible to harmful bacteria since they don't develop a strongly acidic pH, which would break the bacteria down. Keep in mind that listeria is rare and more likely to be found in cold cuts or spinach than in cheese, but if you want to play it safe, reach for pasteurized softies and choose only hard raw-milk hunks, such as Cheddar, Gruyère, Manchego, and Parm. Also, buy from reputable sources. For my raw-milk FAQ, please see page 32.

HOW TO CARE FOR YOUR CHEESES AT HOME

Follow these basic instructions, and your cheeses will stay daisy-fresh:

Use the crisper drawers closest to the bottom of your fridge to store cheese—think of these as mini-cheese caves where the temperature and humidity are constant. The ideal temperature for cheese is 35°F to 45°F.

Avoid plastic wrap. It suffocates cheese and imparts a plastic taste over time. Use breathable cheese paper (try Formaticum) or wrap your cheeses in waxed paper or parchment paper, then set them in a plastic bag and leave the bag open so that there's a bit of air flow. If you seal the bag, they'll get sticky.

Soft cheeses with delicate rinds, like bloomy Bries, like to feel the air on their face. Unwrap them and set them in a glass container lined with a paper towel (it will absorb any condensation), then leave the lid open just a smidge so air can circulate. Or, use a cheese dome. Note that you'll want to check on your softies every couple of days to make sure they're not either drying out or getting too damp, depending on your fridge conditions.

Store blues separately. Since blue mold likes to "wander," it's best to put them in a separate bag in a separate drawer from your other hunks.

A KEY TO THE CHEESE LOVER'S FRIDGE (OPPOSITE)

① SPARKLING DRINKS Keep plenty of sparkling wine, hard cider, beer, and bubbly water on hand. They're easy to pair with boards.

② CHEESE DOME A dome goes from table to fridge and makes a snackable cheese easy to access.

③ BLUE CHEESE CONTAINER Store blues separately so the mold doesn't spread to other cheeses.

④ CHEESE DRAWER Dedicate a drawer to cheese—this will function as a humidor and prevent your hunks from drying out.

⑤ MUSTARDS AND CHUTNEYS

⑥ PICKLES AND PRESERVES

SHARING AND SERVING CHEESE

You're ready to party like a casein queen or king. Whether it's a casual soiree, a seated tasting, a picnic, or a wedding buffet, here are tips for setting the scene and arranging boards on a tablescape, plus a tour of every possible tool that could support your future cheese forays.

ALWAYS LET YOUR CHEESE RELAX.

Cheeses taste best at room temperature, so remove them from the fridge an hour or so before you plan to serve them. Longer is fine, too. This step is called "relaxing your cheese," which is a very fun phrase to say to someone over the phone: "Excuse me, I need a little time to relax my cheese." If you're worried about your hunks drying out, cover them with cheesecloth or a clean dish towel.

WORK WITH NATURAL SURFACES.

Think of your surface as a runway. Needless to say, a plastic cutting board can work in a pinch, but a wooden cutting board or piece of slate or marble will look and feel more appetizing. I often use several small wooden boards to create little cheese-pairing islands. Usually I choose the boards first, then I figure out how I'm going to arrange the cheeses and accompaniments. For a party where you don't want to spend a lot of money on special platters and boards, try using large square tiles—just make sure they are food safe. Tiles that look like natural stone or terra-cotta look great under cheese.

ARRANGE YOUR CHEESES ON A BOARD FROM SOFT TO HARD.

In general, soft cheeses are milder than hard cheeses, so organize your board in the order you want guests to try them. Set out your fresh, light cheeses first to awaken their palate, then add triple crèmes, your washed rinds and Cheddars, and finally your flaky aged Goudas and big blues.

USE A DIFFERENT KNIFE FOR EACH CHEESE, AND CUT FROM NOSE TO RIND.

Invest in a set of cheese knives and you can use it at every party. Each cheese knife in the set corresponds to a different cheese texture, so they're very handy. (For more about tools, see page 216.) When you cut into a cheese, just remember that you want guests to experience every part of it, from the center to the rind. So, start your blade at the "nose" or point of a triangular cheese, then cut toward the rind. For blocks of cheese, cut long slices.

If I'm offered a good cheese board I know I'm in safe hands.

—PATRICIA MICHELSON, *THE CHEESE ROOM*

FOR PAIRINGS, ADD ONE ACCOMPANIMENT FROM EACH CATEGORY.

The more you taste cheese, the more confident you'll feel about creating pairings. Don't hesitate to raid your fridge or pantry as you experiment. You never know what amazing combination you might discover by surprise. (How do you think Pop Rocks and Valençay, an ashy French goat cheese, were first matched up? Yes, it's a thing!) If you need a lifeline, here are three texture categories to guide you in building a balanced board. Choose at least one accompaniment from each category.

CREAMY/GOOEY: honey, jam, jelly, dried fruits or fruit paste, marmalade, apple butter, dulce de leche, citrus curd, mustard, aged balsamic vinegar, olives or olive paste

CRUNCHY: nuts, pretzels, crackers, seeds, popcorn, corn nuts, nut brittle, potato chips, plantain chips, dark chocolate

CRISP: apples, pears, grapes, berries, plums, cucumbers, celery, cherry tomatoes, radishes, cherries, endive, snap peas, cornichons, pickled vegetables

LABEL YOUR CHEESES AND LEAVE THEM WHOLE.

Use a small card to write down the name of each cheese, the farm or place of origin, and the milk type. If you leave your hunks intact, rather than pre-slicing them on a board, they're easier to label and more enticing. C'mon, there is nothing sexy about a cheese cube! Snap a quick shot of your cheese board to chronicle it. That way you can always refresh your memory about what you served, and so can your guests. Btw, don't worry about your hunks going bad: Cheese has longevity! In French cheese shops, for example, many cheeses sit out on the counter all afternoon, often on a cool marble slab. Even cheese caves are not at refrigerator temperature. So, there's no hard-and-fast rule about leaving cheese out as long as your kitchen is cool. If it's a hot summer day, cheeses will begin to melt and sweat fat. The only cheeses that you don't want to leave out for more than a few hours are fresh ones, like ricotta or mozzarella.

CONSIDER AN "APRÈS CHEESE" DRINK TO AID DIGESTION.

After a cheese board, I love to serve an after-dinner drink: A bitter digestif, like an Italian amaro, works well, plus a cup of hot ginger or mint tea made with slices of gingerroot or fresh mint leaves. I learned this trick from cheese-trekking around the Netherlands, where local taverns go all out on using mint (as in a huge bunch jammed down into a glass mug) or long matchsticks of freshly cut ginger. There is nothing better after an epic cheese board than a shot of amaro and a steaming mug of herbal tea. When I'm having people over, I prep all of this on a tray—shot glasses, a bottle of amaro, mugs, lemon wedges, honey, cut ginger, washed mint—and then all I have to do is boil water.

ANIMAL, VEGETABLE, OR *Mineral?*

A CHEESE GAME FOR BEGINNERS

Not sure how to describe what you taste? Don't worry—you're not alone.
I felt the same way at first. Here's a quick game I sometimes play when I teach
total beginners how to taste cheese. With each new cheese you try,
ask yourself which of these three flavors is most dominant:
Animal? Vegetable? Or mineral? Here's how to make those associations:

ANIMAL...	VEGETABLE...	MINERAL...
if you smell/taste barnyard notes, like hay, earth, or bedding	if you smell/taste grassiness or fresh greens, like spinach or lettuce	if you smell/taste wet stone or pavement
if you smell/taste roasted meat, like beef stew, bacon, lamb chops, or broth	if you smell/taste spicy notes of garlic or horseradish	if you smell/taste something that reminds you of a cave or basement
if you smell/taste leather	if you smell/taste steamed asparagus, turnips, cauliflower, or caramelized onions	if you smell/taste salinity, like salt or sea water, or even oysters

TABLESCAPING TIPS

Go for a Grazing Table

The key to a beautiful spread is creating visual layers, which requires serving vessels of different heights. For a large party, cake stands and cheese domes work well for a dramatic display that runs the length of a table or sideboard. The garnishes should be colorful and of varying size, so scout around for fabulous-looking fruit and pick a variety, like small pears and kumquats, which you can tuck amid bunches of grapes or branches of rosemary, alongside pomegranates, figs, and apples. Tiny Lady apples are fun to work with in the fall, when they're in season.

- Start by arranging your boards, cake stands, and cheese domes on the table.

- A few yards of cheesecloth can be wound around the bases or used as a runner, for a rustic effect.

- To add height, fill a few vases with breadsticks, branches, or greens. Set these toward the back.

- Set out your cheeses: Consider three large hunks and two large rounds. You can also add a trio of small round cheeses on a single cake stand for an opulent look.

- Cover the cheeses with cheesecloth while you garnish the table.

- Drape grapes or boughs around the boards and stands to create a serpentine effect.

- Stagger larger fruit and jars and bowls of condiments along the table.

- Tuck in your smaller fruits last, using them for pops of color.

- Make sure to set out cheese knives by the cheeses and spoons by your condiments.

- Note: You can also create a grazing table that looks like one big mandala (see page 219).

Suggested Cheeses for a Grazing Table or Party

GOAT CHEESE
Choose Leonora (page 266) or Monte Enebro (page 267). Both are beautiful loaf-shaped cheeses that can be served whole or sliced like pound cake. Alternatively, buy a high-quality log of fresh goat cheese and roll it in fresh herbs and pink peppercorns, or wind cucumber ribbons around the length of it and gently press a few orange nasturtiums here and there.

ONE LUSH CREAMY CHEESE OR BARK-WRAPPED BEAUTY
For a large party, order a whole wheel of Délice de Bourgogne. Or set out a trio of softies, like bark-wrapped Harbison, and peel back the top rinds so people can dip baguette rounds or sliced veg into it.

TWO RUSTIC HARD CHEESES
Pick from the following: a clothbound Cheddar; a wedge of aged Gouda or Parmigiano-Reggiano so that everyone can eat a few crystalline shards; a firm sheep's milk cheese like Pecorino Toscano (broken up into shards and served with honey).

ONE GLOWING ORANGE STINKER

A lush square of Taleggio or a couple of small-format washed rinds, like Tiger Lily from Tulip Tree Creamery or Red Hawk from Cowgirl Creamery, will bring color and meaty flavor to the table.

ONE BLUE OR TWO!

A hunk of Stilton or Birchrun Blue (page 10) are my go-tos. Their natural rinds always add a rustic vibe. If there are blue fans among your set, add a second blue, like Roquefort (page 270) or Blu di Bufala.

TOOLS
↓
Boards, Knives,
AND NEXT-LEVEL GADGETS

Of course, you don't need any special tools to create an experience—any flat surface and a knife will do, even a book and a butter knife. But if you enjoy sharing cheese with others, it's lovely to open a drawer and lift out just the right tool.

CURVED SPREADER
(for schmearing super-soft cheese, like chèvre)

SKELETON KNIFE
(for gooey cheese; the holes prevent the paste from sticking!)

HOOKED KNIFE
(for cutting firm cheese, then hooking a hunk to pass to your lover)

STILETTO
(for breaking hard cheese into chunks or shards)

SLATE OR WOODEN CHEESE BOARD

SMALL DISHES
(for honey, olives, nuts, etc.)
Note: You can always use egg cups or shot glasses!

**CHEESE DOME
WITH A MARBLE BASE**
(for keeping softies cool
and covered)

CHEESE LABELS

CHEESE WIRE
(for making clean,
even slabs)

CHEESE PLANE
(for paper-thin slices)

CHEESECLOTH
(great for draping over
cheese before guests
arrive)

CHEESE PAPER
(for storing cheese like
a pro and sending leftover
hunks home with guests)

CHEESE GROTTO
(a home aging cave with
air vents and a clay brick
that you soak in water to
generate humidity)

RACLETTE OVEN
(Just throw some
sheepskins over your
kitchen chairs to re-create
an Alpine chalet vibe for
a night of melted cheese.)

FONDUE POT
(Go for a traditional
ceramic pot with Sterno
or candles, or there are
electric pots.)

GOING ALL OUT
↓
Four Ways to Style a Board

1 Cheese Mandala à la Lilith Spencer

When Lilith Spencer (@cheesemongrrl), formerly of Cheesemongers of Santa Fe cheese shop, began posting pics of patterned cheese plates laden with tile-like cheese slices and accompaniments, she changed cheese boards forever. Her ability to fishbone carefully cut cheese rectangles and to interlace triangles of Gouda into seashell-like whorls called to mind meditation mandalas—dizzyingly colorful and creative. Today, she has inspired a throng of cheese caterers and Instagrammers to apply her techniques to their own swirling, curling creations. If you like origami or geometry, give this a try. Start with a large plate or tray, cut up a lot of cheese, and give yourself a wide color palette of accompaniments.

- Use an odd number (one or three) of soft cheeses or dishes of condiments as "anchors."

- Slice firm cheeses into triangles or rectangles, and layer them to create interesting lines.

- Tuck swaths of rolled or folded cured meat alongside cheese or in a couple of zones.

- Arrange your smallest accompaniments last to fill in empty space.

Your Condiment Color Palette

cornichons, olives, pickled okra or green beans, pistachios, candied cashews, walnut halves, dried fruit (apricots, dates, figs, kiwi, white raisins), fresh berries, grapes, sliced peaches or nectarines, cured meats, cucumber slices, sliced radishes, cherry tomatoes, peppadew peppers, ground cherries, edible flowers

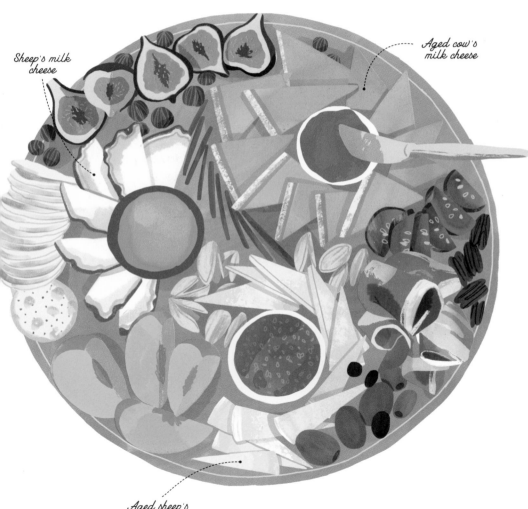

Sheep's milk cheese

Aged cow's milk cheese

Aged sheep's milk cheese

2 Long Rustic Board with Herb Garnishes

A single board works well for showcasing an odd number of cheeses—try a trio of goat cheeses or a row of cheeses with different textures. Use sprigs of fresh herbs, like sage, rosemary, or bay leaves, and weave them around the cheeses to add color. A trio of condiments in small dishes alongside looks lovely.

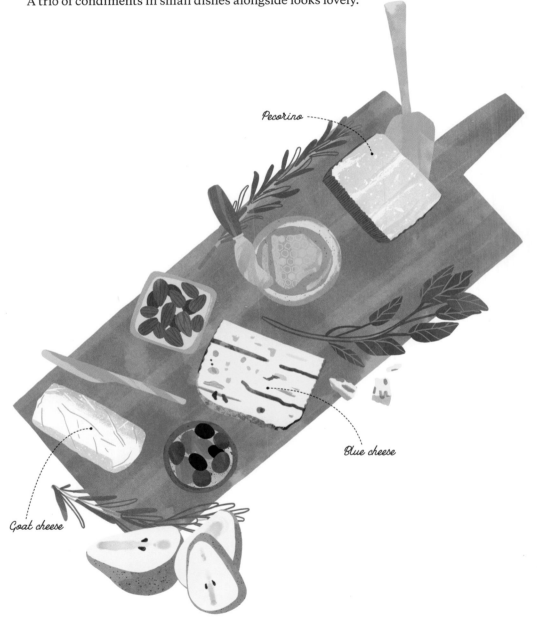

Pecorino

Blue cheese

Goat cheese

3 Slate Board with a Clockwise Selection

For four to five cheeses, try a large slate or a big circular board and arrange cheeses from soft/mild to hard/bold. Then group small accompaniments on the corners or edges and place something eye-catching in the center, like a trio of jams or a tufty mound of prosciutto with black grapes and rosemary sprigs. The effect should look casual but opulent—I like to let something spill off the board so that it doesn't look too pristine, like a few stray pistachios or a gaggle of grapes.

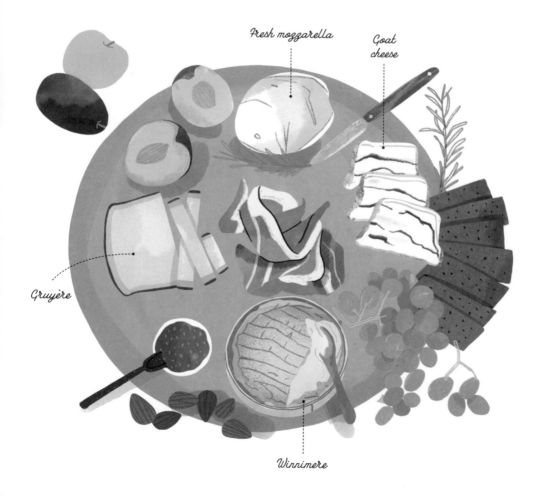

Fresh mozzarella

Goat cheese

Gruyère

Winnimere

Small Pairing Boards

Want to guide guests through a series of pairings? Set out some small boards or plates. You can place these around a room, or you can stack several small plates on top of one large wooden board and set it out on a counter or coffee table. This can be fun for a party or a presentation of different wines or beers.

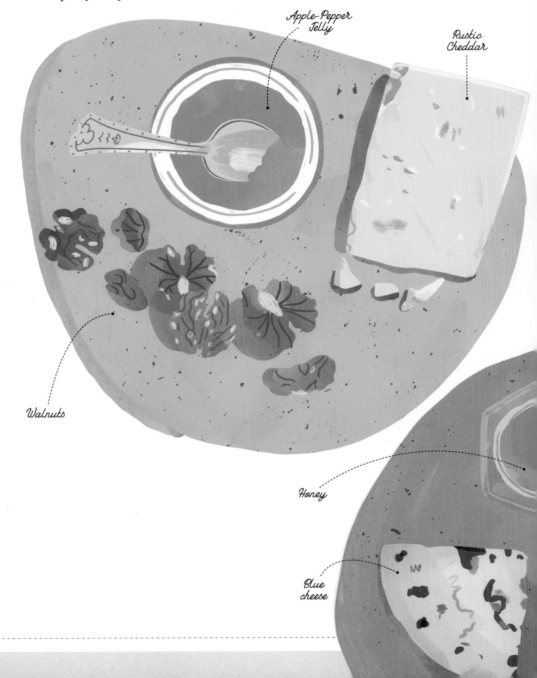

Apple-Pepper Jelly

Rustic Cheddar

Walnuts

Honey

Blue cheese

Brie

Lemon Curd

Pistachios

Dark Chocolate

TOP TIPS FOR PAIRING CHEESE AND DRINKS

Brie and Champagne? Blue cheese and barley wine? Goat cheese and green tea? If you've ever ventured into a cheese-pairing class or bobbed around a wet bar with a cheese board on your own, you know that pairings can be transcendent. They also cause a lot of consternation, so don't overthink it. If you've got an interesting bottle in your cupboard, break it out with your next board. You can learn as much from tasting a pairing that doesn't work as one that does.

WHAT GROWS TOGETHER GOES TOGETHER.
When in doubt, pair a cheese with a beverage from the same region. This is old-school pairing advice, but it often holds true—Camembert de Normandie, for example, is splendid with Norman cider.

BUBBLES CLEANSE THE PALATE.
Effervescence cuts through richness, so you can almost never go wrong with a bottle of bubbly, beer, or sparkling cider as a cheese pairing. The same holds true for nonalcoholic drinks. A glass of kombucha or fizzy water topped off with bitters or a splash of pomegranate juice makes for lovely sips between bites.

LIKE ATTRACTS LIKE.
Pair mild cheeses with mellow bevs, like pilsners, light whites, and dry ciders. Tart or tangy can also tango together: Try a bold Cheddar with a bold, hoppy beer, or try an herbaceous cheese with an herbaceous gin. Sweet aged cheeses with caramel notes (think Gouda) also pair well with sweet, malty notes in dark beers, rum, or bourbon.

CONTRAST IS COMPELLING.
Salty cheeses love sweet pairings—this is why a rugged Pecorino pairs so well with honey and why feta is fab with watermelon. Apply the same principle when you're picking out a bottle to pair with these cheeses. Pair salty cheeses with jammy wines, malty beers, and fruit-forward cocktails to create balance.

Five Bottles That Work with Most Cheeses

Heading to the beach with a bunch of different cheeses? Don't sweat it in your cabana. Pick one of these bottles for any picnic or party, and it will almost always pair beautifully.

SPARKLING WINE
Think Prosecco, Cava, Crémant, even Lambrusco. Avoid anything too brut (dry), as a little sweetness will rock your cheese world a lot more, especially if you have some salty aged hunks on the board.

GEWÜRTZTRAMINER
It's pronounced guh-VURTZ-trah-meen-ur. It's high in alcohol and full of fruity aromas like peaches and lychees (and sometimes a hint of smoke). Why is it magical? It loves salty cheeses and cured meats. So, it's kind of like pineapple on a pizza—it just works.

SAISON
Lots of carbonation and a little spice make a saison super-drinkable. Try Saison Dupont with any cheese and it's hard to go wrong. The Belgians know what they're doing.

GIN (AND TONICS)
Herby gin underscores grassy flavors in cheese, and fizzy tonic cleanses the palate. Pass the Pecorino.

GINGER KOMBUCHA OR GINGER BEER
Look for a kombucha that's not too sour, and enjoy invigorating sips between bites of cheese and cured meat. Ginger beer, and ginger in general, is great with Cheddars and aged Gouda.

The Flavor Wheel for Hard and Soft Cheeses

Curious to learn more? Check out the flavor wheel created by the Center for Dairy Research: cdr.wisc.edu/sensory-resources.

AT-A-GLANCE
Drink Pairings

HARD CIDER	
DRINK	CHEESE
BONE DRY/ DRY	→ fresh goat, fresh cow
OFF-DRY*	→ decadent cheeses, aged goat, aged sheep
TART	→ tangy goat, aged Cheddar
FUNKY	→ clothbound Cheddar, stinkers
BITTER, HOPPED	→ Cheddar
SEMISWEET	→ Gouda, aged sheep
ICE CIDER	→ blue, aged sheep (salty)

SPIRITS	
DRINK	CHEESE
VODKA	→ feta, fresh cow
GIN*	→ fresh or aged goat, fresh or aged sheep, stinkers
WHISKEY, BOURBON	→ Alpines, aged sheep, sweet blue
SCOTCH	→ clothbound Cheddar, aged sheep
RUM (DARK)	→ aged Gouda, aged sheep
TEQUILA	→ smoked cheese, fresh cow
MEZCAL	→ buffalo cheese

BEER

DRINK		CHEESE
LIGHT	→	fresh cow's milk (mozzarella)
WHEAT	→	goat cheese
HOPPY	→	Cheddar, blue
SAISON*	→	most cheese, esp. clothbound Cheddar
SOUR	→	aged goat
NUT BROWN/BOCK	→	Cheddar, Gouda, aged sheep
STOUT	→	smoked cheese, stinkers, blue
FRUIT	→	decadent cheeses, blue

NON-ALCOHOLIC

DRINK		CHEESE
GREEN TEA	→	chèvre
JASMINE TEA	→	Brie, triple crèmes
BLACK TEA	→	Cheddar, Gouda, aged sheep
APPLE CIDER	→	clothbound Cheddar, Alpines
GINGER BEER	→	Cheddar, Gouda
MILD KOMBUCHA	→	most cheese, esp. stinkers

WINE

DRINK		CHEESE
SPARKLING	→	decadent cheeses, aged cow
CRISP WHITE	→	fresh goat, fresh sheep
AROMATIC WHITE*	→	most cheese, esp. stinkers
MED-BODIED WHITE	→	Alpine, Cheddar, aged sheep
ROSÉ	→	fresh goat, fresh cow
LIGHT, FRUITY RED	→	Alpine, mild stinkers
EARTHY MED-BODIED RED	→	aged sheep, aged cow
POWERFUL FULL-BODIED RED	→	aged sheep, aged buffalo
DESSERT WINE	→	blue, aged cow, aged sheep
VERMOUTH (SWEET)	→	Alpines, aged sheep

SHERRY

DRINK		CHEESE
DRY SHERRY (FINO, MANZANILLA)	→	fresh or aged goat or sheep (Spanish)
OLOROSO SHERRY	→	aged cow, smoked sheep (Spanish)

*Pairs with most cheese

SUGGESTED CHEESES FOR EASY BEVERAGE PAIRINGS

Need a quick idea for the suggested cheeses in the At-a-Glance Drink Pairings? Here are a few recommendations, along with the page numbers where you can find more cheese information.

FRESH GOAT: chèvre (page 261)

FRESH COW: mozzarella (page 267), ricotta (page 269)

AGED GOAT: Brabander Gouda (page 259), Midnight Moon (page 266)

AGED COW: Comté (page 262), Parmigiano-Reggiano (page 268)

AGED SHEEP: Manchego (page 266), Pecorino Toscano (page 268)

BUFFALO: Mozzarella di Bufala (page 267), Casatica di Bufala (page 31)

STINKERS: Taleggio (page 271), Grayson (page 264)

SMOKED: Idiazábal (page 265)

THE LACTIC LEXICON: HOW TO TALK ABOUT CHEESE TASTES AND TEXTURES

Learning to describe cheese can broaden your horizon, just as learning a few words in a foreign language empowers you to travel more deeply in another country. Some of the descriptors below may not make sense to you yet, but as you take risks on new cheeses and expand your palate, you'll discover a wide spectrum of flavors. Once you identify and name them, you'll be able to order cheeses with confidence and pair them more easily at home.

Use the "yoga breath of cheese" (page 196) when you studiously taste cheese, and practice on the list of fifty incredible cheeses on pages 200–201.

TASTES

Milky	Tropical fruity
Buttery	Grapey/winey
Grassy	Boozy
Herbaceous	Earthy
Clean	Woodsy
Bright (lemony)	Piney/resinous
Tart/yogurty	Tobacco-y
Floral	Musty
Flinty	Cave-y
Mineraly	Leathery
Mushroomy	Smoky
Vegetal/cabbagey	Funky
Yeasty	Beefy
Doughy	Barnyardy
Toasty	Bitter
Nutty	Spicy
Sweet	Peppery
Toffeelike	Salty
Butterscotchy	Brothy
Malty	Umami
Fruity	Prickly (highly acidic)

TEXTURES

Airy
Spreadable
Moussey
Pillowy
Creamy
Lush
Plush
Luxurious
Springy
Smooth
Waxy
Supple
Claylike
Chalky
Fudgy
Squidgy
Oozy
Gooey
Sticky
Firm
Hard
Dry
Crumbly
Grainy
Flaky
Crystalline

Part Four

KEEP
LEAR

232 Why Cheese Travel?

235 Cheese Festivals and Happenings

240 Exploring Artisan Cheesemakers Around the United States

244 Cheesemaking Classes and Experiences

248 Twenty Wild Cheeses to Explore Around the World

NING

HELLO, WHEYFARER! This is the part of the journey where you get to divine your dairy destiny. Will you plan a road trip to Maine to eat your way through one of the fastest-growing cheese states, stopping at small farms and farmers markets? Will you set off for Sicily, one of the great cheese-producing islands of the world, with an expert guide? Or, perhaps you long to meet other cheese lovers who are as devoted to cheese as you are, in which case you'll want to hightail it to a conference or festival. Get ready to receive some serious intel about cheese travel, classes, guilds, and guides. Blaze your own cheese trail, and by all means, send me a postcard.

But first, I want to let you in on a little secret: Visiting a cheese counter wherever you travel is usually a fabulous way to learn about the region—better than going to the bureau of tourism. You can pick up local snacks for your hotel room and usually glean some choice recommendations about restaurants, bars, breweries, even local bands. Whenever I drop into a new city, my first stop is always the independent cheese shop. It's my North Star, and I've never been steered wrong.

WHY CHEESE TRAVEL?

I always feel that I am most at home in a place when I am eating local cheese.

In 2009, when I started a cheese blog, I made a point of seeking out local cheeses wherever I traveled. Before I visited a new city, I'd sniff out a few cheese haunts, like cheese shops, cheese-centric restaurants, and local markets. Farmers markets in foreign countries are gold. On my first day in Paris, for example, I stumbled upon a small market near Montmartre where I met a vendor who sold terra-cotta crocks full of her own fresh sheep's milk yogurt. After I bought several, she pointed me toward an old man who harvested forest honey and a woman who picked mountain blueberries. Boom, I had a week of wonderful yogurt bowls to enjoy on the balcony of my little apartment.

> I always feel that I am most at home in a place when I am eating local cheese.

Another technique: If I'm walking through a town and I spot an old granny with sensible shoes and a shopping basket, I'll follow her for a few blocks and sometimes I'll get lucky, inadvertently drawn into a bakery on a side street or an out-of-the-way fromagerie. That's one of the best ways to come upon some lovely rolls and a hunk of local cheese you might never find otherwise.

Finally, if I'm on the hunt for a hotel or hostel, I try to pick the smallest one possible, someplace where I can strike up a casual conversation with the person behind the front desk, who, ideally, owns the place or lives nearby. I make no secret about my mission. "I'm here to explore cheese," I'll tell them. "I'm a writer on a quest for the most delicious, unusual cheeses possible. Where should I start?" Usually, I get raised eyebrows. "Cheese? Oh, let's see . . ." Then, a smile appears. I can't tell you the number of times this question has invited mysterious wheels into my life. Once, the mayor of a small Italian village sent a chef over with a wheel of local Pecorino. Another time, I was staying at a ranch in Sicily, and I looked up from a seat on the back porch to see a man in a cowboy hat crossing a field with a giant wheel of goat cheese in his hands. We cut into it, and he showed me how he liked to panfry slabs of it in oil, then eat the hot cheese drizzled with acacia honey.

As I always say, cheese people are the best people.

Tips for Getting Cheese Through Customs

At the end of each escapade, there are the cheese souvenirs one must bring back. When I am settled at home with my secret stash, nothing extends a journey or transports me like sitting on my stoop and unwrapping a cheese from somewhere I've just been. The paper around it looks different, and even the way it's wrapped feels special, folded by faraway fingers. Sure, you can bring home chocolates, jams, oils, wine, whatever you like, but there is nothing quite like the smell and taste of a cheese souvenir, especially one that's handmade from a small market or little shop where someone has said to you, "Take this—you won't find it anywhere but here."

SNEAK IT IN.
As long as it's for your own enjoyment, not for resale, you can smuggle cheese in your suitcase or carry-on. It's legal. Just remember: no cured meats or fresh produce. I fly with cheese all the time and have never had an issue.

STAY FIRM.
Firm and hard cheeses fare best. Softies can spoil, though I have flown many a time with weepy Bries and oozy bark-wrapped cheeses like Vacherin Mont d'Or. The key is to buy these cheeses when they're on the young side so that they are still a bit firm. That way they won't be perceived as liquids. On occasion, a few friends of mine have had gooey loot confiscated at the airport.

KEEP IT COOL.
If you're worried about a soft cheese like Brie on a long flight, freeze a few T-shirts the night before, and wrap them around your wheel right before you head to the airport. Another tip: Buy a little bit of cheese at the airport. I just did this in France and was given a nice cooler bag and a couple of ice packs. After I left the shop, I added my other cheese stash to this little treasure chest. *Parfait.*

WRAP IT UP.

Many cheese shops abroad have a vacuum sealer, so they can pack up your pack up your cheeses for you—just ask. If your cheeses are shrink-wrapped, they will stay fresh and you won't have to worry about them melting all over your good walking shoes. Just be sure to remove the plastic when you get home so your cheeses can breathe.

KEEP IT CLOSE.

In summer, pack cheeses in your carry-on—you never know if your suitcase will get stuck on a hot tarmac or stashed somewhere hot.

Just make sure your carry-on curds are well sealed so they don't get too whiffy (supposedly, wrapping them in newspaper absorbs the smell). Otherwise, your seatmates may hate you.

CHEESE FESTIVALS AND HAPPENINGS

From the Cheesemonger Invitational (page 184) to Australia's Mould: A Cheese Festival, there are more and more dairy-centric showcases all over the globe. Also, a number of regions offer cheese maps (see the list of Sample Cheese Trails & Dairy Road Maps in the United States page 243) or host regional festivals to celebrate their most beloved cheeses. Why not pack your bags for Portugal and check out the Serpa Cheese Festival, held in the walled village of Serpa, home of the gloriously gooey Queijo Cheese World Cup (aka Mundial do Queijo do Brasil), which launched in 2019.

Here are a few fantastic places to try new cheeses and meet people in every part of the industry.

VERMONT CHEESEMAKERS FESTIVAL

vtcheesefest.com

One of my all-time favorite festivals is held each summer at Shelburne Farms in Shelburne, Vermont. You can sample and buy incredible artisan cheeses and accompaniments on the banks of Lake Champlain, plus attend workshops about tasting and pairing cheese. Homey and welcoming, this daylong event is worth a road trip to Vermont. Be sure to eat at least one maple creamie (maple soft serve) along the way, and don't forget to pack your picnic blanket and cooler. If you plan ahead, you can stay at the beautiful Inn at Shelburne Farms, which is on the grounds of the festival and a wonderful place to relax, sip cocktails, peruse the library, and eavesdrop on cheese conversations over dinner. For an enthusiast, this is *the* ultimate Vermont cheese getaway. There's also an excellent Vermont Cheese Map, if you want to visit creameries along your route.

AMERICAN CHEESE SOCIETY (ACS) ANNUAL CONFERENCE

cheesesociety.org

Every summer, the ACS hosts a multiday summer conference that attracts cheesemakers, cheesemongers, shop owners, chefs, and enthusiasts from across North America. Held in different cities, it draws legions of curd nerds and is the best way to dip a serious toe into the scene. Everyone you could hope to meet is there, from goat breeders to cheese company reps to cheese shop owners. Plus, there is an epic lunch where you can taste *alllll* the butters. And a breakfast where you can taste *alllll* the yogurts. Small farms, large farms—you get to try products made at every scale. If you can't spring for the entire conference, volunteer behind the scenes for a day or two—it's an incredible way to get an overview of the American cheese landscape.

> **Cheese invites the world into us.**
>
> —SIMRAN SETHI, FOOD JOURNALIST

CALIFORNIA ARTISAN CHEESE FESTIVAL

artisancheesefestival.com

Spend a weekend in Sonoma sniffing out some of the best cheeses from around the state, home to so many great creameries, including Bohemian Creamery, Fiscalini Farmstead Cheese, Cypress Grove, Cowgirl Creamery, Point Reyes Farmstead Cheese Co, Bellwether Farms, and more. Meet makers, attend pairing workshops, and drink plenty of Cali wine. This much-loved festival is a great way to connect with cheesemakers and cheesemongers on the West Coast.

GOOD FOOD MERCANTILE

goodfoodfdn.org

The Good Food Foundation is a nonprofit devoted to supporting and empowering makers of all kinds who might be overlooked or underserved by other trade shows in the food industry. Curious to meet small-batch cheesemakers and dairies devoted to socially responsible farming? You'll meet them at the Good Food Mercantile, held three times a year on the East Coast and West Coast. The Mercantile is also a great place to source amazing cheese accompaniments, from crackers to jams, and a marvelous place to feel inspired if you are thinking about starting a small food business. Hop online to find out about Good Food members and their members' summit.

WORLD CHAMPIONSHIP CHEESE CONTEST

worldchampioncheese.org

Held every other year in Madison by the Wisconsin Cheese Makers Association, this showcase is a chance to check out a huge range of cheeses from around the world, submitted in more than 130 categories. Most of the judging takes place behind closed doors, but you can still hobnob with other curd nerds and taste wheels you'd never encounter otherwise.

SALON DU FROMAGE

salon-fromage.com

Held every other year in Paris, the Salon du
Fromage is an epic showcase of French cheese.
Brush up on your French pronunciation of Selles-
sur-Cher and plan to crawl your way back to
the metro after dosing yourself with some
of the country's most renowned
cheeses, yogurts, and butters.
The event takes place in
February at the Paris Expo and
often coincides with Fashion
Week, so book a hotel early
and get ready to double down
on fromage and couture.

CHEESE

cheese.slowfood.it/en

Think of this as the Burning Man of cheese. Also known as the Slow Food Cheese
Festival, it attracts small makers from around the globe, who take over the tiny
Italian village of Bra, not far from Turin, to celebrate rare cheeses you won't see
anywhere else. Bra is home to Slow Food, an organization that runs counter to fast
food by highlighting small makers and nearly extinct traditions. Wander the streets
of Bra during Cheese, and you'll meet Sicilian shepherds who coat their wheels with
clay, alongside the last makers of Monteboré—a triple-layered cheese that looks
like a wedding cake and was allegedly Leonardo da Vinci's favorite. While you're in
town, be sure to visit the University of Gastronomic Sciences. Walk through its epic
Wine Bank, where you can sip wine and study the soil samples of each vineyard, and
check out the extensive food library.

THE CHEESEMONGER INVITATIONAL

cheesemongerinvitational.com

Competitive cheesemongering? Oh, yes, it's a thing. Via separate championships in New York, San Francisco, and Chicago, cheese-shop team members from around the United States throw down their most delicious pairings and demo their best knife skills before a roaring crowd. Join the fun and meet a variety of makers from around the globe who table at this annual event.

ALKMAAR CHEESE MARKET

kaasmarkt.nl

If you're traveling in the Netherlands, don't miss this old-world cheese market that takes over the village square of Alkmaar, a town not far from Amsterdam, each summer. You'll see members of the local cheese guild, a historic men's club, ferry giant wheels of Gouda to the weighing house and re-create the process of grading and bargaining for cheese. This spectacle is a reenactment of the town's once robust cheese trade, which operated via local canals. Although the scene is mostly replayed for tourists, it's fascinating and very festive. Take a tour with one of the guild members (they wear white gloves and straw hats), and you can try your hand at being a cheese runner. There are also local museums devoted to cheese and to beer.

EXPLORING ARTISAN CHEESEMAKERS AROUND THE UNITED STATES

If you're road-tripping, why not check out some cheeses from local creameries along the way, or order the taste of a state in advance to prepare your palate for the terroir ahead? Many makers use social media to post about farm tours, farmers markets, and workshops if you're curious to connect with them along your route. Just know that most of these are tiny family-run operations, so they may not have regular hours for tours, though many have farm shops where you can pick up picnic fare. Also, I compiled this list from creameries I've visited and creameries that make cheeses I enjoy, so it's by no means comprehensive. May it whet your appetite to seek out more.

East

CONNECTICUT
Arethusa Farm (Litchfield)
Cato Corner Farm (Colchester)
Mystic Cheese Co. (Groton)

MAINE
Crooked Face Creamery (Skowhegan)
Fuzzy Udder Creamery (Whitefield)
Josh Pond (Whiting)
Lakin's Gorges Cheese LLC (Waldoboro)
Seal Cove Farm (Lamoine)

MASSACHUSETTS
Cricket Creek Farm (Williamstown)
Great Hill Dairy (Marion)
The Grey Barn and Farm (Chilmark)
Westfield Farm (Hubbardston)

NEW YORK
Churchtown Dairy (Hudson)
Four Fat Fowl (Stephentown)
Lively Run Goat Dairy (Interlaken)
Old Chatham Creamery (Groton)
Nettle Meadow Farm and Artisan Cheese (Warrensburg)

NEW JERSEY
Bobolink Dairy & Bakehouse (Milford)
Cherry Grove Farm (Lawrence Township)
Valley Shepherd Creamery (Long Valley)

PENNSYLVANIA
Alpine Heritage Creamery (Paradise)
Amazing Acres Goat Dairy (Elverson)
Birchrun Hills Farm (Chester Springs)
Calkins Creamery (Honesdale)
Caputo Brothers Creamery (Spring Grove)
Goat Rodeo Farm & Dairy (Allison Park)
Goot Essa (Howard)
Hidden Hills Dairy (Everett)
Keswick Creamery at Carrock Farm (Newburg)
Linden Dale Farm (Ronks)
Merion Park Cheese Co (Merion Station)
Perrystead Dairy (Philadelphia)
Shellbark Hollow Farm (Honey Brook)
Valley Milkhouse (Oley)

RHODE ISLAND

Narragansett Creamery (Providence)

VERMONT

Blue Ledge Farm (Salisbury)

Cabot Creamery (Waitsfield)

Grafton Village Cheese Co (Brattleboro)

Consider Bardwell Farm (Pawlet)

Fairy Tale Farm (Bridport)

Jasper Hill Farm (Greensboro)

Lazy Lady Farm (Westfield)

Neighborly Farms of Vermont
   (Randolph Center)

Parish Hill Creamery (Westminster West)

Shelburne Farms (Shelburne)

Sage Farm Goat Dairy (Stowe)

Twig Farm (West Cornwall)

Vermont Creamery (Websterville)

Vermont Shepherd (Putney)

Von Trapp Farmstead (Waitsfield)

Woodcock Farm (Weston)

Midwest

IOWA

Maytag Dairy Farms (Newton)

Milton Creamery (Milton)

Reichert's Dairy Air (Knoxville)

INDIANA

Capriole Goat Cheese (Greenville)

Jacobs & Brichford Cheese (Connersville)

Tulip Tree Creamery (Indianapolis)

MICHIGAN

Idyll Farms (Northport)

Leelanau Cheese (Suttons Bay)

Zingerman's Creamery (Ann Arbor)

MINNESOTA

Caves of Faribault (Faribault)

Redhead Creamery (Brooten)

MISSOURI

Baetje Farms (Bloomsdale)

Green Dirt Farm (Weston)

Hemme Brothers Farmstead Creamery
   (Sweet Springs)

Dashboard Cheese Board

Expert traveler Anna Juhl of Cheese Journeys, a food tour company focused on artisan cheese (see page 244), taught me the key to van life: Spread a kitchen towel on the dash, pull a wooden cutting board out of your glove compartment, grab a hamper off the back seat, and you've just turned a rainy day on the road into a gourmet banquet of delights. Fellow travelers never fail to be astonished. Make it a habit, and you'll always be invited on beach trips and foraging adventures.

NEBRASKA

Dutch Girl Creamery (Lincoln)

OHIO

Canal Junction Farm (Defiance)

Yellow House Cheese & Meats (Seville)

WISCONSIN

Blakesville Creamery (Port Washington)

Bleu Mont Dairy (Blue Mounds)

Carr Valley Cheese (La Valle)

Cedar Grove Cheese (Plain)

Crave Brothers Farmstead Cheese (Waterloo)

Dreamfarm (Cross Plains)

Hidden Springs Creamery (Westby)

Hook's Cheese Company (Mineral Point)

Landmark Creamery (Paoli)

Marieke Gouda (Thorp)

Roelli Cheese Haus (Shullsburg)

Saxon Creamery (Malone)

Uplands Cheese (Dodgeville)

Widmer's Cheese Cellars (Theresa)

South

ALABAMA

Working Cows Dairy (Slocomb)

GEORGIA

Hobo Cheese Co. (Keith Valley)

Sweet Grass Dairy (Thomasville)

KENTUCKY

Kenny's Farmhouse Cheese (Austin)

NORTH CAROLINA

Boxcarr Handmade Cheese (Cedar Grove)

Chapel Hill Creamery (Chapel Hill)

Goat Lady Dairy (Climax)

Looking Glass Creamery (Columbus)

Prodigal Farm (Rougement)

OKLAHOMA

Lovera's Market (Krebs)

TENNESSEE

Blackberry Farm (Walland)

Sequatchie Cove Creamery (Sequatchie)

TEXAS

Mozzarella Company (Dallas)

Pure Luck Farm & Dairy (Dripping Springs)

VIRGINIA

Meadow Creek Dairy (Galax)

Twenty Paces (Charlottesville)

West

CALIFORNIA

Andante Dairy (Petaluma)

Bellwether Farms (Petaluma)

Central Coast Creamery (Paso Robles)

Cowgirl Creamery (Point Reyes Station)

Cypress Grove (Arcata)

Fiscalini Farmstead (Modesto)

Laura Chenel (Sonoma)

Marin French Cheese Co. (Petaluma)

Point Reyes Farmstead Cheese Co. (Point Reyes Station)

Stepladder Ranch & Creamery (Cambria)

COLORADO

Haystack Mountain
(Longmont)

James Ranch (Durango)

MouCo Cheese Company
(Fort Collins)

IDAHO

Lark's Meadow Farms
(Rexburg)

OREGON

Briar Rose Creamery
(Dundee)

Don Froylan (Salem)

Pholia Farm Nigerian
Dwarf Goat
(Rogue River)

Rivers Edge Chèvre
(Blodgett)

Rogue Creamery
(Central Point)

UTAH

Beehive Cheese (Uintah)

WASHINGTON

Beecher's Handmade Cheese
(Seattle)

Cherry Valley Dairy
(Seattle, New York)

Samish Bay (Bow)

Try Cheese Trails and Dairy Road Maps!

Many state tourism boards now promote dairy-tripping. Before you hit the open road, look for a cheese map or cheese trail for the state where you're going. You'll find these abroad, too. This is a mere smattering to get you started.

Berkshire Cheese Trail
berkshirefarmandtable.org/taste-trails-cheese/

California Cheese Trail
cheesetrail.org

Maine Cheese Map
mainecheeseguild.org

Pennsylvania Cheese Map
pacheeseguild.org/pennsylvania-cheese-trail-map

Vermont Cheese Trail
vtcheese.com

If you're looking for cheese contacts in a particular state, Google around to find a "cheese guild." Regional and state cheese guilds usually list upcoming events and maker maps on their websites. If you join your local guild, you'll be able to plug into cheese news and find out about happenings, from farm potlucks to cheesemaking workshops. Some states with active guilds include California, Maine, and Massachusetts. There's also a Southern Cheese Guild.

CHEESEMAKING CLASSES AND EXPERIENCES

A number of cheesemakers offer workshops, ranging from farm stays where you can milk goats and make morning ricotta to short afternoon workshops where you can learn to stretch mozz while you drink wine. Talk to local cheesemakers at farmers markets to see what they offer, or fold one of these special experiences into your travel plans. There's little more restorative than a cheese sojourn.

ACADEMY OF CHEESE
England
academyofcheese.org
Take courses online or in person with cheese professionals from around Europe. This nonprofit offers a multi-level certification program for anyone seeking to become a Master of Cheese.

ACADEMIE MONS
Saint Haon le Châtel, France
mons-formation.com
For an incredible experience at one of France's greatest aging houses, check out the class list on everything from affinage to cheesemaking to cheesemonger essentials.

CENTER FOR DAIRY RESEARCH IN WISCONSIN
Madison, WI
cdr.wisc.edu/short-courses
From short courses on cheese grading to pasteurization and sanitation, this well-respected research center on the University of Wisconsin campus offers a huge range of fascinating intensives all year long. The program has been running since 1890.

CHEESE JOURNEYS
Various locations
cheesejourneys.com
Cheese travel maven Anna Juhl hosts tours around the United States and

Europe for both professionals and enthusiasts, using her background as a former cheese shop owner to guide guests through key cheesemaking regions, including Somerset, England, the Savoie region of France, northern Italy, and Vermont. As a longtime cohost for this company, I can't recommend these tours enough. If you're looking to meet some of the world's best cheesemakers and affineurs, Cheese Journeys offers not just tours of cheese rooms and cheese caves but also a chance to sit down at the table for supper with these artisans to learn about their philosophy and their craft.

THE CHEESE SCHOOL OF SAN FRANCISCO
San Francisco, CA

thecheeseschool.com

From a cheese and wine pairing class to a Camembert-making intensive to a deep dive into how to open your own cheese shop, this institution attracts great educators from around the Bay Area to create unique cheese-driven experiences that run pretty much nonstop. Take a class next time you visit San Francisco.

THE CHEESEMAKING WORKSHOP
Coffs Harbor, Australia

thecheesemakingworkshop.com.au

Learn to make cheese at home from cheesemaker, author, and teacher Lyndall Dykes at her cheese shop and cheesemaking facility in New South Wales. Lyndall has been making cheese since the 1970s and has experience making just about every kind of cheese in a home kitchen, including camel's milk Halloumi. Her affordable daylong workshops include a deep dive into soft cheeses, such as quark and Camembert, plus an advanced course in firm cheeses, from Havarti to blues.

MURRAY'S CHEESE BOOT CAMP
New York, New York

murrayscheese.com/boot-camp

This Greenwich Village institution offers a two-day dairy intensive covering cheese styles, counter culture, and flavor analysis. Expect readings and an exam.

NEAL'S YARD DAIRY
London, England

nealsyarddairy.co.uk

Pop into London's premier aging house and cheese shop for a lesson in Cheesemaking Fundamentals, a history lesson in British cheese, or a "From Pasture to Plate" tasting. There's an impressive list of weekly workshops and cheese tasting nights—not to mention seasonally inspired cheese board workshops leading up to the holidays.

NEW ENGLAND CHEESEMAKING SUPPLY
Williamsburg, MA

cheesemaking.com

Sarah Carroll, daughter of the famed "cheese queen" Ricki Carroll, who has sold cheesemaking supplies to American cheesemakers for years.

SHEPHERDS AND FOOD CULTURE WORKSHOP
Puglia, Italy

messors.com

This annual workshop is offered by cultural guide Tonio Creanza, a Puglia native who has deep contacts in the world of shepherding and cheesemaking. His eight-day workshop is an immersive experience into traditional cheeses of the region—including burrata, scamorza, Pecorino, and giuncata (morning cheese)—but also includes much more, from foraging to olive oil tastings in the field to visits to his local butcher and baker friends. Home base is a rural masseria (a fortified farmhouse) with exquisite pastures and plenty of animals. An unforgettable place.

TULIP TREE CREAMERY
Indianapolis, IN

tuliptreecreamery.com/classes

Education is a tenet of this urban creamery, where lively two- to three-hour classes focus on make-at-home recipes, from buttermaking to homemade burrata. Private workshops for groups are also available.

WESTMINSTER ARTISAN CHEESEMAKING
Westminster West, Vermont

dairyfoodsconsulting.com

Cheesemaking legend Peter Dixon teaches multiday in-depth classes around the country but also at his home creamery, Parish Hill.

ZINGERMAN'S CREAMERY
Ann Arbor, MI

zingermanscreamery.com

Master mozzarella, take a production tour, or sit down for any number of pairing classes involving cheese and hard cider, wine, beer, or chocolate.

TWENTY WILD CHEESES TO

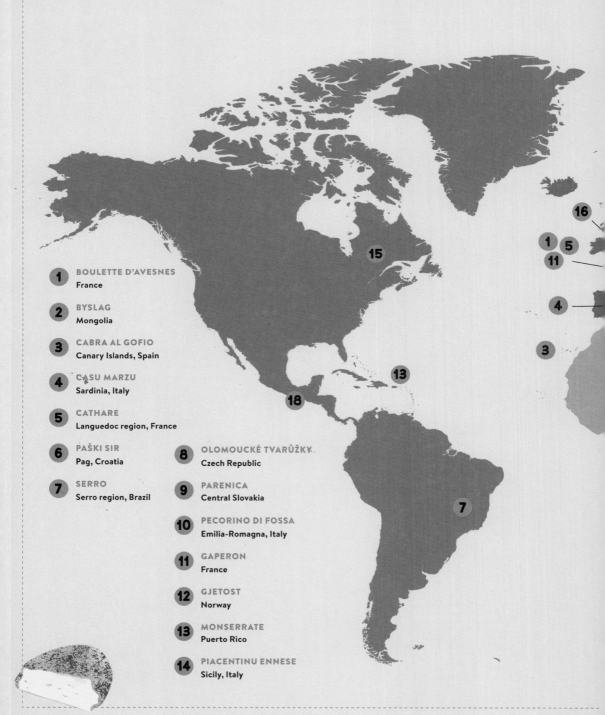

16

1 **5**
11

4

3

15

13

18

7

1	**BOULETTE D'AVESNES** France
2	**BYSLAG** Mongolia
3	**CABRA AL GOFIO** Canary Islands, Spain
4	**CASU MARZU** Sardinia, Italy
5	**CATHARE** Languedoc region, France
6	**PAŠKI SIR** Pag, Croatia
7	**SERRO** Serro region, Brazil

8	**OLOMOUCKÉ TVARŮŽKY** Czech Republic
9	**PARENICA** Central Slovakia
10	**PECORINO DI FOSSA** Emilia-Romagna, Italy
11	**GAPERON** France
12	**GJETOST** Norway
13	**MONSERRATE** Puerto Rico
14	**PIACENTINU ENNESE** Sicily, Italy

EXPLORE AROUND THE WORLD

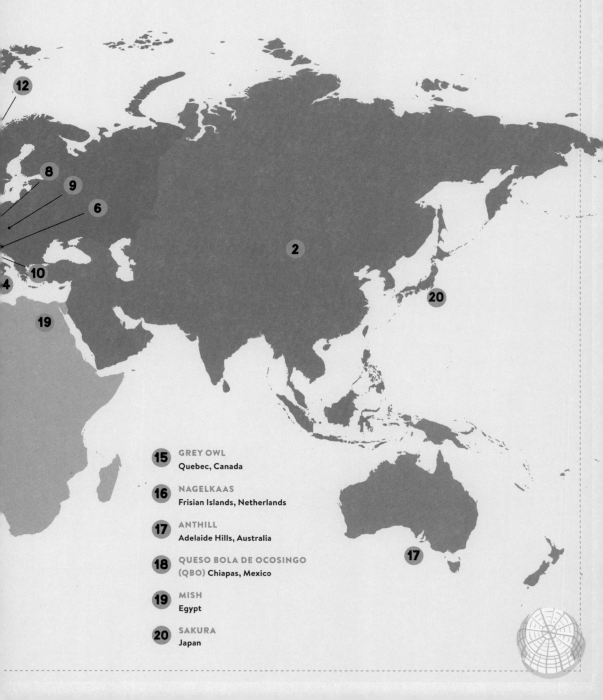

12

8

9

6

2

10

4

19

20

17

15 **GREY OWL**
Quebec, Canada

16 **NAGELKAAS**
Frisian Islands, Netherlands

17 **ANTHILL**
Adelaide Hills, Australia

18 **QUESO BOLA DE OCOSINGO**
(QBO) Chiapas, Mexico

19 **MISH**
Egypt

20 **SAKURA**
Japan

BOULETTE D'AVESNES
France

Otherwise known as le suppositoire du diable (the devil's suppository), this conical cheese mixed with fresh herbs and dredged in reddish-brown paprika is made from the leftover scraps of a famous local stinker called Maroilles. It was, as you might guess, invented by a monk. If you travel to France, you can easily find Boulette in Paris cheese shops (page 72).

 BYASLAG
Mongolia

Otherwise known as Mongolian yak cheese, Byaslag is a ricottalike cheese made in large blocks that are wrapped in cloth and pressed under piles of rocks to squeeze out moisture, resulting in a mild-tasting dry cheese that can be eaten fresh or aged. Served with tea, it's popular at Mongolian weddings or as a travel staple for nomads on the go. Alas, you'll have to go to Mongolia to find it.

 CABRA AL GOFIO
Canary Islands, Spain

This aged goat cheese is made on the island of Fuerteventura, using a traditional method of coating the rind in toasted corn flour (gofio). The local dairy, Grupo Ganaderos de Fuerteventura, works primarily with Majorero goat's milk from local farmers and its own herd. The taste is milky and mild with notes of sweet corn along the rind. You can find this gem in the United States, thanks to intrepid cheese hunter Michele Buster. Check out her company Forever Cheese (forevercheese.com).

 CASU MARZU
Sardinia, Italy

If you're a fan of travel shows, you've no doubt heard of "maggot cheese." The paste of this Sardinian sheep's milk cheese contains live insect larvae. Although it's technically illegal, according to European Union rules, intrepid cheese travelers report that it can still be found. No, I haven't tried it. But supposedly, it's delicious. To find it, you'll have to befriend a local villager with deep roots in Sardinia.

 CATHARE
Languedoc region, France

Every round of this delicate raw-milk goat cheese from southwestern France is rolled in ash, then imprinted with the Occitane cross—a symbol of the Cathars, a medieval religious group that settled the area around the time of the Crusades. This is one of the most beautiful cheeses to see (and eat—it's fresh and herbaceous tasting) in person. Look for it in cheese shops around Paris and London.

 PAŠKI SIR
Pag, Croatia

From the windswept island of Pag, Paški sir is made from a unique breed of Paška Ovca sheep, which are small and known for their rich, salty milk.

Why salty? The animals graze on woody grasses and herbs laced with dried salt from the heavy winds that are known as the Pag bora, making for a hard rustic cheese that is savory and herbaceous.

 QUEIJO DO SERRO
Serro region, Brazil
Gold explorers started artisan cheese production in Brazil's Serro region during the second half of the eighteenth century, creating Queijo do Serro. Beloved by locals, it's one of the country's oldest cheeses and still made by hand from pasture-raised raw cow's milk and native starter cultures, known as pingo. Often sold fresh or aged for eight to sixty days, Serro cheese can go from mellow and yogurty, when it's still young, to buttery and slightly piquant when aged for more than twenty days. This cheese has been inducted into Slow Food's Ark of Taste.

 OLOMOUCKÉ TVARŮŽKY
Czech Republic
What looks like a translucent golden doughnut is actually a pungent ring that tastes like gooey sautéed garlic. Originally made in the area around the city of Olomouc, the capital of Moravia, this centuries-old recipe is now protected by the European Union. A museum devoted to "Olomouc cheese" is in the town of Loštice.

 PARENICA
Central Slovakia
Parenica is a spiral-shaped, steamed string cheese that looks like a pair of fused cinnamon rolls. Mild and milky, it's made by shepherds in the villages of Slovakia's Podpol'anie region, using raw milk of the local sheep (though cow's milk is sometimes added). The technique of scrolling this cheese is passed from father to son. To find it, book a trip to Slovakia!

 PECORINO DI FOSSA
Emilia-Romagna, Italy
Since the twelfth century, cloth bags of lumplike sheep cheese have been buried in subterranean caverns, called fossa, from roughly mid-August to November (originally, this was to hide local cheese from Saracen pirates). On November 25, this dense, tangy cheese is unearthed with great gusto for the Feast Day of Saint Catherine of Alexandria. You can sometimes find this cheese in the United States at cheese shops, though it's rare. As you might imagine, it tastes wildly earthy.

 GAPERON
France
Farmers in the Auvergne used to hang this cheese flavored with garlic and peppercorns over their hearths to cure; legend has it that the number of these rounds hanging over a fireplace helped to determine the size of the dowry for the daughters of the house.

Today, Gaperon is still tied with yellow ribbon and given as a wedding gift. You can sometimes find this round wonder in the United States. It tastes like the world's best cheese ball.

 GJETOST
Norway

Sold under the Ski Queen label, this brown cube of sticky soft brown cheese is made from cooking down whey until it caramelizes. Norwegians love to eat it with sliced apples and often pack it on ski trips for when they need a quick boost. The merit of this candylike cheese, whose name is pronounced yay-toast, is oft-debated at curd nerd parties—people either love it or detest it. Sold in a shiny red wrapper, the cube-shaped cheese is easy to find year-round at many grocery stores.

 MONSERRATE
Puerto Rico

This black-wax-coated cheese is one of the only hard cheeses you'll find on the island of Puerto Rico. It's named after an old power station, and it's made by Wanda Otero, a microbiologist turned pioneering cheesemaker, who ran her own milk testing lab until 2006, when she saw firsthand how Puerto Rico's economic crisis was hurting women in the dairy industry. Instead of charging her clients for milk testing, she began accepting milk as payment. After experimenting in her kitchen and then attending cheesemaking classes, she

built her own creamery, Vaca Negra (black cow), where she makes cheese from local milk and teaches classes. Take a tour if you visit Hatillo!

 PIACENTINU ENNESE
Sicily, Italy

Made with sheep's milk, saffron, and whole peppercorns, Piacentinu (pee-uh-chen-tin-oo) was designed by a king, Ruggero the Norman (1095–1154), as a cure for his wife's depression. Saffron was thought to be uplifting to the spirit, and peppercorns were treasured. Hunt for this glowing, golden cheese if you travel to Sicily, or you may see its golden light from time to time at cheese counters in the United States.

 GREY OWL
Quebec, Canada

When Grey Owl was ordered for a dinner party surrounding Prince Harry's wedding in 2018, it made international news, and suddenly this little fascinator from Quebec was in high demand. Besides being one of Duchess Meghan Markle's favorites, Grey Owl is a stunning soft goat cheese with an ashy rind from a small creamery, Fromagerie le Détour, run by husband-and-wife team Ginette Bégin and Mario Quirion. The silver rind looks feathery, hence the name.

16 NAGELKAAS
Frisian Islands, Netherlands
This hard Gouda-style cheese is studded with whole cloves. The Dutch word for clove is kruidnagel, which means "spicy nail." This sweet cheese tastes like winter spices and is especially tasty when paired with a cup of chai. Look for it in the Netherlands, or seek out Marieke Gouda Clove from Wisconsin.

 17 ANTHILL
Adelaide Hills, Australia
Chèvre encrusted with dried green ants and dried lemon myrtle leaves? Yes, that's right. Maker Kris Lloyd of Woodside Cheese Wrights claims that the ants add a citrusy kick (not to mention a delicate crunch) to her award-winning chèvre. Only thing is, you'll have to pop over to South Australia to find this gem.

 18 QUESO BOLA DE OCOSINGO (QBO)
Chiapas, Mexico
An unusual artisan cheese from Chiapas made by stuffing a soft cheese into a firm cheese that forms a crust (think the turducken of cheese) to form a sphere. The first branded cheese of Mexico, it must be made from the raw milk of local Zebu-Brown Swiss cows. Prepare to travel to Chiapas for a taste!

 19 MISH
Egypt
This spiced cheese made in earthenware pots is thought to be similar to cheeses found in pharaohs' tombs dating back to 3200 BCE. The recipe calls for covering cheese curds with whey, salt, and a mix of red pepper, cumin, and fenugreek seeds, and letting the mixture ferment in jars sealed with mud paste for months or even years. Today, this salty, pungent mixture is still made mostly by home cheesemakers in Egypt.

 20 SAKURA
Japan
Made only during Japan's cherry blossom season in April and May, Sakura is a tiny Camembert-like cheese topped with a pickled cherry blossom, from Kyodo Gakusha Shintoku Farm in Hokkaido. These delicate wheels are aged for ten days on cherry blossom leaves, making them wonderfully aromatic, plus delicate and creamy. *Note:* This cheese was designed to look like the Japanese flag.

BOOKS FOR YOUR
LACTIC LIBRARY

The first cheese book I ever read was *The Cheese Room*, by Patricia Michelson, which was recommended to me by cheesemonger Zeke Ferguson, one of my first over-the-counter mentors. It inspired me to travel to London to visit the Cheese Room—a cool, dim spa-like space within Michelson's shop, La Fromagerie, which functions as a giant glass cheese humidor. From there, I read every cheese book I could get my hands on and built a little cheese library in my house. May this list of recommendations fuel your passion and help you find the hunks of your dreams.

Science & History

Butter: A Rich History
BY ELAINE KHOSROVA

Everything you ever wanted to know about the history and production of this famous fat, from sacred Buddhist butter sculptures to grass-fed vs. grain-fed butters. Author Elaine Khosrova crosses three continents, takes you inside farms and factories, and provides a bevy of baking tips and recipes.

Cheese and Culture: A History of Cheese and Its Place in Western Civilization
BY PAUL KINDSTEDT

A comprehensive look at the traditions and impacts of cheesemaking, from 6500 BCE to the present, this is a fabulous book for archaeology buffs, future cheesemakers and cheesemongers, or anyone interested in the development of fermented foods.

A Cheesemonger's History of the British Isles
BY NED PALMER

Want a history book you can cozy up to while munching a Cheddar and chutney sandwich? Jazz pianist turned cheesemonger Ned Palmer shares his infectious passion for British cheese and storytelling with a book that rolls through the eras, wheel by wheel, making this a must-read for turophiles and trivia nuts.

The Life of Cheese: Crafting Food and Value in America
BY HEATHER PAXSON

MIT anthropologist Paxson embeds herself within the artisan cheese movement after falling hard for a hunk of Hooligan, a small-batch stinker from Cato Corner Farm in Connecticut. Academic in tone but wonderfully readable, this well-researched volume takes you into the kitchens and creameries of rural entrepreneurs for a better understanding of how visionary cheesemakers are changing the landscape of American cheese.

Milk: A Local and Global History
BY DEBORAH VALENZE

Historian Valenze delves into digestion, milk myths, depictions of milk maids, cultural shifts, and controversial claims—all of which make for a fascinating overview of how western civilization has worshipped, consumed, corporatized, and politicized cow juice.

The Oxford Companion to Cheese
EDITED BY CATHERINE DONNELLY

A comprehensive tome with alphabetized entries covering a massive range of topics, from cheese mites to wine pairings. If you work in the industry, get this essential reference, and flip through it in your free time. It's full of fascinating information about cheesemaking and also includes an incredible variety of cheeses you've likely never heard of.

The Science of Cheese
BY MICHAEL H. TUNICK

Want to know how cows digest grass to produce milk? Or how surface molds on cheese affect flavor? Researcher Tunick delves under the rind and offers illuminating facts and anecdotes in a book that is both serious in terms of content and yet rather playful in tone—an unexpectedly delightful read.

Cheese Guides

The Art of the Cheese Plate: Pairings, Recipes, Style, Attitude
BY TIA KEENAN

Full of sumptuous photos, this next-level cheese plate guide offers advanced pairing ideas and thematic plates from a chef-turned-queen-cheesemonger at Murray's in New York. If you're keen to move beyond your basic apples-and-apricots approach to cheese boards in favor of caramel and Tandoori Cashews, this book is filled with enticing recipes.

The Book of Cheese: The Essential Guide to Discovering Cheeses You'll Love
BY LIZ THORPE

If you want to arm yourself with new ideas next time you hit the grocery, check out this book. Thorpe organizes each chapter around a common "gateway" cheese (such as Manchego), then points you toward an array of similar cheeses. Tasting notes and brand recommendations accompany each entry, and Thorpe offers useful insights from her years working as a cheesemonger.

Cheese: Exploring Taste and Tradition
BY PATRICIA MICHELSON

A beautifully written memoir by the owner of London's La Fromagerie, this book is a great example of passionate storytelling. It begins with Michelson's decision to open a cheese shop (made while she was skiing) and is full of seasonal suggestions, homey recipes, and tales about visiting European cheesemakers. File this under lactic romance—it will make you want to dump your day job and sell cheese for a living.

Cheese & Wine: A Guide to Selecting, Pairing, and Enjoying
BY JANET FLETCHER

This easy-to-follow guide from longtime journalist and cookbook author Janet Fletcher offers pairings for seventy cheeses, along with tasting tips and storage suggestions. It's a useful resource for hosting tastings or pairing special bottles with special cheeses.

Cheese Sex Death: A Bible for the Cheese Obsessed
BY ERIKA KUBICK

Chicago "Cheese Preacher" Kubick delivers dairy evangelism with a devilish smile, winning over neophytes with gooey blog pics and titillating texture references. Clever and crafty, her book of commandments will help you not only develop a worshipful approach to cheese but also understand how to buy the best Brie on a budget and melt it into manna.

The Flavor Thesaurus: A Compendium of Pairings, Recipes and Ideas for the Creative Cook
BY NIKI SEGNIT

While this isn't a cheese book per se, it's incredibly handy when you're trolling for pairing ideas—just look up goat cheese or blue cheese for a list of workable matches, many of which are a bit unexpected. Goat cheese and lemon curd? Why not?!

Mastering Cheese: Lessons for Connoisseurship from a Maître Fromager
BY MAX MCCALMAN AND DAVID GIBBONS

A fantastic entry into serious cheese study, written by the first master cheese sommelier in the United States, if you will (McCalman launched the Artisanal Bistro and Artisanal Premium Cheese Center in New York). The explanations of raw milk, terroir, and breed differences are invaluable, as are the lists of must-try cheeses. If you're a pro cheesemonger or cheese boarder, you'll want to devour a copy.

The New Rules of Cheese: A Freewheeling & Informative Guide
BY ANNE SAXELBY

The late great owner of Saxelby Cheese writes passionately and succinctly about how to buy and serve cheese in this manifesto. Need to know how to cut, wrap, or select cheese for a party? Saxelby offers practical advice as well as insights into the business.

Stuff Every Cheese Lover Should Know
BY ALEXANDRA JONES

Think of this as the pocket guide to cheese— all the essentials, succinctly explained, by a cheesemonger and food journalist with a keen understanding of the artisan American cheese realm.

That Cheese Plate Will Change Your Life: Creative Gatherings and Self-Care with the Cheese by Numbers Method
BY MARISSA MULLEN

A vivid visual guide created by Instagram cheese whiz Marissa Mullen (@thatcheeseplate). It's terrific for theme parties, color theory principles, and playful approaches to serving cheese.

How-To Books and Stories from the Field

American Cheese: An Indulgent Odyssey Through the Artisan Cheese World
BY JOE BERKOWITZ

One man's mission to glean everything he possibly can about cheese in one year, from attending conferences and competitions to working behind a counter. It's an illuminating and amusing odyssey through contemporary cheese culture.

Di Palo's Guide to the Essential Foods of Italy: 100 Years of Wisdom and Stories from Behind the Counter
BY LOU DI PALO

Want to go deep into mozzarella, Parmigiano-Reggiano, and Pecorino, not to mention things that pair well with them, like olive oil and aged balsamic? Lou Di Palo, owner of the longstanding family-run Italian specialty food shop in Little Italy, NYC, shares fascinating insights about how he selects his products.

Get Your Goat: How to Keep Happy, Healthy Goats in Your Backyard, Wherever You Live
BY BRENT ZIMMERMAN

Everything you ever wanted to know about goats, from raising different breeds to making cheese.

Home Cheese Making: From Fresh and Soft to Firm, Blue, Goat's Milk, and More
BY RICKI CARROLL

In the late 1970s, Carroll launched a cheesemaking supply catalogue (copies were 25 cents), becoming the United States's first real source of cheesemaking ingredients and equipment. Since then, she has coached thousands of novice cheesemakers (often over the phone) and become a legend in the business. This book of her recipes and techniques remains a classic.

Reinventing the Wheel: Milk, Microbes, and the Fight for Real Cheese
BY BRONWEN PERCIVAL AND FRANCIS PERCIVAL

The Percivals peer behind industrial cheese practices to find traditional recipes and the people who are reviving them. For anyone interested in British cheese, raw milk, and native starter cultures, this book is an essential read.

DAIRY DOSSIER
AT-A-GLANCE CHEESE PROFILES

For your next cheese shop visit or online ordering,
here's a quick reference to all the cheeses featured on
the cheese boards in the book.

ALP BLOSSOM Rolled in flowers and herbs inspired by the meadows where the cows graze, Austria's Alp Blossom may be the industry's most festive cheese. It's creamy and full of umami flavor, a stunner on a cheese board. Think Alpine cheese meets Funfetti.

ALPHA TOLMAN Jasper Hill Farm's Alpha Tolman is an Alpine-style cheese made in Greensboro, Vermont. An excellent table cheese or melter, it's named after a generous dairy farmer from the 1930s who helped build the local library. Many cheesemongers swear by this wheel for a great grilled cheese sandwich.

APPLEBY'S CHESHIRE Once a hugely popular British table cheese, Cheshire originates in the English county bearing its name. Today, this farmstead version produced by the Appleby family at Abbey Farm is championed as one of the finest and most traditional versions. It's made in cylindrical drums, wrapped in calico, and served as a table cheese. Try it with plum jam and toast or scones.

ASIAGO D'ALLEVO (PDO) Asiago d'Allevo comes from the highest part of northern Italy's Asiago plateau in the Veneto region.

Made at cooperative dairies with the raw milk of local cows, it's an excellent cheese for a tasting or a board. Apricoty and buttery, it's a far cry from deli-case sliced Asiago. Look for milky, pliable Mezzano (three months) or the more aged and complex Vecchio (nine months).

BAYLEY HAZEN BLUE Think Vermont Stilton. Made at Jasper Hill Farm in Greensboro, this raw-milk blue has a natural rind and loads of character. Imagine complex notes of toasted walnut, grass, butter, and even licorice. The name Bayley Hazen refers to a military road near the farm.

BEEMSTER XO A good choice for anyone in search of a high-quality supermarket Gouda, Beemster XO is made from grass-fed milk and humanely raised cows. Note that Holland's Beemster label includes a number of varieties sold at different ages. For the ultimate caramelized crunch-buster, look for Beemster XO, which is aged for at least twenty-six months.

BELPER KNOLLE This cheese looks like a freshly dug turnip still covered in earth; the "dirt" is a thick crust of crushed peppercorns enrobing a hard cheese crammed full of garlic. Shave it over pasta (use a truffle grater if you have one, or a cheese plane), and you've got an incredible topping that's fun to share at the table. Made from raw milk, this is one of the most unique cheeses from Switzerland.

BIRBABLU From Piedmont, this boozy cow's milk blue is soaked in local craft blonde ale and coated with malted wheat. The result is a hoppy, fruity, slightly crunchy cheese that beer lovers must try. It's made by the Rosso family at Caseificio Rosso near Biella. A rare find, this blue is worth seeking out for your next beer and cheese tasting.

BLEU MONT DAIRY BANDAGED CHEDDAR Made by renegade Swiss cheesemaker Willi Lehner of Blue Mounds, Wisconsin, this legendary raw-milk clothbound has a cult following. It's a mythical creature—difficult to find but so worth it. Lehner uses pasture-based milk from his rock-star neighbor, Andy Hatch over at Uplands Cheese (Hatch makes Pleasant Ridge Reserve and Rush Creek), then hand-makes this clothbound Cheddar in small batches and ages it himself.

BLOCK CHEDDAR Unlike clothbound Cheddar, which is made in round cylinders (or drums), the standard method for maturing most Cheddar involves cutting the cheese into cinder-block-like rectangles and sealing them in plastic. The shape makes them easy to stack and to store for aging. Quality and flavor varies widely, since there is no protected status for block Cheddar.

BLUE BRAIN Imagine an ice cream scoop of cheese with a wrinkly silver-blue surface. Yes, it really does look like a little brain. Created by Jumi Cheese in Switzerland— a company with a notoriously delicious

sense of humor—this spreadable blue is sweetly fruity and sharp. Forget all other cheese balls, and use this as a centerpiece for crackers and crudités at your next ghoulish bash.

BRABANDER This beautifully balanced goat's milk Gouda from the Netherlands is matured by star affineur Betty Koster of Fromagerie L'Amuse in Amsterdam (see page 36). Nutty and sweet, with just a touch of brightness, it's an ideal cheese for packing in lunches or putting on a cheese board. If you like this one, look for the more mature version, Brabander Reserve, which has even more toffeelike notes and crunchy crystals.

BREAD CHEESE Known in Finland as juustoleipä or leipäjuusto, this fresh cheese was dried like beef jerky to preserve it and later warmed over a fire. Today, several American cheesemakers market "bread cheese," which is dried, baked, then packaged for sale so it can be heated at home. Note that it does not contain bread; it simply looks like a toasted crust. In fact, the gluten-free community has embraced this cheese as a bread substitute because it's easy to top and toast in the oven. *Note:* It does not melt and lose its shape, since it's been dried and contains little to no moisture.

BREBIROUSSE D'ARGENTAL This French cheese is pure sheep's milk custard. With its fiery orange rind, it looks wild, but it's pleasurably mild—the orange coloring comes from the annatto plant. Silky and delicate, this is one of the few spreadable sheep's milk cheeses on the market. Prepare to weep.

BRIE FERMIER Brie is a soft, mild, bloomy rind cheese with origins in France, close to Paris. Since anyone can make a cheese and label it brie, the easiest way to distinguish a really good French version is to look for the French word *fermier*, which indicates French farmhouse production (rather than factory production). To be clear, it's a label—not a brand.

BRIN D'AMOUR "Breath of Love" from Corsica is a little sachet of soft sheep's milk cheese rolled in herbs from the island (rosemary, fennel, juniper) and the occasional pop of red chili. Young, it's whipped and fluffy with a fresh, slightly tart taste—like the Boursin of your dreams. As it ages and the paste absorbs oils from the herbs, it becomes more savory. *Note:* This cheese also goes by the name Fleur de Maquis.

BUCHERON A classic log of goat cheese with a bloomy rind and a soft clay-like center, this French beauty is full of bright acidity and minerality. Try serving it on a cheese board, where the slices will look like tree rings and add visual interest. Or serve a few moons on top of a beet salad.

BUTTERKÄSE German Butterkäse is simple and delectable. It looks like a big ol' pat of butter, and it tastes like one, too. Mild and sweetly milky, it melts well on sandwiches or makes a great snack with just about any accompaniment, from fresh tomatoes to more exotic pairings like dried pineapple and dark rum.

CABOT CLOTHBOUND CHEDDAR Inspired by the great British clothbounds, this beauty began as a collaboration in 2003 between two Vermont cheese companies,

Cabot Cooperative and the Cellars at Jasper Hill. The cheese is made at Cabot from the milk of one farm, then toted to the Cellars, where it is bandaged and carefully matured by a team of affineurs. Each cheese is tasted, sensory notes are recorded, and then the cheeses are classified based on a series of flavor profiles that Jasper Hill has developed over the years. Often grassy and butterscotchy, this is a real American gem—a must-try for all US Cheddar heads.

CABRALES (PDO) Wickedly spicy, Cabrales is a leaf-wrapped blue cheese produced in northern Spain. It's made from raw cow's milk and aged in limestone caves, which lend minerality to this famously sharp and savory cheese. Try a bite and chase it with a cold shot of vodka. Not kidding. Don't expect to be able to feel your tongue for at least fifteen minutes.

CACIO DI BOSCO AL TARTUFO From Tuscany, this Pecorino flecked with truffles is delicate and aromatic. Milky sweet and full of gentle caramel notes, this is a wonderful cheese for special-occasion snacking—truffle pound cake? Also, Cacio di Bosco al Tartufo tends to be moister and more delicate than other truffled sheep's milk cheeses, such as Moliterno al Tartufo, which is drier and saltier.

CACIOCAVALLO A fascinating gourd-shaped cheese that hangs from a rope to age, caciocavallo means "cheese on horseback"—which is how it was originally taken to market (over the back of a saddle). Made from either cow's or sheep's milk, this Italian classic is essentially a large aged mozzarella ball, hence the slightly thready texture. Sliced, it's wonderful paired with olives and charcuterie. *Note:* There's a PDO version, Caciocavallo Silano, along with Caciocavallo Podlico—which has a special designation from Slow Food. Try these two if you can find them!

CAMBOZOLA BLACK LABEL Imagine a Camembert crossed with Gorgonzola, and you get Cambozola. A triple crème blue from Germany, this may be one of the most photogenic cheeses. It has a silver rind and sapphire specks embedded within a creamy paste. Produced by dairy company Käserei Champignon, Cambozola Black Label looks great on a board and tastes fabulous on a cheesesteak.

CAMEMBERT D'ISIGNY Since true raw-milk Camembert de Normandie (see below) is not legal for sale in the US market, this is a reliable (pasteurized) alternative that's easy to find in the United States. It's produced in Normandy by the cooperative Isigny Sainte-Mère, using milk from family-owned farms. Mushroomy and lush, it's wonderful paired with Norman hard cider and toasted walnuts—a traditional French trio.

CAMEMBERT DE NORMANDIE (PDO) Camembert is a soft, bloomy cheese originating in Normandy, France. Although there are many Camemberts on the market, any cheese labeled Camembert de Normandie must be made in Normandy, using at least 50 percent raw milk (au lait cru) from local Normande cows. Satiny in texture, with notes of hay, sautéed mushrooms, and steamed cauliflower, a real Camembert de Normandie is a thing of beauty.

CAMPO Imagine a silky-soft square of cow's milk that tastes like bacon, and you've got Campo—a creamy, cold-smoked washed-rind cheese from North Carolina. Made

in small batches at Boxcarr Handmade Cheese—a small sister-brother operation in Cedar Grove—this is the ultimate camping cheese. Eat it by the bonfire with a flask of bourbon.

CASHEL BLUE Ireland's Cashel Blue is a buttery fantasy that is as spreadable as frosting. Created by the Grubb family in Tipperary, it's made with grass-fed cow's milk from the family's herd and from the milk of neighboring farms within twenty-five kilometers. Distributed by Kerrygold (makers of grass-fed Irish butter), this cheese tends to be easy to find at supermarkets, a real plus.

CHEESE CURDS Curds are the building blocks of all cheese—they're milk solids that are separated from the whey (liquid) during cheesemaking. Bags of fresh cheese curds are often sold at farmers markets, and when they are truly fresh, they squeak between your teeth. You can enjoy them as a snack or melt them in dishes, such as poutine.

CHÈVRE Chèvre is the French word for goat. In the cheese world, this term is used to refer to fresh goat cheese. Chèvre is typified by a light, bright taste (think lemon zest and fresh snowfall) and a spreadable consistency.

CHIRIBOGA BLUE A great gateway blue, this subtle stunner with minimal blue veining is a cheesemonger favorite, especially for winning over the hearts of blue cheese novices. It's named after cheesemaker Anton Chiriboga, an Ecuadorian who created this cheese while living in Bavaria. Try this sweet blue with dried figs and toasted pecans.

CLOTHBOUND CHEDDAR: AMERICAN (see Cabot Clothbound, Flory's Truckle, Bleu Mont Dairy Bandaged Cheddar)

CLOTHBOUND CHEDDAR: TRADITIONAL BRITISH (see Montgomery's, Keen's, Westcombe, Pitchfork, Quicke's, Isle of Mull)

COLSTON BASSETT STILTON (PDO) The gold standard for perfect Stilton, this rustic blue is made in the English village of Colston Bassett and aged at Neal's Yard Dairy in London. Buttery and crumbly with notes of walnuts, pipe tobacco, and leather, it is perhaps the ultimate fireside cheese for the winter months. Try it with an after-dinner tipple, like port or Madeira.

COMTÉ (PDO) One of the most popular aged French cheeses, Comté is known for being supple, sweet, and savory. Made primarily from the raw milk of pasture-raised Montbéliard cows in the Franche-Comté region of eastern France, it's sold at different ages to highlight flavor notes that develop over time. Eighteen-month and twenty-four-month Comté are especially prized. Look for the Marcel Petite brand.

CORNISH YARG Wrapped in a coat of overlapping emerald-green nettle leaves, Cornish Yarg wins the prize for being one of the most stunning cheeses ever created. Dense and lemony, this cow's milk cheese from Cornwall, England, is perfect for a picnic board. It's named after creator Alan Gray, who developed the recipe in the 1980s (Yarg is his name spelled backward).

COUPOLE Shaped like a scoop of vanilla ice cream, this brainy-looking French-style goat cheese was developed by pioneering artisan cheesemaker Allison Hooper of Vermont Creamery, one of the country's first small-batch producers. Inspired by her travels in France, she created this award-winning dome, which has a veil-thin rind and a silky smooth interior. Today, the company is owned by Land O'Lakes, and cheeses are made under the direction of longtime French cheesemaker Adeline Druart.

CRÉMEUX DES CITEAUX A decadent triple crème with a whipped texture from Burgundy, France, this bloomy cheese is mild and buttery, great for breakfast or for a cheese board. It has the added status of being matured under the watchful eye of premier French affineur Rodolphe Le Meunier—you'll see his name on the label.

DÉLICE DE BOURGOGNE A cheesecake-thick triple crème with a moussey texture, this ultra-buttery cheese is made by the French company Lincet. Good for entertaining, this easy-to-find crowd pleaser is available at many American specialty food shops and supermarkets.

EMMENTALER (PDO) A renowned cheese from Switzerland that is easily identified by its large holes, Emmentaler is produced by village creameries of the Emmental region, near the Swiss capital of Bern. Nutty and sweet with a buttermilky hook, it's an excellent melter and table cheese. It's also strictly regulated to ensure that Emmentaler PDO is made only with pasture-based milk.

ÉPOISSES (PDO) One of the great French stinkers! Legend has it that the monks at the Abbaye de Citeaux first made Époisses in Burgundy beginning in the seventeenth century. The monks washed their cheeses in local Marc de Bourgogne, producing a washed-rind cheese with an intense meaty taste—a perfect addition to their humble vegetarian diet. To enjoy a round of Époisses, set it out in its box and peel back the rind. Then dip warm bread or boiled potatoes into it.

EWEPHORIA Think dried pineapple and bourbon—this may be the sweetest aged Gouda you'll ever try. Its punny name is a key to its milk source (sheep's milk), making it an especially lush cheese. Try pairing it with dark spirits and enjoy every bite of this crunch bomb from the Netherlands (it's loaded with crystals).

FETA (See sheep's milk feta)

FINGER LAKES GOLD RESERVE One of the great aged goat cheeses of the East Coast, this Gouda-style cheese is made at a small family creamery in the Finger Lakes region of New York State. Addictively nutty and crunchy with a perfect balance of sweetness and saltiness, it's a must-try artisan American cheese.

FLORY'S TRUCKLE Fiendishly likeable, Flory's Truckle is a great gateway Cheddar for anyone wanting to explore clothbounds, thanks to its brown-sugary sweetness (some would say the sweetness is not exactly authentic to this style, but there's no downplaying this cheese's deliciousness). It's made in Missouri by the Flory family, where cheesemaking is overseen by Jennifer Flory, the eldest of eight daughters. Then the Truckles are sent to Milton Creamery in Iowa for cave-aging.

FROMAGE BLANC Meaning white cheese in French, fromage blanc is a fresh, spreadable cheese made from cow's milk. Originally, the recipe called for skim milk, but now cream is often folded in for a surge of richness. Mild and spoonable, it's great for spreading on bread with jam or for topping soups and desserts.

FUJIYAMA This iconic Japanese goat cheese shaped like Mount Fuji has a bloomy white peak and an ashy base, thanks to creative inventor Mirasaka Fromage. Highly prized but rarely found outside of Japan, Fujiyama is worth launching an adventure to find—and to explore other exquisite Japanese showpieces.

GLACIER BLUE Aged in an underground lava tube (a hardened vent formed after a volcanic eruption), this stunner from Washington State is made by John and Marci Shuman, a young couple who decamped from Portland to apprentice with a local dairy farmer and eventually make cheese. Fudgelike in texture, with beautiful complexity, this blue is probably as close to a cave-aged French Roquefort as you'll ever find in the United States; it's made from raw cow's milk (not sheep's milk), but the lava tubes and volcanic soil lend a similar minerality.

GORGONZOLA DOLCE (PDO) A spoonable and sweet blue, mild Gorgonzola Dolce is often displayed in cheese shops as a whole wheel, cut open, with an ice cream scoop resting in its liquidy center. Dolce, which means sweet in Italian, is the operative word here. Try serving this racy specialty from Lombardy and Piedmont for dessert with a side of toasted walnuts, dark chocolate, and cherries—like a blue cheese sundae bar!

GORGONZOLA PICCANTE (PDO) Savory and intense, Gorgonzola Piccante is the opposite of Gorgonzola Dolce (see above). Piccante means spicy in Italian. Matured longer than its sweet stepsister, this peppery cow's milk blue is full of intricate indigo veins, making it a beautiful slab for topping salads, burgers, and steaks.

GOUDA WITH FENUGREEK SEEDS (ALSO KNOWN AS GOUDA FOENEGREEK) Gouda is a style of cheese that develops caramel notes as it ages. Named after the village of Gouda in South Holland, where it was traded for centuries, it remains one of Holland's biggest exports. The Dutch often incorporate spices—thanks to their early role in the spice trade—such as cloves, caraway seeds, and others. Fenugreek seeds, which are nutty and slightly bitter, are a perfect counterbalance to Gouda's natural sweetness.

GRANA PADANO (PDO) Dense, sweet, and granular (the Italian word *grana* means grain), Grana Padano is an excellent cheese for snacking, grating, or cooking. It bears similarities to Parmigiano-Reggiano but is generally viewed as less complex in flavor and also more of a "good value" cheese, since it's made in much larger quantities and with fewer strict regulations. For pesto, it's ideal.

GRAYSON Revered as the first real artisan American stink bomb, this glorious raw-milk creature from Meadow Creek Dairy in Virginia is made by mother-daughter team Helen and Kat Feete using milk from their small herd of pasture-raised Jerseys on a sustainably run farm abutting the Blue Ridge Mountains. This is a beloved American classic—handmade, in small batches. A must-try.

GRUYÈRE D'ALPAGE (PDO) Made around the small town of Gruyères and produced in village dairies around western Switzerland, this funky, herbaceous cheese is based on a traditional recipe dating back to 1115. Only the handmade Alpage versions are still made high up in the Alps, which is what makes these wheels so prized. They are a completely different breed from other versions on the market, sold simply as Gruyère.

HANFMUTSCHLI Loaded with hemp seeds toasted in hemp oil, this raw-milk cheese from Switzerland is famous for the giant pot leaf on its label. (Although hanfmutschli means "the joint" in Swiss German, the cheese has no groovy psychotropic properties.) Word has it the cheesemaker's wife found a hemp plant growing in her garden and decided to experiment. The seeds add toasty notes to an otherwise deeply creamy and rather mellow cheese.

HARBISON This soft, scoopy cow's milk cheese wrapped in spruce bark is the ultimate chip dip (yes, dip potato chips into it—you won't be disappointed). Made at Jasper Hill Farm in Vermont, this American classic is now available at many cheese shops and supermarkets. Peel back the top rind and dunk away!

HAVARTI From Denmark, Havarti is a buttery cheese inspired by an 1800s recipe created by a well-known cheesemaker named Hanne Nielsen. She pioneered the style at her farm near Copenhagen (it's now a landmark), and later it became a supermarket staple. Mild and milky with a springy texture, it's perfect for open-faced sandwiches, a Danish favorite. You'll also find versions studded with dill or caraway seeds. Note that there are two kinds of Havarti: regular and cream Havarti, which is extra-plush.

HOOLIGAN A wild yawp of a cheese made in Connecticut, this raw-milk funk bomb is made by legendary mother-son team Elizabeth MacAlister and Mark Gillman. She's the herdswoman, he's the cheesemaker. Fudgy in texture and full of meaty taste, Hooligan rivals the best French Muenster.

IDIAZÁBAL (PDO) Smoked over local wood, this Spanish sheep's milk cheese is one of the all-time great smoky cheeses from Europe. It hails from the Basque Country and the Navarre, where local shepherds stored their wheels by their bonfires at night. Today, it's still made with milk from two local breeds, the Latxa or Carranzana. Rich and gently smoky, with caramel notes, it's a great pairing with red wine or whiskey.

ISLE OF MULL CHEDDAR This Scottish stunner from the Isle of Mull is an unusual clothbound Cheddar; it's made from the milk of cows that are fed spent barley malt from a Scotch distillery near the dairy. When you taste this delicious cheese, you can actually detect a hint of booze. It's like a hunk of Cheddar and a shot of whisky rolled into one.

KEEN'S CHEDDAR Made at Moorhayes Farm in Somerset, England, since 1898, Keen's Cheddar is one of the great traditional artisan clothbound Cheddars from the area. Made according to strict specifications that govern Somerset's four artisan Cheddar makers, raw-milk Keen's Cheddar is legendary among connoisseurs and beloved for its creamy texture and layers of flavor. Today, it's made by fifth-generation maker Nick Keen.

KUNIK A voluptuous artisan American triple crème, this flavorful cream bomb is crafted from a combination of pasture-based goat's milk and Jersey cow cream. It's made at Nettle Meadow Farm, a small creamery in Warrensburg, New York, that is also known for its animal sanctuary (all of the creamery's dairy animals live out their full lives here). Sold in small rounds at specialty cheese counters, it's worth seeking out for a decadent evening. Pair it with bubbles and berry jam.

L'AMUSE SIGNATURE GOUDA A top-of-the-line Gouda, L'Amuse Signature is aged by beloved Dutch cheese queen Betty Koster, a cheese shop owner and affineur in Amsterdam who hand-selects wheels from makers around the Netherlands. Betty's aging process brings out the deep butterscotch notes in her cheeses, which pair beautifully with complex dark beers, red wines, and even Madeira.

LABNEH This fresh Lebanese cream dream is made by straining and salting yogurt. Sometimes a small amount of rennet is added to thicken the texture. Spreadable and slightly tart, it's a great substitute for cream cheese, or you can eat it like yogurt. It's especially good topped with honey, walnuts, and pomegranate seeds.

LANGRES (PDO) A concave cupcake from the plateau of Langres in northeastern France, Langres is designed to hold a splash of bubbly (Champagne is made nearby, FYI). Bright orange in color and silky in texture, its stench is impressive for such a small round.

LEONORA Think of this as the ice cream cake of goat cheese. From León, this head-turner is fresh tasting and citrusy with just a hint of white pepper in the rind. Buy a slice (this loaf-like cheese is the size and shape of a Baked Alaska) and serve it with fresh berries and lemon curd. Of all the goat cheeses on the market, Leonora has one of the most striking textures—a fluffy rind, followed by an oozy creamline, and a center that's like hard-pack ice cream.

L'ETIVAZ D'ALPAGE (PDO) Produced in the Alps from May to October, this waxen raw-milk cheese is still made over open fires by a handful of cheesemakers around the canton of Vaud in Switzerland who maintain a highly traditional approach to their craft. A rare find, this cheese is known for its complexity of flavors, including Alpine herbs, nuts, and stone fruit.

MANCHEGO (PDO) Manchego, from the La Mancha region in Spain, is a popular table cheese that is typically grassy and nutty. Traditionally made from the milk of Manchega sheep who graze on wild pastures of limey-clay soils, these wheels are sometimes rolled in rosemary to play up the herbaceous notes in the milk. Manchego is easily identified by the herringbone pattern of its rind, which was originally an imprint from reed baskets. For the best Manchego, look for Manchego PDO.

MARCO POLO RESERVE From Beecher's Handmade Cheese in Seattle, this extra-aged clothbound Cheddar is studded with green and black peppercorns, which add perfume and pop. In 2021, this cheese won gold in the flavored cheese category at the World Cheese Awards—a major win. Zesty and flaky, Marco Polo Reserve is named after the explorer who is thought to have introduced peppercorns to Europe. It's not easy to find, but you can look for it on the website for Beecher's Handmade Cheese.

MARIEKE GOUDA (SMOKED) One of the few Goudas smoked over actual wood, this hickory-smoked wonder is a cheese counter favorite. It's made by Marieke Penterman, an award-winning Dutch cheesemaker who settled in Wisconsin and makes farmstead cheese. Her line of Dutch Goudas includes some of the best made in the United States.

MASCARPONE The richest of all fresh cheeses, mascarpone contains 80 percent fat, making it a good stand-in for whipped cream or sour cream. Use it to top soups, baked potatoes, French toast, or fruit crisps. Italian in origin, it's also known as "the tiramisu cheese" for its use in that popular dessert.

MIDNIGHT MOON This goat's milk Gouda is a sweet alternative to cow's milk Goudas and an easy-to-find wedge in many groceries. Dense and crystalline, it's full of caramel notes, making it a good choice for a dessert board or for kids.

MIMOLETTE With its round shape and glowing orange hue, French Mimolette often gets trotted out in cheese shops around Halloween (some cheesemongers have even been known to carve it like a pumpkin). Nutty, sweet, and slightly tart, it was developed as a response to popular Dutch cheeses like Edam and Gouda. Note that young versions are pliable and mellow, and aged versions become dense and butterscotchy.

MOLITERNO AL TARTUFO Dry and woodsy, this dense and powerfully truffley Pecorino from Sardinia can be served on a cheese board with a touch of honey. It's also a beloved sheep's milk cheese for grating over risotto or warm pasta. Note that Moliterno without truffles is also available for a smooth, ivory sheep's milk cheese that is rich and sea-salty.

MONTE ENEBRO Produced by sibling makers in Spain who trained with their father, legendary cheesemaker Rafael Baez, this stunning goat cheese looks like a silver river stone. The surface is dusted with ash and *Penicillium roqueforti* to lend color and flavor. Produced near Madrid, it's one of the freshest-tasting, most balanced goat cheeses you'll find. Try it with honey.

THE MOONRABBIT From Chris Gentine of Deer Creek Cheese in Wisconsin, this sweet, creamy Cheddar is bathed in Green Chartreuse, a French liqueur that adds a pop of herbal flavor around the rind. Gently herbaceous with bright acidity, this fascinating Cheddar is part of Deer Creek's innovative line of spirituous cheeses. Try pairing it with Chartreuse . . . or absinthe!

MOZZARELLA AND MOZZARELLA DI BUFALA Mozzarella is a soft, fresh cheese that can be made from any milk. Water buffalo milk, used in traditional Italian mozzarella making (and associated with Italy's Campania region, home to Mozzarella di Bufala PDO), is considered the most prized: The result is featherlight but especially plush from the richness of the milk. Serve Mozzarella di Bufala (literally "buffalo mozzarella") in the summer with sliced fresh tomatoes or peaches, along with olive oil, fresh basil, and a sprinkle of sea salt.

MONTGOMERY'S CHEDDAR Considered by many to be the top clothbound Cheddar of the world, this raw-milk cheese is produced by James Montgomery at Manor Farm in Somerset, England. Made from the family's long-standing herd of two hundred Friesian cows, Montgomery's is one of just four farmhouse Cheddars still being made in Somerset. It's beloved for its complex flavors and long-lasting taste.

NABABBO A unique goat's milk Taleggio, with pleasant sourdough notes and a hint of minerality, this cheese is made by casArrigoni in Lombardy, Italy. Try out this rose-toned beauty on goat cheese skeptics; it is mellow with just a hint of sour-cream tang.

NEGRONI BLUE An Italian blue marinated in an Italian cocktail? Why not? Blue cheeses often pair well with bitterness, and a Negroni is nothing if not bitter. Creamy and covered in candied orange slices, this is an eye-popping, showstopping cheese to throw down on a party board.

OSSAU-IRATY (PDO) From the French Basque region, this firm sheep's milk cheese is one of the all-time great wheels for pairing with red wine (sheep's milk can handle tannins). Expect notes of warm butter, almonds, and sometimes a touch of herbs. The name refers to two areas where the cheese is produced: the Iraty Forest and the Ossau Valley. Both are in the foothills of the Pyrénées.

PARMIGIANO-REGGIANO (PDO) Italy's "king of cheese" is an exquisite, crystalline cheese that dates back to the Middle Ages. Today, a consortium oversees the production of every wheel to assure authenticity and quality. Full of umami notes and sweetness, true Parmigiano-Reggiano is a delicacy, not just a grating cheese. Italians often enjoy it at the table with Prosecco or red wine.

PECORINO SARDO (PDO) From Sardinia, Pecorino Sardo is made from the island's indigenous Sarda sheep that clamber around the rocky terrain. It's sold in two versions: dolce, or sweet; and maturo, which is a little spicy. Rustic and wild, Pecorino Sardo is a beloved Italian cheese, best enjoyed with a drizzle of honey. Note that Fiore Sardo, a type of Pecorino Sardo, is a connoisseur's favorite—it's lightly smoked and tends to be rather sheepy.

PECORINO TOSCANO (PDO) Typified by sweetness rather than saltiness, Pecorino Toscano is the ultimate table Pecorino—perfect for pairing with red wine, charcuterie, and olives. Made from sheep's milk, it's sold as either a fresco, or fresh, young cheese, which is moist and milky; or in a staggianato version, which is drier and nutty. Both are great for snacking.

PECORINO GINEPRO A fabulous Pecorino to pair with gin, this sheep's milk cheese from Italy is bathed in balsamic vinegar and rolled in juniper berries. Aromatic and gently herbaceous, with a pop of acidity around the rind, this is a truly special cheese. Try it on a board with honey.

PITCHFORK CHEDDAR Made by Trethowan's Dairy in Somerset, England, this star is a recent addition to the area's artisan Cheddars. It's produced by a pair of brothers, Todd and Maugan Trethowan, who produced a traditional cheese in Wales, called Gorwydd Caerphilly; when they moved their operation to England, near the village of Cheddar, they felt inspired to produce a traditional English cheese. The name Pitchfork refers to a Cheddar-making tool that is traditionally used to toss the curds as they are being salted.

PLEASANT RIDGE RESERVE One of the most decorated artisan cheeses made in the United States, this award winner is made from raw, pasture-based milk at Uplands Cheese in Wisconsin. Inspired by French Beaufort, it's firm, nutty, and gently fruity.

POINT REYES ORIGINAL BLUE Made from the raw milk of cows that graze along the Northern California coast, Point Reyes Original Blue is a sea-salty situation. Creamy and pungent, it's an excellent salad topper or burger blue. It's produced at Point Reyes Farmstead Cheese Co. under the oversight of the farm's four daughters.

PONT-L'ÉVÊQUE (PDO) One of Normandy's oldest cheeses, Pont-l'Évêque is the perfect bridge to enjoying washed-rind cheeses. It's medium-whiffy and very sultry, thanks to rich Normandy cream. It was also Hemingway's favorite cheese, which should put you in the mood to read a book and eat a cheese in a little square box, alongside a stiff drink, though the French usually serve this titillating hunk with a funky Norman cider.

PORT SALUT A gentle, creamy crowd pleaser with origins in Brittany, this mellow French cheese was once produced at a local abbey. Today, it's factory made and can be found in many supermarkets. Mild, soft, and doughy in taste, its bright orange rind (from natural annatto) adds color to a cheese board. Try pairing it with hard cider or light beers.

QUICKE'S CHEDDAR In Devon, England, the Quicke family has farmed the same land for five hundred years. Their pasture-based Cheddars—especially the bold, zingy clothbound version—are well distributed in the United States and full of complex flavor. Note that this is one of the few English clothbounds that is pasteurized.

RACLETTE This fantastic Swiss melter is made in both Switzerland and France, though only Swiss Raclette du Valais—a raw-milk version from the Alpine canton of Valais—holds PDO status. Funky, creamy, and rich, Raclette is typically melted over boiled potatoes and served with onions and cornichons as part of a traditional mountain meal.

RAGUSANO (PDO) A specialty of Sicily, this unusual cheese is made in large blocks and hung from ropes in local caves to age. One of the island's oldest cheeses, it's made in the provinces of Siricusa and Ragusa, using the milk of local Modicana cows. As it ages, it turns sweetly buttery and a bit spicy.

RED HAWK This ruddy little washed-rind cheese made by Cowgirl Creamery in California is considered an American classic. It's beloved for its rich texture (it's a triple crème) and full-bodied funky taste. Note

that there is often a faint taste of peanuts on the finish, making this a great pairing for chocolate stout.

RED ROCK An interesting hybrid, Red Rock is a Cheddar/blue cross created by cheesemaker Chris Roelli of Roelli Cheese Haus in Wisconsin. Bright orange (from annatto) with lightning bolts of blue mold, it was designed to look like the red rock around Roelli's home in Lafayette County. A former firefighter with a family history of cheesemaking, Roelli is credited with developing a truly original American cheese. Mellow and snackable, Red Rock is a cheesemonger favorite.

RICOTTA (see sheep's milk ricotta)

ROBIOLA LA ROSSA From Italy's Piedmont region, this unusual soft goat cheese comes wrapped in cherry leaves. The leaves hold this delicate beauty together (its rind is very thin) and impart a slight fruity, earthy taste. This is a stunning cheese on a board.

ROBIOLA TRE LATTI A classic northern Italian soft cheese made of three milks: goat, cow, and sheep. The pleasure here is that you can taste all three—sweetness from cow's milk, a little tartness from the goat's, and subtle herbaceousness from the sheep's milk. With its thin white rind and complex flavor, this is one of the best soft cheeses around. Worth a trip to Piedmont for the raw-milk version, for sure! Note that there is also a Due Latti—made with just two milks.

ROCKET'S ROBIOLA Inspired by Piedmont's soft, pillowy robiolas, this artisan American version from sibling-owned Boxcarr Handmade Cheese in North Carolina is made from cow's milk and dusted with ash. It's supple and creamy, great for spreading on a baguette. Handmade in small batches, this is a cheese shop favorite.

ROGUE RIVER BLUE From Oregon's Rogue Creamery, this fantastic blue bears the distinction of winning Grand Champion at the 2019–2020 World Cheese Awards. Each wheel is wrapped in organic biodynamic Syrah grape leaves that have been soaked in pear spirits, making for an incredibly complex, moist, and aromatic blue cheese that's known for exhibiting notes of truffle and toffee.

ROGUE CREAMERY SMOKEY BLUE Cold-smoked over Oregon hazelnut shells, this unique American blue has a cult following. It's sweetly spicy with a remarkable candied bacon note. Try pairing it with bourbon.

ROQUEFORT (PDO) Punchy French Roquefort is an incredibly supple blue, thanks to sheep's milk. France's first-ever name-protected cheese must be made from the milk of the Lacaune breed and aged at the world-famous caves of Combalou in southern France. Fissures in the rock allow sea air to humidify the space and lend Roquefort its sea-salty pop. Look for Carles Roquefort, produced by a small family operation that still harvests blue mold (*Penicillium roqueforti*) from rye bread—the traditional method of Roquefort production, which dates back to 1070.

RUSH CREEK RESERVE Made only in autumn, this much-anticipated gooey round from Andy Hatch of Uplands Cheese in Wisconsin is a tribute to Jura cheesemakers in France and Switzerland who produce Vacherin Mount d'Or each fall in time for the holidays. Like Vacherin, Rush Creek is made from exceptional raw milk and bound in bark.

SBRINZ ALPAGE (PDO) Sometimes called "Swiss Parmesan," Sbrinz has been produced in central Switzerland since the thirteenth century and is often enjoyed in thin curls that look like manicotti; the best versions of Sbrinz hail from about ten small dairies high in the Alps—these are the rare Alpage versions. At thirty-six months of age, these wheels are prized for their buttery, slightly floral flavor notes.

SELLES-SUR-CHER (PDO) A classic French goat cheese from the town of Selles-sur-Cher in the Loire Valley, each saucer-sized wheel is dusted in vegetable ash, which encourages a rumpled rind to form. At peak ripeness, a thin creamline forms just below the surface, making this young cheese incredibly supple. Try it with raspberries or raspberry jam.

SHEEP'S MILK FETA Feta is a fresh cheese (think no rind) that is preserved in brine, a saltwater solution. Although it can be made from any milk, the richness of sheep's milk makes it the most desirable style in terms of creamy texture. Many cultures make feta-style cheese, but feta PDO comes from Greece, where the cheese must be made from at least 70 percent sheep's milk (the other 30 percent can be goat's milk).

SHEEP'S MILK RICOTTA *Ricotta*, which means recooked, is traditionally made by recooking whey that is left over from cheesemaking and skimming off any tiny remaining curds. Ricotta can be made from any milk, but ricotta made from sheep's milk is especially rich and fluffy.

In Italy, it's a staple and is often sold at markets in small baskets.

SHROPSHIRE BLUE Colored with annatto—a natural plant dye used in some Cheddars and Goudas—this is essentially "gold Stilton." On a cheese board, it pops with color, making it a favorite around the holidays. Like Colston Bassett Stilton, its sister cheese (they're made at the same dairy), it is a full-flavored blue.

SOFIA Back-to-the-lander Judy Schad moved to Indiana with her husband in the 1970s and began raising goats, then created a small company called Capriole Farm in 1988, where she started making delicate one-of-a-kind goat cheeses, many of them named after female family members and friends. Sofia bears a pair of ashy stripes and is a tribute to the great goat cheeses of the Loire Valley.

SOTTOCENERE This rich, creamy cheese from Italy's Veneto region is lightly flecked with truffles, then dusted with winter spices and ash. The combination shouldn't work, but it does! The ash and spices give the rind a velvety sheen, making it a beautiful wedge for a board, and they add interest to a very decadent cheese. Sottocenere is a cold-weather favorite.

SPARKENHOE RED LEICESTER A gentle cheese that is infinitely nibble-able, Sparkenhoe was created in Cheshire County, England, in 1745. The original recipe was recently resurrected by husband and wife team David and Jo Clarke, a pair of Cheshire County dairy farmers who love their cows and wanted to create a special cheese. Although British Leicester (pronounced "lester") is abundant in supermarkets, Sparkenhoe is decidedly different—more rustic, naturally dyed with annatto, and bound with cloth that turns speckled silver and pink as the cheese cave-ages over time.

STICHELTON This is raw-milk Stilton—as it was originally made in the 1700s, long before legislation around Stilton production required makers to pasteurize their milk. Meaty and mushroomy, this beautiful blue is made at a farm in Nottinghamshire by cheesemaker Joe Schneider—an American cheesemaker, no less, who is passionate about preserving the traditional recipe for Stilton. Stichelton was a favorite cheese of the late Anthony Bourdain.

TALEGGIO PDO From Lombardy, this terra-cotta-colored church tile of a cheese is easily recognizable by its square shape and four circles stamped on the rind. Gooey and deliciously funky, this washed-rind cow's milk cheese is an Italian classic. It's traditionally served with mostarda, a northern Italian condiment made with cooked fruit and mustard oil.

TÊTE DE MOINE (PDO) From Switzerland, the name of this cylinder-shaped cheese literally means "head of a monk." A special tool, called a girolle, has been developed to shave the cylinder into rosettes, which mimics shaving the top of a monk's head. The cheese itself is bold and beefy, though slivering it into thin curls diminishes its intensity (and makes it really fun to eat).

TUNWORTH An outstanding small-batch Camembert-style cheese made in England? Believe it! Developed by Australian-born Stacey Hedges of Hampshire Cheese Co., Tunworth is considered to be one of the most flavorful and rich soft cheeses in this style. Whereas the milk for traditional Camembert is partially skimmed to make butter, Hedges leaves all the cream in her vat, making for an extra-luscious bloomy rind cheese that, when ripe, tastes like cauliflower custard.

UBRIACO The Italian word for drunk, Ubriaco is traditionally made by storing a wheel of cheese in a barrel of wine (rosé, Chianti, Merlot, and so on). Although the wines may vary, Ubriaco is typically a firm, uncomplicated cow's or mixed milk cheese. The wine saturates the rind, giving the outer edge of the cheese a boozy kick—a great choice for a wine pairing. Look for spirit-saturated cheeses in this same category such as Occelli Testun al Malto D'Orzo e Whiskey or Occelli Testun con Frutta e Grappa di Moscato.

UP IN SMOKE Maple leaves are misted with bourbon, then wrapped around small bundles of naturally smoked goat cheese. The result is exquisite, thanks to the ingenuity of Pat Morford at Rivers Edge Chèvre in Oregon. Made in small batches, these are rare finds but well worth asking for at a local cheese shop—or ordering online.

VACHERIN MONT D'OR (PDO) A seasonal bark-wrapped cheese from Switzerland made with autumn milk from the same cows that are used to produce Gruyère in the Alps each summer, this delicacy is available only in fall and winter once the cows are moved off of high pastures and fed straw and fodder. Soft and gooey inside, it's sold in a balsa-wood box and is typically served warm alongside boiled potatoes or toasted baguette. *Note:* There's also a French version, simply called Mont d'Or.

VALDEÓN (PDO) Made with a mix of cow's milk and goat's milk, this complex Spanish blue is wrapped in sycamore leaves, then aged in caves across the Valdeón Valley of Castilla y León. Dense, earthy, and flinty, it's a wonderful blue to serve on a steak.

VALENÇAY (PDO) This young ashy French goat cheese is most notable for its shape, which looks like a truncated pyramid. According to legend, Napoleon contributed to the shape of this Loire Valley classic by lopping off the tip with his sword (it reminded him of the pyramids in Egypt, where he suffered military defeat). Herbaceous and light, it pairs well with honey and fresh fruit.

VAMPIRE SLAYER Think of this as the best pepperjack you'll ever eat, plus there's a Halloween hook. Vampire Slayer from tiny Calkins Creamery in Honesdale, Pennsylvania, tastes like a moist jack cheese studded with garlic, ginger, onion, and paprika. A coating of black wax forms its cape. Maker Emily Bryant uses the milk from her family's herd to create this much-loved pasture-raised fireball.

WEINKÄSE LAGREIN Sometimes called "the salami of cheese," Weinkäse Lagrein from Italy's Alto-Adige region is loaded with garlic and black pepper, then bathed in local Lagrein red wine. Bold and boozy, it pairs well with big reds and looks great on a cheese board.

WENSLEYDALE A mild, slightly tart English cheese popularized by the Claymation series

Wallace and Gromit, this wheel originates in Wensleydale, North Yorkshire, where it was originally developed by Cistercian monks. Today, Hawes Wensleydale is considered one of the best examples of this style. Try pairing it with chutney.

WESTCOMBE CHEDDAR One of four distinguished artisan clothbound Cheddars from Somerset, England, Westcombe Cheddar is made at Lower Westcombe Farm and bears the distinction of being matured in a high-tech cheese cave modeled after the Cellars at Jasper Hill Farm in Vermont. Cheesemaking at Westcombe draws on a rich tradition of dairying that involved Edith Cannon, an influential local figure who taught cheesemaking at a school for Cheddar makers in the late nineteenth to early twentieth century. An exceptional raw-milk cheese.

WESTFIELD FARMS CLASSIC BLUE LOG
This flagship goat cheese from Westfield Farm in Massachusetts contains a touch of blue mold on the rind, giving it a hint of Roquefort flavor. Try sharing it with blue cheese fans or with those who are keen to explore very delicate blues. With its silvery blue-black exterior, this log looks gorgeous on a cheese plate, especially alongside honey.

WILDE WEIDE One of the great raw-milk cheeses of the Netherlands, Wilde Weide (wild meadow) is made on a tiny island where the only inhabitants are the Dutch cheesemaker, his family, and his herd of cows—they literally graze around his kitchen window. Made in very small batches, this Dutch darling is sweetly complex and loaded with crystals.

WINNIMERE The more robust of Jasper Hill Farm's two bark-bound cheeses, this lush custard is all bacon and spruce. Modeled after Switzerland's Vacherin Mont d'Or, it is girdled with bark and produced only seasonally, in fall and winter. Each year, it's eagerly awaited by cheese counters.

INDEX

A

aam papad, 183
Adopt an Alp program, 129
affinage, 23, 34
affineurs, 23, 34, 37
aged cheese, 138–55. *See
    also specific cheese
    types*
  accompaniments, 148
  cheese board detours,
    149
  creating cheese board
    for, 144–49
  crystals in, 138, 153–55
  exploring in the kitchen,
    150
  overview, 138
  pairing with drinks, 148
  pressed cheeses, 139
  primary types of, 140–43
  sheep's milk cheese, 147
Alkmaar Cheese Market,
    239
Alpage cheese, 118–19, 124
Alp Blossom, 125, 258
Alpha Tolman, 127, 258
Alpine cheese, 116–35. *See
    also specific cheese
    names*
  accompaniments, 126
  Adopt an Alp program,
    129
  Alpage, about, 118–19, 124
  Alp Blossom, 125
  caciocavallo, 127
  cheese board detours, 127

Comté, 122
  at the Comté Cathedral,
    130–35
  creating cheese board for,
    120–27
  Emmentaler, 122
  exploring in the kitchen,
    128–29
  fondue cheeses, 116
  industrially produced,
    118
  overview, 116
  pairing with drinks, 126
  Raclette, 123
  Tête de Moines, 125
American Cheese Society
    (ACS) Conference, 236
American Farmstead Cheese
    (Kindstedt), 153
Androuet, 76–77
Androuet, Henri, 77
animal rennet, 23
Anthill, 253
Appleby's Cheshire, 107, 258
ash, for rind growth, 61
Asiago d'Allevo, 147, 258

B

baguettes, for cheese, 76
bark-wrapped cheeses, 87
Barthélémy, Nicole, 75
Bayley Hazen Blue, 178, 183,
    258
Beecher's block Cheddar,
    104
Beemster, 140, 146

Beemster XO, 89, 258
beer and cheese pairings,
    227
Behr, Edward, 119
BelGioso's American Grana,
    141
Belper Knolle, 163, 258–59
Big Bluff Tomme, 169
BirbaBlu, 179, 259
Birchenough, Alyce, 170
Birchrun Blue, 10
Birchrun Hills, 25–27
Bleu Mont Dairy Bandaged
    Cheddar, 105, 259
block Cheddars, 99, 104,
    204–5, 259
bloomy cheese, 60, 61, 66, 71
bloomy rind, 60
Blue Brain, 181, 259
blue cheese, 174–87. *See also
    specific types*
  accompaniments, 180
  booze-infused, 179
  cheese board detours, 181
  creating a cheese board
    for, 176–81
  exploring in the kitchen,
    182–83
  fiercely-flavored, 179
  how they are made, 174
  intensely-flavored, 178
  mellow-flavored, 178
  overview, 174–75
  pairing with drinks, 180
  pre-crumbled, note
    about, 175
Blue de Basque, 175

boerenkaas, 140
Boulette d'Avesnes, 250
Brabander, 146, 259
bread cheese, 51, 259
Brebirousse d'Argental,
    149, 259
Brevibacterium linens, 82
Brie:
    breakfast with, 70
    compared to Camembert,
        63
    de Meaux, 66, 79
    de Melun, 79
    fermier, 66, 260
    more adventurous picks,
        204–5
    Noir, 73
    in Paris, 72–78
Brin d'Amour, 163, 260
Briquette du Nord, 78
Brix meter, 12
Bucheron, 149, 260
buffalo milk cheeses, 49
Buffalo Mozzarella, 49, 260
Butterkäse, 181, 260
Byaslag, 250

C

Cabot block Cheddar, 104
Cabot Clothbound Cheddar,
    105, 260
Cabra al Gofio, 250
Cabrales, 175, 179, 260
caciocavallo, 127, 261
Cacio de Bosca al Tartufo,
    162, 260
calcium lactate
    pentahydrate, 155
California Artisan Cheese
    Festival, 237
Cambozola, 204–5
Cambozola Black Label,
    178, 261
Camembert, 63, 71

Camembert de Normandie,
    66, 79, 261
Camembert d'Isigny, 66, 261
Campo, 162, 261
Capriole Goat Cheese, 159
Carles Roquefort, 193
Cashel Blue, 178, 261
Casu Marzu, 250
Cathare, 250
Cellars at Jasper Hill, 93,
    153
Certified Cheese
    Professionals, 192
cheddaring, defined, 98
Cheddars, 98–113. *See also
    specific cheese names*
    accompaniments, 106
    block, about, 99
    cheese board detours, 107
    clothbound, about,
        99–101
    creating cheese board for,
        102–7
    crystals on, 155
    exploring in the kitchen,
        108–9
    overview, 98
    pairing with drinks, 106
    variations from tradition,
        105
cheese. *See also specific
    cheese types*
    at-a-glance cheese
        profiles, 258–73
    at-a-glance drink
        pairings, 226–28
    beginner tasting tips, 212
    bringing through
        customs, 234–35
    budget-conscious
        choices, 198–99
    buying at cheese shops,
        192–94
    buying directly from
        cheesemakers, 191

buying for a party, 195
buying online, 190–91
buying through cheese
    clubs, 191
and dental health, 171
for easy beverage
    pairings, 228
farmstead and
    handcrafted, 13
fifty must-try, 200–201
flavor wheel for, 225
for a grazing table or
    party, 214
high quality,
    characteristics of, 11–12
identifying tastes and
    textures, 229
kosher, 207
for lactose-intolerant,
    206
local, seeking out, 232–33
from pasture-raised
    dairy, 11–12
raw-milk, 32–33, 207
serving tools, boards, and
    knives, 216–17
storing instructions, 208
table-scaping tips, 213–14
tasting like a pro, 196–97
tips for sharing and
    serving, 210–11
top tips for drink
    pairings, 224–25
twenty, to explore around
    the world, 248–53
useful terms, 34–35
vegetarian, 203, 206
Cheese and Culture
    (Kindstedt), 153
cheese boards:
    cheese mandala à la
        Lilith Spencer, 218–19
    fresh cheese, 46–51
    long rustic, with herb
        garnishes, 220

planning, for beginners, 204–5

slate, with a clockwise selection, 221

slate or wooden, 216

small pairing boards, 222–23

template for, 8–10

tools for, 216–17

cheese caves, 34, 37, 94–95

cheese crystalographer, 153–55

cheese curds, 53, 261

cheese festivals and happenings, 235–39

cheese iron, 133–34

cheesemakers:
  a day in the life, 25–27
  in Japan, 69
  United States, 240–43

cheesemaking:
  basics of, 20–21
  books for, 254–57
  brief history of, 14–19
  classes and experiences, 244–46
  a day in the cheesemaker's life, 25–27
  life cycle of, 21
  variables in, 22–23

cheese maps or trails, 243

Cheesemonger Invitational (CMI), 184–87, 239

cheesemongers:
  defined, 34
  learning from, 192–94
  second-career, 110–13
  vegetarian, 203

cheese portraits, 169–70

cheese shops, 75, 192–94

Cheese (aka) The Slow Food Cheese Festival, 238

chèvre (goat cheese), 48, 89, 261

Chez Virginie, 72, 74

chhundo, 183

Chiriboga Blue, 178, 262

Clark, Christine, 112

clothbound Cheddars:
  about, 99–101
  American, 105, 262
  traditional British, 104, 262

Colston Bassett Stilton, 107, 175, 178, 262

Comté:
  about, 262
  crystals in, 155
  Marcel Petite, 122, 132
  sampling, 122

"Comté Cathedral," visit to, 130–35

cooked pressed cheeses, 139

Copper Kettle Parmesan, 141

Cornish Yarg, 163, 262

Coulommiers, 79

Coulon, Pierre, 77

Coupole, 66, 262

Cowboy Coffee, 158

cows, Montébeliard, 133

cows, pastured, 14

cow's milk, 30

cow's milk cheese, fresh, 48

Cravero Parmigiano-Reggiano, 147

creamery, defined, 34

creamline, defined, 34

Creanza, Tonio, 55–57

Crémeux des Citeaux, 67, 262

Crooked Face Creamery, 159

crystals, 34, 138, 153–55

curds, cheese, 53

curds and whey, defined, 35

Cypress Grove, 159

D

Deer Creek Cheese, 159

DeGoulet, Fabien, 132, 134–35

Délice de Bourgogne, 67, 262

Di Bruno Bros., 193

Don Quixote, 141

drunk cheeses, 89, 272

Drunken Goat, 89

Dubois, Laurent, 74

Dutch Gouda, 146

E

Emmentaler, 122, 262–63

Époisses, 87, 263

Essex Manchego, 147

Ewephoria, 146, 263

eyes (in cheese), defined, 35

F

farmers' cheese, 140

feta, sheep's milk, 49, 271

field guides:
  meeting a cheese crystalographer, 153–55
  meeting a cheesemaker, 25–27
  meeting a cheese painter, 169–70
  meeting an affineur, 37
  meeting a second-career cheesemonger, 110–13
  meeting a vegetarian cheesemonger, 203
  meeting a washed-rind cheese specialist, 93–95

Fike, Hunter, 193

Finger Lakes Gold Reserve, 146, 263

flavored cheese, 158–71.
  See also specific types
  accompaniments, 164
  cheese board detours, 165
  creating cheese board for,
    160–67
  exploring in the kitchen,
    166–67
  herby, 163
  overview, 158–59
  pairing with drinks, 164
  smoked, 162
  spiced, 163
  truffled, 162
flavor wheel for cheese,
  225
Flory's Truckle, 105, 113,
  263
Fondue, Swiss, 117
fondue cheeses, 116
Fort St. Antoine, 130–35
Fountainebleau Ardéchois,
  76
French Roquefort, 174, 179
fresh cheese, 44–57. *See also*
    specific types
  accompaniments, 50
  bread cheese, 51
  buffalo milk cheeses, 49
  cheese board detours, 51
  cheese curds, about, 53
  cow's milk cheeses, 48
  creating cheese board for,
    46–51
  exploring in the kitchen,
    52–53
  goat cheeses, 48
  identifying quality in,
    45
  overview, 44
  pairing with drinks, 50
  sheep's milk cheeses, 49
  tasting ricotta in Puglia,
    54–57
  where to find, 45

fromage blanc, 48, 263
Fromagerie Hardouin-
  Langlet, 77–78
Fromagerie Laurent Dubois,
  73, 74
Fromagerie Nicole
  Barthélémy, 75
Fujiyama, 69

G

Gaperon, 251–52
Geno, Mike, 169–70
Geotrichum candidum,
  60, 61
Gjetost, 252
Glacier Blue, 149, 178, 263
goat cheese (chèvre), 48,
  89, 261
goat milk, 30–31
Good Food Mercantile,
  237
Gorgonzola Dolce, 178,
  264
Gorgonzola Piccante,
  179, 264
Gouda:
  aged, crystals in, 154
  Dutch, 37, 140, 146
  with fenugreek seeds
    (Gouda Foenegreek),
    165, 264
  more adventurous picks,
    204–5
  variations, 146
Grana Padano, 141, 147,
  155, 264
grana-style cheese,
  140–41
Grayson, 86, 264
grazing tables, 213–14
Grey Owl, 252
Gruyère, 155, 264
Gruyère d'Alpage,
  124, 264

H

Hanfmutschli, 264
Harbison, 8, 69, 264–65
Harbutt, Juliet, 140
hard cider and cheese
  pairings, 226
Hardouin, Madame and
  Monsieur, 78
Hatch, Andy, 12
Havarti, 165, 265
Haver, Olivia, 93–95
herby cheese, 163
Hook's, 104
Hooligan, 87, 265
Hooper, Allison, 60
Hostettler, Caroline, 129
Hughes, John, 153
Humbolt Fog, 186

I

Idiazábal, 159, 162, 265
ikaite crystals, 153–54, 155
Indian snacks, 183
Isigny Sainte-Mère, 66
Isle of Mull Cheddar, 104,
  265

J

Japanese cheeses, 69
Jasani, Mansi, 183
Jasper Hill Farm, 93, 153
Jumi Cheese, 123, 181

K

Keen's Cheddar, 101, 104,
  265
Kehler, Andy and Mateo,
  93
Kindstedt, Paul, 153–55
Kindstedt lab, 153–54
Knight, Aimee, 55

kosher cheese, 207
Koster, Betty, 37
Kraft cheese slices, 19
Kunik, 67, 265

L

labneh, 48, 52, 266
Lakin, Allison, 159
Lakin's Gorges, 159
La Laiterie de Paris, 77
L'Amuse, 37
L'Amuse Signature Gouda,
    10, 37, 89, 146, 265
Lane, Malory, 69
Langres, 87, 266
Larkin Cold Storage, 185
Leonora, 149, 266
L'Etivaz d'Alpage, 124, 266
L-leucine, 155
L-tyrosine, 154, 155

M

Mahón, 158
Manchego, 89, 141, 147,
    204–5, 266
Marcel Petite Comté, 122,
    132
Marco Polo Reserve, 105,
    266
Marieke Gouda (smoked),
    146, 266
mascarpone, 48, 266
Matsubara, Masanori, 69
McGee, Harold, 171
Meilleur Ouvrier de France,
    185
microbe wrangling, 20
Midnight Moon, 146,
    266–67
milk:
    cow, 30
    fall and winter, 29
    goat, 30–31

raw, 32–33
seasonal variations,
    28–29
sheep, 31
spring and summer, 28
water buffalo, 31
Miller, Sue, 25–27
Mimolette, 151, 155, 267
Mirasaka Fromage, 69
Mish, 253
mold, in cheese, 174
Moliterno al Tartufo, 162,
    267
monks, and cheesemaking,
    82–83
Monserrate, 252
Montébeliard cows, 133
Monte Enebro, 181, 267
Montgomery, James, 101
Montgomery's Cheddar, 101,
    104, 267
MoonRabbit, 105, 267
Moskowitz, Adam, 185
Mount Fuji, 267
Mozzarella di Bufala, 49,
    267
Murray's (NYC), 111–13

N

Nababbo, 86, 267
Nagelkaas, 253
Negroni Blue, 179, 267
nose (in cheese), defined, 35

O

Occelli al Barolo, 89
Olomoucké Tvarůžky, 251
Oma, 93
On Food and Cooking
    (McGee), 171
Ossau-Iraty, 127, 268
The Oxford Companion to
    Cheese (Behr), 119

P

Parenica, 251
Paris, Brie in, 72–78
Parmigiano-Reggiano:
    about, 140–41, 268
    authentic, 142–43, 147
    crystals in, 155
    with fresh cheese board,
        51
Paški Sir, 250–51
paste (in cheese), defined,
    35
pasteurization, 22, 32, 33
peak ripeness, defined, 35
Pecorino:
    de Fossa, 251
    Ginepro, 163, 268
    Romano, 141
    Sardo, 147, 268
    Siciliano, 141
    Toscano, 141, 147, 268
Penicillium camemberti, 60
Penicillium candidum, 60
Pepperjack, 204–5
Perdido, 169
Petite, Marcel, 132
Piacentinu Ennese, 252
Pitchfork Cheddar, 101, 104,
    268
Pleasant Ridge Reserve, 12,
    14, 268
Point Reyes Creamery, 159
Point Reyes Original Blue,
    179, 268
Polowsky, Pat, 154
Pont-L'Éveque, 86, 268–69
portraits, cheese, 169–70
Port Salut, 86, 269
Powell, Greselda, 111–13
pressed cheeses, 139
Protected Designation of
    Origin (PDO), 35
Puglia, ricotta in, 54–57
Puigpédros, 113

Q

quark, 53
Querry, Claude, 133–34
Queso Bola de Ocosingo
   (QBO), 253
Quicke's Cheddar, 104, 269

R

Raclette, 123, 269
Ragusano, 147, 269
raw milk, 32–33, 35
raw-milk cheese, 32–33, 207
Red Hawk, 69, 86, 269
Red Rock, 105, 269
rennet, 23
ricotta, sheep's milk, 49,
   54–57, 270
rind, defined, 35
Rivers Edge, 162
Robiola la Rossa, 62, 67,
   269
robiolas, 62, 67
Robiola Tre Latti, 67, 269
Rocket's Robiola, 67, 269
Rockweed, 167
Rogue River Blue, 113, 179,
   270
Rogue Creamery Smokey
   Blue, 165, 270
Roquefort, 69, 174, 179, 270
Roth Sriracha Gouda, 169
Rowbottom, Amy, 159
Rush Creek Reserve, 8, 12,
   13, 14, 87, 270

S

Saint Maure de Touraine,
   74
Saint Nectaire, 79
Saisons, 78
Sakura, 253
Salon du Fromage, 238

Sbrinz Alpage, 155, 270
Schie, Jan van, 186
"scraping the face," 192
Selles-sur-Cher, 66, 270
Serro, 251
sheep milk, 31
sheep's milk cheese:
   aged, 141, 147
   feta, 49, 271
   fresh, 49
   ricotta, 49, 54–57, 270
Shelburne Farms, 104, 111
Shropshire Blue, 178, 271
smear-ripened cheese, 155
smoked cheese, 159, 162
Sofia, 66, 271
soft cheese, 60–79. See also
   specific types
   accompaniments, 68
   cheese board detours,
      69
   creating cheese board
      for, 64–69
   eating rinds on, 61
   exploring in the kitchen,
      70–71
   five must-try, 79
   French bloomy-rind, 66
   from Japan, 69
   overripe, 62
   overview, 60
   pairing with drinks, 68
   rind styles, 60–61
   ripening process, 62
   robiolas, 62, 67
   tasting Brie in Paris,
      72–78
   triple crèmes, 62, 67
   wrinkly-rind, 66
Somerset Cheddar, 101
Sottocenere, 162, 271
Sparkenhoe Red Leicester,
   107, 271
Spencer, Lilith, 218
spiced cheese, 163

spirits and cheese pairings,
   226
starter cultures, 23
Sterling College, 111
Stichelton, 178, 271
Stilton, 175
stinky cheese, 82–95. See
   also specific types
   accompaniments, 88
   bark-wrapped, types of,
      87
   certifiably stinky, types
      of, 86
   cheese board detours,
      89
   creating cheese board for,
      84–89
   exploring in the kitchen,
      90–91
   mildly whiffy, types of,
      86
   overripe, 83
   overview, 82–83
   pairing with drinks,
      88
   rank, types of, 87
   ripening process, 83
   washed-rind cheese
      specialist, 93–95
struvite crystals, 155
Sturman, Susan, 75
Sweet Home Farm, 170
Swiss Fondue, 117

T

tablescaping tips, 213–14
Taka & Vermo, 76
Taleggio, 86, 95, 271
teeth, and cheese, 171
terpenes, 119
terroir, 22
Tête de Moine, 125, 271–72
thermization, 33
triple crèmes, 62, 67

truffled cheese, 51, 162
Tunworth, 107, 271

U

Ubriaco, 51, 89, 272
uncooked pressed cheeses, 139
United States of Cheese project, 169–70
Up in Smoke, 162, 272
Uplands Cheese, 12–14
Uplands Pleasant Ridge Reserve, 127
Up North, 159

V

Vacherin Fribourgeois, 78
Vacherin Mont d'Or, 87, 272
Valdeón, 175, 178, 272
Valençay, 66, 127, 272
Vampire Slayer, 163, 272
vat pasteurization, 33

vegetable rennet, 23
vegetarian cheesemonger, 203
vegetarian cheeses, 203, 206
vein (in cheese), defined, 35
Vermont Cheesemakers Festival, 111, 236
Vermont Creamery, 60
Verofsky, Adam, 203

W

washed curd cheese, 140
washed-rind cheese specialist, 93–95
washed rinds, about, 82. See also stinky cheese
water buffalo milk, 31
water buffalo milk cheeses, 49, 260
Weinkäse Lagrein, 163, 272
Wensleydale, 107, 272

Westcombe Cheddar, 101, 104, 273
West Country Farmhouse Cheddars, 101
Westfield Blue Log, 181, 273
whey, defined, 35
Wilde Weide, 146, 186, 273
wine and cheese pairings, 227
Winnimere, 87, 93, 153–54, 155, 273
World Championship Cheese Contest, 239
World Cheese Awards, 185
The World Cheese Book (Harbutt), 140
wrinkly-rind cheese, 60–61, 66

Y

Yescas, Carlos, 186
"yoga breath of cheese," 196–97

ACKNOWLEDGMENTS

Like all things in the realm of cheese, this book is the result of lavish love. It would never have been possible without Anna Juhl of Cheese Journeys who invited me to cohost cheese tours around Europe and see so much artisan cheesemaking firsthand, my PA cheese gang (the Rennet Rough Riders) for joining me at the table for so many tastings, the kindness of everyone at our cheese clubhouse (Martha) in the Kensington neighborhood of Philadelphia where I've been able to BYO my own cheese to experiment with pairings at the bar, the friendship of cheesemaker Sue Miller who kidnaps me periodically for cheese road trips, the hospitality of Peter Dixon and Rachel Fritz Schaal in Vermont, the cider intelligentsia (Ben Wenk and Imogen Wirth-Granlund of Ploughman), bread support from Pete Merzbacher and the crew at Lost Bread Co., the incredible cheesemongers at Di Bruno Bros. who always teach me new things and give me free range to graze, not to mention the wonderful staff at Tria who read early drafts of this book as part of their training manual.

This book has been a five-year odyssey. It started with a pitch to write an updated guide to American cheeses, then swerved into an international project, took several wrong turns thematically, became roadblocked by the COVID-19 pandemic, and was waylaid by a thief who stole my laptop in Luxembourg. Maintaining momentum would not have been possible without serious roadside assistance! Huge thanks to my stalwart agent Clare Pelino for believing in this project from start to finish, to editor Kylie Foxx McDonald for her wild enthusiasm, to Peggy Paul Casella for shepherding me through a drastic revision, to copy editor Laurel Robinson for working her fact-checker mind like a metal detector on this manuscript, to illustrator Aly Miller, designers Laura Palese and Becky Terhune, typesetter Barbara Peragine, production editor Kate Karol, and everyone at Workman Publishing who got this book printed and onto shelves and into hands.

Countless people in and around the cheese community shared their time with me to help shape this book. Huge thanks to Hunter Fike, Emilio Mignucci, Julia Birnbaum, Stefania Patrizio, Malachy Egan, Jason Hinds, David Lockwood, Sam Frank, Susan Sturman, Lindsey Tramuta, Veronica Cassidy, Jennifer Greco, Leah Gilles, Fabrice Gepner, Pierre Coulon, Raw Cheese Power, Andy Hatch, Mike Geno, Matt Buddah, Emiliano Tatar, Yoav Perry, Carlos Yescas, Erika Kubick, Brie Best, Jill Tardiff, Alyce Birchenough, Janee' Muha, Michelle Vieira, Camilla Bojsen-Møller, Sylvain Jamois, Romain Alinat, Samantha Kane, Rachel Juhl, Ana Caballero, Wolf, Alexis Siemons, Marissa McClellan, and Margaux Kent.

Huge thanks to the people in my daily life who have supported my cheese and writing habit for so many years: my parents, Sonja Darlington and Mahlon Darlington; my brother, André Darlington; Todd Stregiel; Emily Geddes and Anthony Mazza; Leonardo De Paoli and Tommaso Gagliardi; and my colleagues and students in the English Department at Saint Joseph's University in Philadelphia.

ABOUT THE AUTHOR

Tenaya Darlington serves as Cheese Director for two wine bars in Philadelphia, both called Tria, and is a member of the writing faculty at Saint Joseph's University. When she's not teaching cheese workshops under the name "Madame Fromage," you can find her circumnavigating the globe as a guide for Cheese Journeys—a dairy-centric food tour company. She is also the author of *Di Bruno Bros. House of Cheese* and coauthor of four cocktail books, including *Booze and Vinyl*, written in collaboration with her spirits-expert brother, André Darlington. Her writing has appeared in *Cooking Light*, the *Philadelphia Inquirer, Edible Philly, Fermentation*, and *Culture Magazine*. You can find her on social media as @mmefromage.